THE HIDDEN PLACES OF
DEVON

By Joanna Billing

Regional Hidden Places

Cambs & Lincolnshire
Chilterns
Cornwall
Derbyshire
Devon
Dorset, Hants & Isle of Wight
East Anglia
Gloucs, Wiltshire & Somerset
Heart of England
Hereford, Worcs & Shropshire
Highlands & Islands
Kent
Lake District & Cumbria
Lancashire & Cheshire
Lincolnshire & Nottinghamshire
Northumberland & Durham
Sussex
Thames Valley
Yorkshire

National Hidden Places

England
Ireland
Scotland
Wales

Hidden Inns

East Anglia
Heart of England
Lancashire & Cheshire
North of England
South
South East
South and Central Scotland
Wales
Welsh Borders
West Country
Yorkshire
Wales

Country Living Rural Guides

East Anglia
Heart of England
Ireland
North East of England
North West of England
Scotland
South
South East
Wales
West Country

Published by: Travel Publishing Ltd, 7a Apollo House, Calleva Park, Aldermaston, Berks, RG7 8TN

ISBN 1-902-00789-1

First published 1989, second edition 1992, third edition 1996, fourth edition 1998, fifth edition 2000, sixth edition 2003

Printing by: Scotprint, Haddington

Maps by: © Maps in Minutes ™ (2002)
© Crown Copyright, Ordnance Survey 2002

Editor: Joanna Billing

Cover Design: Lines & Words, Aldermaston

Cover Photograph: Willmead Farm, near Bovey Tracey
© www.britainonview.com

Text Photographs: © www.britainonview.com

Foreword

The ***Hidden Places*** is a collection of easy to use travel guides taking you in this instance on a relaxed but informative tour of Devon, a delightful county endowed with green rolling hills, bright fresh streams tumbling through wooded valleys and picturesque little villages. Devon is home to the National Parks of Dartmoor and Exmoor (which it shares with Somerset), two areas of outstanding natural beauty with bleak uplands and isolated moorlands stretching out towards the impressive coastlines in the north and south of the county.

The covers and pages of the ***Hidden Places*** series have been comprehensively redesigned and this edition of ***The Hidden Places of Devon*** is the third title to be published in the new format. All ***Hidden Places*** titles will now be published in this new style which ensures that readers can properly appreciate the attractive scenery and impressive places of interest in Devon and, of course, throughout the rest of the British Isles.

Our books contain a wealth of interesting information on the history, the countryside, the towns and villages and the more established places of interest. But they also promote the more secluded and little known visitor attractions and places to stay, eat and drink many of which are easy to miss unless you know exactly where you are going.

We include hotels, inns, restaurants, public houses, teashops, various types of accommodation, historic houses, museums, gardens, and many other attractions throughout the area, all of which are comprehensively indexed. Most places are accompanied by an attractive photograph and are easily located by using the map at the beginning of each chapter. We do not award merit marks or rankings but concentrate on describing the more interesting, unusual or unique features of each place with the aim of making the reader's stay in the local area an enjoyable and stimulating experience.

Whether you are visiting the area for business or pleasure or in fact are living in the county we do hope that you enjoy reading and using this book. We are always interested in what readers think of places covered (or not covered) in our guides so please do not hesitate to use the reader reaction forms provided to give us your considered comments. We also welcome any general comments which will help us improve the guides themselves. Finally if you are planning to visit any other corner of the British Isles we would like to refer you to the list of other ***Hidden Places*** titles to be found at the rear of the book and to the Travel Publishing website at **www.travelpublishing.co.uk.**

Travel Publishing

Devon
Somerset
Cornwall
Chapter 3
Chapter 2
Chapter 1
Chapter 4
Chapter 5
Chapter 6
Chapter 7

Contents

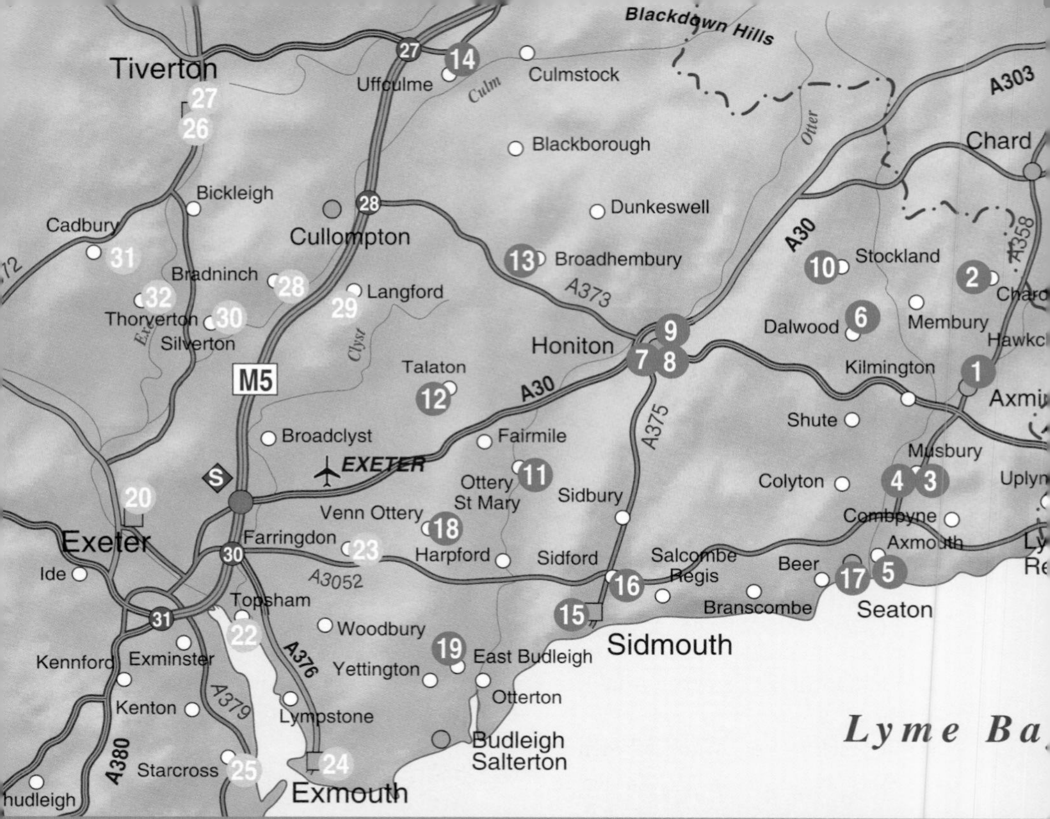

PLACES TO STAY, EAT AND DRINK

The Castle Inn, Axminster	1	Pub with Food	p5
The George Inn, Chardstock, Axminster	2	Pub, Food and Accommodation	p6
The Golden Hind, Musbury, Axminster	3	Pub with Food	p8
Kate's Farm B&B, Musbury, Axminster	4	Bed and Breakfast	p9
The Harbour Inn, Axmouth, Seaton	5	Pub with Food	p9
Burrow Farm Gardens, Dalwood, Axminster	6	Gardens	p11
The Honiton Wine Bar, Honiton	7	Wine Bar with Food	p12
Carlton Inn Restaurant, Honiton	8	Pub and Restaurant	p13
Allhallows Museum, Honiton	9	Museum	p13
The Kings Arms Inn, Stockland, Honiton	10	Pub, Restaurant and Accommodation	p14
Cadhay Manor, Ottery St Mary	11	Historic House and Gardens	p16
The Talaton Inn, Talaton, Exeter	12	Pub with Food	p17
Lane End Farm, Broadhembury, Hontion	13	Bed and Breakfast	p18
Coldharbour Mill, Uffculme, Cullompton	14	Historic Attraction	p20
Norman Lockyer Observatory, Sidmouth	15	Scientific Attraction	p22
The Rising Sun, Sidford	16	Pub with Food	p23
The Bay Tree Guest House, Seaton	17	Guest House	p26
Stable Cottage, Venn Ottery, Ottery St Mary	18	Self Catering	p27
Bicton Park Botanical Gardens, East Budleigh	19	Gardens and Museum	p28

● Denotes entries in other chapters

1 East Devon and the Heritage Coast

This is a beautiful and often overlooked part of Devon, as many pass through here on the motorway for destinations deeper into the southwest. However, this area has much to offer those willing to leave the main roads: there are ancient market towns, picturesque villages, beautiful and tranquil valleys, elegant resorts and spectacular coastline.

Dating back to Roman times, when it was a major stopping place on the Fosse Way, Honiton is still considered as the gateway to the far southwest. Although, like many West Country towns, its prosperity was built on wool it is for its lace, first hand-made here in the late 16th century, that the town has become famous all over the world. Just to the east lies another market town, whose roots too go back to Roman times, and Axminster has, since the mid 1700s, become synonymous with luxuriously woven carpets that are still made here today. It was in this area of east Devon that one of the West Country's most famous sons, Sir Walter Raleigh, was born, near Yettington, in 1552 and he is said to have never lost his soft Devon burr – a regional accent that was regarded by 16th century London sophisticates as uncouth and he was greatly mocked by his enemies at the court of Elizabeth I. The Raleigh's family pew can still be seen in Yettington parish church whilst the famous picture by Sir John Everet Millais, *The Boyhood of Raleigh*, was painted on Budleigh Salterton's beach. Meanwhile, Ottery St Mary, one of

Broadhembury

Devon's most ancient towns, was, in the mid 18th century, the birthplace of the celebrated poet, Samuel Taylor Coleridge.

Beer Village

Three river valleys, those of the Axe, Sid and Otter, cut through the rolling hills and rich farmland of inland east Devon to meet the sea at Lyme Bay and they provide the only openings in this magnificent stretch of coastline that is dominated by rocky beaches and rugged cliffs. Virtually the only settlements to be found along the seaboard are those that developed around the mouths of the rivers, Seaton, Sidmouth and Budleigh Salterton, as the intervening cliffs discouraged human habitation and, even today, the only way to explore most of this coastline is on foot by taking the superb South West Coast Path. For centuries these little towns subsisted on fishing and smuggling until the days of the Prince Regent whose fad for sea bathing brought an influx of comparatively affluent visitors in search of healthy relaxation. Their numbers were augmented by many others who, accustomed to holidaying on the continent, were, due to Napoleon's domination of Europe, forced to find English alternatives. Between them, they transformed these modest places into fashionable resorts and the gentility that was characteristic of that era still lives on today in the elegant villas, peaceful gardens and wide promenades.

Holiday Cottage, Sidmouth

Axminster

Found in the beautiful countryside of the Axe Valley, a designated Area of Outstanding Natural Beauty, Axminster grew up around the junction of two major Roman roads, the Fosse Way (from Axmouth to Lincoln) and Icknield Street (from Exeter to London). By the time of the Middle Ages, this little town had become an important religious centre with a Minster (now a ruin) standing beside the River Axe, from which the town takes its name. However, it is as a centre for the manufacture of carpets that Axminster is best known and, in particular, luxuriously woven carpets, which bear the town's name, that first appeared in the early 1750s. Whilst wandering around London's Cheapside market, an Axminster weaver, Thomas Whitty, was astonished to see a huge Turkish carpet, 12 yards long by 8 yards wide, and, on returning to the sleepy market town where he was born, Whitty spent months puzzling over the mechanics of producing such a seamless piece of work. By 1755, he had solved the problem and, on Midsummer's Day, the first of his fabulous carpets was revealed to the world.

The time and labour involved was so great that the completion of each carpet was celebrated by a procession to St Mary's Church and by the ringing of a peal of bells. Ironically, one distinguished purchaser of an Axminster carpet was the Sultan of Turkey who, in 1800, paid the colossal sum of £1,000 for a particularly fine specimen. Unfortunately, the inordinately high costs of producing the exquisite hand-tufted carpets crippled Whitty's company and, in 1835, the looms were sold to a factory at Wilton.

Carpets are still manufactured in the town, using the latest computerised looms, and the Axminster Carpets Showroom has a wide selection from

The Castle Inn

Castle Hill, Axminster, Devon EX13 5NN
Tel: 01297 34944

Situated on Castle Hill, right in the heart of Axminster, **The Castle** is a traditional mid 18th century inn that has, in its time, also been a wine merchants. In fact, the history has been traced back through local archives and one of the earliest innkeepers registered at the premises was a Robert Hook in the early 1800's. Today's hosts, Tracey and Miles Wheller, each with almost twenty years experience in the licensed trade, have maintained the friendly atmosphere of a pub that is well known for its warm hospitality.

Along with three real ales, and a choice of lagers and stout, there is also a real cask cider available at the well stocked bar. This too is a destination for food as a good selection of hot and cold traditional pub meals are available between noon and 8pm throughout the week (except Sunday, when the popular roast dinner is available on a pre-booked basis only). To further add to customers' enjoyment, live entertainment is laid on every Saturday night, a monthly blues club is gaining widespread recognition, and many regulars while away a Sunday afternoon by taking part in the weekly quiz.

The George Inn

Chardstock, near Axminster,
Devon EX13 7BX
Tel: 01460 220241
e-mail: infogeorgeinn@ol.com

Dating back to at least the early 14th century, **The George Inn**, in the centre of the charming village of Chardstock, has been at the heart of village life for over 700 years. Originally a Church house where parishioners would retire after attending service to take a glass or two of the Church brew, this remains a welcoming and popular place with both locals and visitors alike. It is also a popular place for ghosts and, in particular, there is Copeland, a one time parson, who is said to haunt the entrance passage and the cellar.

As its age would suggest, The George is a rambling building with numerous intimate corners and it has a particularly cosy atmosphere in winter when roaring fires add an extra warmth. Keen observers will notice, in the snug, the graffiti carved into the stone window frames that dates from 1648 whilst, at one end of the bar, the walls are adorned with the works of the inn's resident poet, Arthur Lord.

Whilst historical interest and a welcoming atmosphere are important, landlord Andy Webster also ensures that visitors to The George receive the very best in traditional English inn hospitality. There is always a good choice of real ales available from the bar and the inn too has a select wine list along with the more usual lagers, ciders and spirits. However, it is for its cuisine that the inn is best known. The two skilled house chefs create a wide variety of dishes each day ranging from the lunchtime snack list through to the à la carte restaurant menu. While the dishes vary from freshly cut sandwiches and traditional grills to such delights as honey glazed rack of lamb and pan fried chilli chicken, visitors here can rest assured that the same care and attention to detail is taken whatever their choice and that only the freshest of ingredients are used.

Along with satisfying customers admirably with food and drink, Andy also organises a series of live music events most weekends through the Summer months and these further add to customers enjoyment though diehards here find it hard to leave their games of pool and skittles. Finally, The George has several excellent en-suite guest rooms that are let on a bed and breakfast basis and can be found in a converted barn adjacent to the inns courtyard.

which to choose and welcomes visitors. Situated close to Whitty's old factory is **St Mary's Church**, the oldest building in the town, which, after pealing its bells in celebration of the finished carpets, finally got its own and, inside, the pews are set back so that visitors and the congregation can admire the richly woven carpet in all its glory.

The town's old Police Station and Courthouse, found opposite the church, is now home to the **Axminster Museum**, which holds a varied collection including agricultural tools, archaeological finds and old photographs as well as, of course, an exhibition on Axminster carpets. The museum, which has a café, is open from the end of May to the end of September every day except Sundays and Bank Holiday Mondays.

The **Axe Vale Festival of Gardening and Crafts** is held every June, on the showground just outside the town, and it draws people from all over the southwest and beyond. A traditional horticultural show the festival also includes a craft marquee, antiques fair and numerous amusements for the children.

Around Axminster

Chardstock

3½ miles N of Axminster off the A358

This is a delightful village, centred on a 19th century church, that is surrounded by a varied landscape of pasture and woodland that stretches to the county border with Somerset.

Hawkchurch

3 miles NE of Axminster off the B3165

Known as 'the village of roses', this pretty place of picturesque cottages has, not surprisingly, an ancient village church, found in an attractive setting, which contains several unusual carvings dating from the Norman era. Footpaths from Hawkchurch extend into the surrounding countryside and, from here, there are superb views of not only Devon but also of neighbouring Dorset and Somerset.

Uplyme

4 miles SE of Axminster on the B3165

Found in the valley of the River Lym and surrounded by woodland, Uplyme is an ancient settlement – the remains of a Romano-British villa were uncovered nearby in 1850. Meanwhile, the village Church of St Peter and St Paul is believed to have been founded in the 9th century although the 14th century tower is the oldest part of the present building.

Combpyne

4 miles S of Axminster off the A3052

A tiny and scattered hamlet, set deep in one of Devon's prettiest combes, Combpyne has a 12th century church, which contains ancient wall paintings and bells, and a beautiful medieval manor house that overlooks the village pond – known locally as The Harbour.

Just to the south lies **Rousdon**, a relatively new village that was established around the Peek family's mansion in the 19th century and it was Rousdon School, founded by Sir Henry Peek, that was the first school in England to provide a hot midday meal. In 1839 the coastal cliffs south of Rousdon gave way in an extensive landslip and this area, between Axmouth and Lyme Regis, is now known as the **Undercliff**. Managed by English Nature, this area offers some of the most interesting coastal walks in the south.

Musbury

3 miles SW of Axminster off the A358

This attractive village is overlooked by **Musbury Castle**, an Iron Age earthwork hill fort, and from its summit, which can be reached by a footpath starting from the parish church, there are spectacular views of the Axe Valley to its estuary at Seaton. The village church is worth a visit, too, as it contains the **Drake Memorial**, which dates from 1611. Musbury is also renowned as the birthplace of John Churchill, a member of the Drake family, who, as one of the country's greatest military leaders, was created Duke of Marlborough after the Battle of Blenheim. He was, of course, an ancestor of another of the country's greatest leaders, Sir Winston Churchill.

Musbury lies on the **East Devon Way**, a 40-mile long footpath and here the path follows a winding section of the Axe Valley that is particularly rich in wildlife and that has, recently, been recognised as a Site of Special Scientific

The Golden Hind

The Street, Musbury, Axminster, Devon EX13 8AU
Tel: 01297 552413
website: www.golden-hind.co.uk

A popular stopping place for walkers and their dogs on the East Devon Way and only 3 miles from the World Heritage Jurassic Coast. **The Golden Hind** dates from Georgian times and is run as a traditional English village pub by owners Cecilia and Roger Adamson providing local ales, keg beers and home cooked food. It has a convenient car park adjacent to the A358.

There is a Public bar for adults only and a seperate lounge which is welcoming to families and has access to an enclosed rear garden with childrens play equipment during the summer months. There are panoramic views over the Axe Valley from the front beer garden.

Kate's Farm Bed & Breakfast

Lower Bruckland Farm, Musbury, near Axminster, Devon EX13 8ST
Tel: 01297 552861

Just a few minutes from the south Devon coast lies Lower Bruckland Farm, a charming 16th century longhouse that is home to **Kate's Farm Bed and Breakfast**. Along with comfortable bedrooms, owner, Kate Satterley offers her guests a superb home-cooked breakfast served in the farmhouse's lounge that not only has its original flagstone floor but also a magnificent inglenook fireplace and bread oven. This organic dairy farm has two trout lakes and there is much to interest the naturalist and walker locally. Children and dogs welcome.

Interest. The much shorter (8 miles) **Axe Valley Local Walk** passes through the peaceful countryside of the East Devon Area of Outstanding Natural Beauty and links with the longer, better known, path.

Axmouth

5 miles SW of Axminster on the B3172

Facing Seaton across the Axe estuary, this picturesque village of thatched cottages and farmhouses is a peaceful place from which to enjoy the estuary's birdlife. The village lies at one end of the **Buzzard Route**, a 100-mile cycle path that passes through the Axe Valley and up into the Blackdown Hills on the border with Somerset.

Kilmington

1½ miles W of Axminster off the A35

A charming village, where cricket is still played on the village green in summer, Kilmington not only has glorious surroundings but also magnificent views out across the Axe valley. Although the parish Church of St Giles was rebuilt in 1862 it incorporates an earlier west tower with six bells and some gruesome gargoyles. There is a pleasant walk

The Harbour Inn

Axmouth, near Seaton, Devon EX12 4AF
Tel: 01297 20371 Fax: 01297 20371

Found just yards from the River Axe and opposite the village church, **The Harbour Inn** is a picturesque thatched pub that dates back over 800 years.

A true family inn that has been owned and personally run by Pat and David Squire for nearly 35 years, this charming olde worlde establishment is not only well known for its excellent range of real ales but it is also a popular place for food and, in particular, the house speciality lamb dishes that use meat reared by the family.

along an old Roman road to the neighbouring village of Shute.

Shute

3 miles W of Axminster off the A35

Surrounded by woodlands, extensive farmland and green hills, this village dates from the 13th century and the remains of Shute Manor House, built in the 14th century can be found nearby. Now known as **Shute Barton** (National Trust), this is an exceptional example of a non-fortified medieval manor house and, whilst only two wings of the original 1380s building still survive, they include some remarkably impressive features. Amongst these is the Great Hall with its massive beamed ceiling, the Great Kitchen with its open fireplace that is believed to be the largest in the country and a Tudor gatehouse. Shute Barton was owned by the Pole family, a local dynasty that is commemorated by some grand monuments in **St Michael's Church** and here can be found an overbearing memorial to Sir William Pole, which depicts the Master of the Household to Queen Anne standing on a pedestal dressed in full regalia. Meanwhile, the 13th century church has an altogether more appealing feature in the 19th century seven-foot high sculptured panel framed in alabaster that shows Margaret Pole greeting her three little daughters at the gates of heaven.

Close to the village is **Lyme Bay Winery** where the traditional craft of making West Country cider is kept very much alive. Using old fashioned locally farmed cider apples, such as Kingston Black, Dabinett and Yarlington Mill, the winery produces a range of ciders and apple-based drinks that can be purchased at the winery shop (open daily in summer and closed weekends in winter).

The Winery includes a range of drinks named after the notorious smuggler Jack Rattenbury (1778-1844), who operated around the Lyme Bay coast between Weymouth and Topsham. Often involved in skirmishes with the Customs and Excise men, Rattenbury, like other smugglers of the time, practiced creeping, a local method of hiding contraband from the authorities by sinking barrels on rafts off the coast and then recovering the goods when Excise men were otherwise employed.

Dalwood

3 miles NW of Axminster off the A35

By some administrative oversight, until 1842 this picturesque rural village was part of Dorset despite it being completely surrounded by Devon. Along with having a fine 15th century church, dedicated to St Peter, which contains an Elizabethan chalice and some early stained glass, the village is home to another fascinating place of worship – **Loughwood Meeting House** (National Trust). One of the earliest surviving Baptist chapels in the country, when the meeting house was built in the 1650s the site was hidden by dense woodland as, at that time, the Baptists were being

Burrow Farm Gardens

Dalwood, near Axminster, Devon EX13 7ET
Tel: 01404 831285 website:
www.burrowfarmgardens.co.uk

The beautifully landscaped **Burrow Farm Gardens** were created over the last 40 years by Mary Benger and, awarded star status in the *Good Gardens Guide*, they will appeal to both plantsmen and those seeking a relaxing walk in a tranquil setting. Along with the fascinating woodland garden created in a Roman clay pit, the sweeping lawns and beds of unusual shrubs and herbaceous plants, there is the most recent addition, the Millennium Rill Garden. Open daily from April to September, the gardens have a coffee shop serving light refreshments and a plant nursery.

persecuted and could only congregate in secret. Under its quaint thatched roof, this charming little building contains a simple whitewashed interior with early 18th century pews and pulpit. In use up until 1833, the chapel was restored by the Trust who acquired it in 1969.

Dalwood is also home to **Burrow Farm Gardens** (see panel above), beautifully landscaped gardens that provide not only a relaxing setting but also fine views of the surrounding countryside. Along with the pergola walk, the new Millennium Rill Garden and the courtyard garden that provides late summer colour, there is a superb woodland garden that features, in particular, wild flowers.

Membury

3 miles NW of Axminster off the A358

Taking its name from **Membury Castle**, a nearby Iron Age earthwork, this pretty village is home to the ancient Church of St John the Baptist, which dates from the 13th century and whose tall, slim tower is unusual in Devon. Also close by is a former Quaker's meeting house (now a hotel) and burial ground whilst, just to the west, lies Beckford Bridge, the oldest packhorse bridge in east Devon, which spans the River Yarty.

Honiton

Thought of as the 'capital of east Devon', this delightful little town in the Otter Valley, is very much a gateway to the far southwest. A major stopping place on the Fosse Way, the great Roman road that struck diagonally across England from Lincoln to Exeter, Honiton's position on the main route to Devon and Cornwall brought it considerable prosperity and its broad, two-mile-long High Street is a testament to its busy past. However, by the 1960s the amount of traffic passing through the town, particularly during the holiday season, had reached appalling proportions but, the construction of a by-pass in the 1970s, has allowed Honiton to resume its true character as an attractive market town.

Surrounded by sheep pastures, Honiton was the first town in Devon to manufacture serge cloth but the town has become much better known for an altogether more delicate material – lace. Lace-making was introduced to east Devon by Flemish immigrants, who arrived here during the early years of the reign of Elizabeth I, and it was not long before anyone who could afford this new and costly material was displaying it lavishly as a signal of their wealth and status. Just over 100 years later, at the end of the 17th century, some 5,000 people were employed in the lace-making industry, most of them working from their own homes making fine 'bone' lace by hand. Such was the demand for lace that children as young as five were sent to lace schools where they received a rudimentary education and also instruction in the art of lace-making. The hand-made lace industry was almost wiped out by the arrival of machinery in the late 1700s but the industry was given a new lease of life when Queen Victoria insisted on Honiton lace for her wedding dress and created a new fashion for lace that persisted throughout the 19th century. The traditional material is still made on a small scale in the town and can be found on sale in local shops.

The town's museum, **Allhallows Museum** (see panel opposite) is one of the few buildings in the town to have survived a series of devastating fires in the mid 18th century. However, the

The Honiton Wine Bar

79 High Street, Honiton, Devon EX14 1PG
Tel: 01404 47889 Fax: 01404 47889
e-mail: honitonwinebar@btopenworld.com

The Honiton Wine Bar, found on the town's main High Street, is certainly one of the places to be seen in – a stylish and sophisticated Wine Bar which is open from 10am in the morning through to 3pm and then from 5.30pm to 11pm. Owned and personally run by local couple, Stephen and Sarah Hodgkins, who took over the ownership in October 2002, the tasteful decor and layout of the Wine Bar creates a very welcoming and friendly atmosphere for the day time,whilst in the evening, when the lights are dimmed and the individual table oil lamps lit, the atmosphere changes to one of intimacy,

In the mornings and from 2pm to 3pm along with teas and coffee, a light snack menu is available ranging from toasted teacakes, toast with jam, bacon baguettes and toasted sandwiches. The lunchtime menu is ideal for a relaxing bite in the middle of a busy day, and also includes Crispy Baguettes and Jacket potatoes with a wide choice of fillings.The evening menu is altogether more sophisticated. Here, such delights include Monkfish tail with shallots and fresh tarragon sauce and Vol au vents topped with Cajun spiced mushrooms. The menus are updated regularly and the homemade dishes all reflect the very best of Devon's produce.

Along with wines from around the world, spirits, soft drinks, draught beers, Guinness and lagers are all available. The Draught Beers are 'Otter Ale' and 'Otter Bitter' brewed locally on Honitons doorstep.

Carlton Inn Restaurant

42 High Street, Honiton, Devon EX14 1PJ
Tel: 01404 42903

Honiton's main street is home to the **Carlton Inn Restaurant**, an old inn that, under the guidance of experienced licensees Julian Davies and Sid Tinworth (a lady), has become a very popular pub and restaurant.

Stylishly decorated and furnished in a way that successfully blends the age of the premises with the modern tastes, this is not only a place for good ale but also a popular place for food - it is essential to book at weekends. Finally, the couple have opened a nightclub on the first floor.

wholesale destruction of the town had the fortunate result that the new buildings constructed were gracious Georgian residences that still give Honiton the pleasant atmosphere of a prosperous coaching town.

Another building that escaped the flames was **Marwood House** in the High Street that was built in 1619 by the second son of Thomas Marwood, one of Elizabeth I's many physicians. Thomas achieved great celebrity when he managed to cure the Earl of Essex after all others had failed and for this he received his Devonshire estate as a reward. He was also equally successful in preserving his own health and he lived to the extraordinary age of 105. Other buildings on the outskirts of the town that are worth a mention include **St Margaret's Hospital**, which was founded in the Middle Ages as a refuge for lepers, an early 19th century toll house known as **Copper Castle** and, on Honiton Hill, there is the massive folly of the **Bishop's Tower**, erected in 1842 and that was once part of Bishop Edward Copplestone's house. To the north of the town lies **Dumpdon Hill** (National Trust), an 850-foot high steep-sided outcrop that is crowned by a sizeable Iron Age hill fort.

Allhallows Museum

Honiton, Devon

The building housing the museum has a very interesting history, being the oldest building in Honiton and starting life as a chapel.It later became a school and then a museum. It dates from before 1327 and was built when the folk from the 'new town' grew tired of climbing the hill to St Michael's and obtained permission to build the chapel.

Fifty years ago the chapel was bought by the townspeople and opened as a museum. It now has three galleries - the Murch Gallery, the Nicholl Gallery and the Norman Gallery, in which are housed selections of an extensive lace collection as well as local antiques.

THE KINGS ARMS INN

Stockland, near Honiton, Devon EX14 9BS
Tel: 01404 881361 Fax: 01404 881732
e-mail: info@kingsarms.net
website: www.kingsarms.net

Found in the centre of the village of Stockland, on the edge of the Blackdown Hill, **The Kings Arms Inn** is a wonderful, traditional inn that is popular with locals and also extends a warm welcome to visitors to the area. Owned and personally run by business partners, Heinz Kiefer, Paul Diviani and John O'Leary, this lovely establishment has a relaxed atmosphere that stems from the very professional approach taken by the partners on the inn's day to day running.

An old and attractive building, The Kings Arms has several bar areas that each provide a different atmosphere so that all who come here can enjoy their visit. Especially popular with the locals, the Farmers' Bar is very much a meeting place for villagers who congregate here and put the world to rights. Visitors are welcome to join in the conversations that take place over a pint or two from the inn's selection of real ales. For relaxed and easy going eating and drinking there is the Cotley Restaurant bar whilst those looking for more formal dining will find the Dining Room more to their liking. Along with the fine selection of ales, beers and spirits at the bar there is an extensive wine list, which acts as an excellent accompaniment to the cuisine served here at both lunchtime and in the evening. Wherever customers choose to enjoy their meal, the menu, which ranges from tasty lunchtime bar snacks through to an evening à la carte, has something for everyone and, on Sundays, the imaginative list includes a traditional roast. Reservations are advisable throughout the week to avoid disappointment. However, The Kings Arms not only offers superb food and drink, there is also live music here every weekend and bank holidays, during the week in the winter, there are regular Skittles Matches.

Finally, The Kings Arms also offers visitors to the area comfortable bed and breakfast accommodation in a choice of three attractive en-suite colour co-ordinated guest rooms. Children are welcome at The Kings Arms as are well behaved dogs although it should be noted that the inn has pet Dobermans who patrol the ground floor of the premises at night.

Meanwhile, back in the town, is the **Thelma Hulbert Gallery**, which holds a series of contemporary exhibitions throughout the year that have included works by David Hockney, Andy Warhol and Roy Lichtenstein. Open daily from February to December (closed Sundays and Mondays), the gallery is housed in the home of local artist Thelma Hulbert who lived and worked here until her death in 1995.

Around Honiton

Dunkeswell

5 miles N of Honiton off the A373

Situated in the heart of the Blackdown Plateau, this little village's main claim to fame is the 900-year-old Norman font in St Nicholas' Church on which is carved a rather crude image of an elephant – the earliest known representation of this animal in England. Almost certainly the stonemason had never seen such a creature but he made almost as good a job of it as he did with his satirical carvings of a bishop and a doctor. The font came, originally, from **Dunkeswell Abbey**, a Cistercian foundation whose ruins lie a couple of miles north of the village. Today, only the 15th century gatehouse of the abbey remains whilst the rest of the site is now occupied by a rather charmless Victorian church.

To the west of the village lies **Dunkeswell Memorial Museum**, a living memorial to the past that stands on the site of the only American Navy Air base commissioned on British soil during World War II. Dedicated to the veterans of the US Fleet Air Wing 7 and RAF personnel who served at the base, the museum explores the special role that the servicemen played during the war through a range of exhibits and displays that include artefacts and photographs. Open from March to November (except non Bank Holiday Mondays) and weekends throughout the winter, there is also a restaurant, a playground for children and a museum shop.

Stockland

6 miles NE of Honiton off the A30

Situated on the southern slopes of the Blackdown Ridge, on the summit of Stockland Hill there are two prehistoric earthworks – **Stockland Great Camp** and **Stockland Little Camp**.

Ottery St Mary

5 miles SW of Honiton on the B3177

Found in the picturesque Otter Valley, this pretty little town is surrounded by some of the most beautiful and least explored countryside in Devon. This is also one of Devon's most ancient towns and, along with being included in the *Domesday Book* (where it is recorded there was a church and three mills), it was mentioned in a Saxon Charter of 1061 as 'Otrei'. The glory of the town is its magnificent 14th century **Church of**

St Mary that was commissioned by Bishop Grandisson of Exeter in 1337 and that was modelled, as he stipulated, on Exeter Cathedral. He also wanted it to be "a sanctuary for piety and learning," so accommodation for 40 scholars was provided. The church's interior remains very striking and its medieval treasures include a brilliantly coloured altar screen, canopied tombs and a 14th century astronomical clock showing the moon and planets that still works using its original mechanism.

Church of St Mary

During the mid 18th century, Ottery's vicar was the Rev John Coleridge whose 13th child became the celebrated poet, Samuel Taylor Coleridge. Born at the family home near the church in 1772, though the house has since been

Cadhay Manor

Ottery Sy Mary, Devon EX11 1QT
Tel?Fax: 01404 812432

"John Haydon, esquire, sometime bencher of Lincoln's Inn, builded at Cadhay a fair new house and enlarged his demenses". So wrote Risdon in his book of Devon published in 1620. Much of the present house was built around 1550 and it remains in all essentials unchanged. Approached by an avenue of limes, Cadhay stands in a magnificent garden and looks out over the original medieval fish-ponds which may have been used by the Warden and Canons of the lovely Collegiate Church of St Mary of Ottery a mile away.

When John Haydon built his impressive mansion, he retained the Great Hall of an earlier building on the site and its fine timber roof, built between 1420-1470, which is still in place. In the early 1600's Haydon's great nephew, Robert Haydon, added an Elizabethan Long Gallery, forming a unique and attractive courtyard. It's known as the Court of Sovereigns because of the statues of Henry VIII, Edward VI, Mary and Elizabeth I which stand over the doors. Robert Haydon married Joan, eldest daughter of Sir Amias Poulett, and interestingly the present owners of Cadhay, the William-Poulett family, are descended from Sir Amias. Cadhay and its gardens are open to the public on the Spring and Late Autumn Bank Holiday Sunday and Monday, then each Tuesday, Wednesday and Thursday during July and August.

demolished, a bronze plaque in the churchyard wall honours the town's most famous son and it depicts the poet's profile, menaced by the albatross that features in his best known poem, *The Ancient Mariner*.

This is a delightful little town in which to wander with narrow twisting lanes that lead up from the River Otter and where there are fine Georgian buildings to be found along with an old wool manufactory – a dignified example of early industrial architecture.

Whilst its famous building and famous son draw people here from far and wide, the town is also well known for the 'Tar Barrel Rolling', an ancient annual ritual that takes place on the Saturday closest to November 5th, when barrels of flaming tar are rolled through the narrow streets. Meanwhile, in the summer, on 'Pixie Day', local children dress up as pixies and attempt to capture the church bell ringers and so gain control of the town.

Just a mile northwest of Ottery St Mary is the historic **Cadhay Manor House** (see panel opposite).

Fairmile

5 miles SW of Honiton off the A30

Just to the north of the village lies **Escot Fantasy Gardens and Parkland**, a vast area of parkland that was originally laid out by Capability Brown in the 18th century but that has been magically brought back to life by the land artist and television gardener Ivan Hicks. Surrounding the ancestral home of the Kennaway family, the gardens and parkland are an ideal place to visit for those who enjoy beautiful flowers, shrubs and trees as well as those who enjoy nature. The Wetland and Waterfowl area was once the ice ponds for the big house and it is now, with the use of natural springs and marshes, a haven for insects and pond life. Children, too, will be delighted to see Britain's only native species of squirrel, the beautiful red squirrel, along with the Birds of Prey and Falconry displays, the otters and the wild boar. Meanwhile, there is also the Stables Craft Centre and, found in a handsome Grade I listed building, the Coach House restaurant.

Blackborough

7 miles NW of Honiton off the A373

Most of the villages in this corner of east Devon nestle in the valley bottoms, but Blackborough is an exception as it stands high on a ridge of the Blackdown Hill. It is also a comparatively new settlement that sprang up when whetstone mining flourished in the area for a period in the early 19th century. RD Blackmore's novel, *Perlycross*, paints a vivid picture of life in these makeshift mining camps where day-to-day living was both harsh and cruel.

Culmstock

9 miles NW of Honiton on the B3391

At the heart of the village, which was once a small market town with a considerable woollen industry, is the parish church that is famous for its yew tree that grows from the top of the church's tower. The tree has been growing here for well over 200 years and, despite the fact that its only nourishment is the lime content of the mortar in which it is set, the trunk has now achieved a girth of more than 18 inches. It is believed that the seed was

carried up in the mortar used to repair the tower then its spire was demolished in 1776. Meanwhile, the church's more traditional treasures include a magnificent embroidered cope of the late 15th century displayed in a glass case; a remarkable 14th century tomb rediscovered during a 19th century restoration of the building; and a richly coloured memorial window designed by Burne-Jones.

Lovers of the novels of RD Blackmore will be particularly interested in Culmstock as it was here that the author lived as a boy during the years when his father was the local vicar. One of his playmates in the village was Frederick Temple, another bright boy, and the two friends both went on to Blundell's School in Tiverton where they shared lodgings.
Blackmore was to become one of the most successful novelists of his time whilst Temple entered the church and, after several years as the headmaster of Rugby School, reached the pinnacle of his profession when he became Archbishop of Canterbury.

A couple of miles east of the village lies **Hemycock Castle** that was built around 1380 but, today, all that remains of the Hidon family's fortified manor house are four turrets, a curtain wall, a moat and a dungeon. A peaceful and evocative setting, the castle ruins stand behind the church and, since it lies close to the head of the lovely Culm valley, this is a popular picnic spot.

Uffculme

10 miles NW of Honiton on the B3440

In medieval times this charming little village, set beside the River Culm, was an important centre for the wool trade and profits from this booming business helped to build the impressive parish Church of St Mary in the mid 15th century. Its splendid rood screen, also paid for by the local trade, is believed to be the longest in Devon.

Close to the village is one of the few surviving reminders of the area's industrial wool trade – **Coldharbour Mill** – which closed down in 1981 but that has since been converted into a living museum (see page 20). Here, in authentic surroundings, visitors can follow the story of woollen cloth production from the early days of hand spinning and weaving in the 18th century through to the brilliant mechanical inventions of the Victorian era and beyond to the present day. The mill's giant waterwheel, boilers and steam engines played a vital role in the mill's development and, now restored, they are an impressive part of the mill tour.

Also at the mill there is a fascinating display of exhibits covering World War II, an outstanding textile craft exhibition, a mill shop and gift gallery and a waterside licensed restaurant and café. Coldharbour Mill is open daily from March until Christmas.

Coldharbour Mill

Coldharbour Mill Trust, Coldharbour Mill, Uffculme, Cullompton, Devon EX15 3EE
Tel: 01884 840960 Fax: 01884 840858
e-mail:Info@coldharbourmill.org.uk
website: www,coldharbourmill.org.uk

In 1698 while visiting Exeter, Celia Fiennes wrote "...the whole town and country is emply'd for at least 20 mile round in spinning, weaving, dressing and scouring, fulling and drying of serges, it turns the most money in a weeke of anything in England...". The woollen industry in the West Country was an incredibly important industry, and the area was famed for producing several types of woollen fabric. One such cloth, Broadcloth, described as the 'best known fabric of all English fabrics', was famous in Europe and America and was fashionable for over 500 years. It seems strange then, that there is such little evidence of the importance in the area now.

Coldharbour Mill working wool museum is one heritage site that is working to revive interest in this part of the West Country's past. The museum is housed in a woollen mill once owned by the Fox Brothers, a Somerset based company. The company began work at the mill in 1799 and continued production of woollen and worsted yarn there until 1981. Coldharbour Mill is one of the most complete industrial heritage sites in the country, with the mill, machinery and buildings still intact. But the story the mill tells is not simply one of process and machinery, but also of the men, women and children who worked there during its 200 year history. Visitors to the museum are taken on a guided tour of the mill, discovering the sights and sounds of a Victorian factory. During the tour they see how a sheep's fleece is turned into knitting wool, and hear the clatter as the machines are switched on. History comes alive for both adults and children as they see just how low a Victorian child would have had to crawl under moving machinery. Visitors can also see the mill's original air raid shelter and to trace the development of 'power' from waterwheel to steam engines and boilers.

Coldharbour mill is also the permanent home of the 'New World Tapestry', a hidden treasure of international appeal. The largest stitched tapestry in the world, it tells the story of the colonisation of the Americas and the part in particular that the West Country played. Tales of exploration, adventure and romance are told through the 23 panels on display, with many famous characters from the past on show, such as Queen Elizabeth I, Sir Walter Raleigh, Sir Francis Drake, Guy Fawkes, Shakespeare, Pocahontas to name a few. The tapestry was designed by Tom Mor in a humorous, cartoon like form, and was stitched by over 250 volunteers in centres across Devon and Dorset, taking 20 years to complete.

The mill runs a special event programme throughout the year, a lively educational programme and offers conference facilities and group discounts. It also produces an exclusive range of Devon and Somerset tartan, worsted knitting wool and woollen floor rugs on site which can be bought at the shop or via e-mail. Set in the Culm valley, visitors are able to enjoy riverside walks, picnics by the river or lunch in the Waterside Restaurant. Open April-October 7 days a week 10.30am - 5pm; November -March Monday to Friday (phone for details).

Sidmouth

View Along The Coast

Like many other English resorts Sidmouth's success has much to do with Napoleon Bonaparte and his conquest of Europe. Barred from the continent and their favoured resorts by the Emperor, the leisured classes were forced to find diversion and entertainment in Great Britain. At the same time sea bathing had suddenly become fashionable so these years were a boom time for the south coast, even as far west as Sidmouth that, until then, had been a poverty stricken village dependent on fishing. However, the village's spectacular position at the mouth of the River Sid, flanked by dramatic red cliffs soaring to over 500 feet high, and its pebbled beach assured its popularity with newcomers. A grand Esplanade, lined with handsome Georgian residences, was constructed and, between 1800 and 1820, Sidmouth's population doubled as the aristocratic and well-to-do built substantial 'cottages' in and around the town. Many of these have since been converted into impressive hotels.

One of the town's earliest visitors was Jane Austen who came here in 1801 and, according to Austen family tradition, it was at Sidmouth that she fell in love with a clergyman whom she would have married if he had not mysteriously disappeared or possibly died. Other novelists to visit the resort include William Makepeace Thackery, who featured the town as Baymouth in his semi-autobiographical work *Pendennis* (published in 1848), and, in the Edwardian

Sidmouth Folk Festival

Norman Lockyer Observatory

Sidmouth, Devon EX10 0YQ
Tel: 01395 512096

There are few public access observatories in Britain; the **Norman Lockyer Observatory** has a planetarium and large telescopes, including those used to discover helium and establish the sciences of astrophysics. Lockyer's achievements include the establishment of meteorology, astro- archaeology, the science journal, Nature, the Science Museum and government departments fro Science and Education. The radio station commemorates the contribution of Sir Ambrose Fleming, a local hero, to the invention of the radio valve. Programme of public events available from local tourist offices and libraries, or contact The Observatory Secretary or phone 01395 512096 for party bookings.

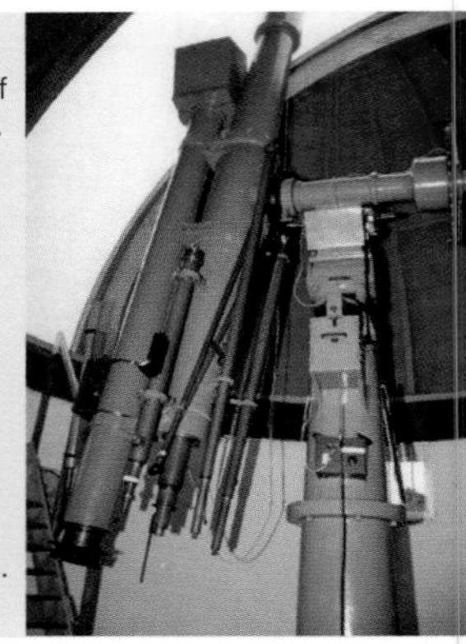

era, Beatrix Potter. In 1819, in order to escape his creditors, the Duke of Kent moved to Sidmouth and his house is now the Royal Glen Hotel. Attempting to keep his whereabouts secret, the duke had his mail redirected to Salisbury and each week he would ride there to collect his letters. However, he could not conceal his delight in his young daughter, Princess Victoria (later Queen Victoria), and he would push her in a little carriage along the Esplanade, stopping passers-by to tell them to look carefully at the little girl "for one day she would be their Queen." Half a century later, Queen Victoria presented a stained glass window to Sidmouth parish church in dutiful memory of her father.

A walk around the town reveals a wealth of attractive buildings and, amazingly for such a small place, Sidmouth boasts nearly 500 listed buildings. Along with the elegant villas and houses and the parish Church of St Giles and St Nicholas, which dates from the 15th century, there is a rather curious structure known as the **Old Chancel** that is a glorious hotch-potch of styles and was built using bits and pieces salvaged from, amongst other buildings, the parish church, when it was renovated by the Victorians.

Close to the seafront is the **Sid Vale Heritage Centre** that portrays the varied history of this elegant resort through old photographs, costumes, Victoriana and artefacts that once belonged to famous residents. The geology and archaeology of the area is also explored. The museum is open daily (except Sundays) from Easter to October and on certain days guided tours of the town leave from here led by the museum staff. Sidmouth seems an unlikely place for an observatory but, in 1912, Sir Joseph Norman Lockyer founded the **Norman Lockyer Observatory** for astronomical and meteorological research. (see panel above).

Just outside the town and set in unspoilt countryside is the **Donkey Sanctuary**, home to around 500 donkeys, which was founded in 1969 by Dr

Elizabeth Svendsen. Open all year round, the sanctuary welcome visitors who can stroll around this serene setting.

Around Sidmouth

Sidford

1½ miles NE of Sidmouth on the A375

As its name suggests, Sidford stands beside a narrow stretch of the River Sid – one of the shortest rivers in England – that rises from spring-fed waters to the east of Ottery St Mary and tumbles and twists down a narrow valley for just four miles before entering Lyme Bay at Sidmouth. The village is famous for its Norman packhorse **Bridge**, dating from the 12th century, which has played an important part in local history over the centuries, not least during the Civil War when there was a skirmish here in 1644.

Sidbury

2½ miles NE of Sidmouth on the A375

A charming and ancient village, Sidbury's **Church of St Peter and St Giles** boasts the unique amenity of a powder room, although in this case the room over the porch was not the preserve of ladies but a place where gunpowder was stored during the days when Napoleon was expected to land in England at any moment. The church is also noted for its Saxon crypt – a rough-walled room just nine feet by ten feet located under the chancel floor that dates from 670 – that was rediscovered during restoration work in 1898. Other treasures include a remarkable 500-year-old font with a square iron lock that was intended to protect the Holy Water in the basin from witches and a number of curious carvings on the Norman tower. In September each year, the church, which is open for guided tours one afternoon a week in the summer, is the setting for the traditional Sidbury Fair.

Sidbury is also home to the last working watermill on the River Sid and, now carefully restored, it is open to the public as **Sidbury Mill and Art Gallery**. Although it is nearly 100 years since the mill's massive waterwheel turned it remains a feature of the village whilst the gallery displays arts and crafts by local artists.

Above the village, to the southwest, stands **Sidbury Castle** that is not, in fact, a castle at all but the site of an Iron Age hillfort and, from here, there are some spellbinding views of the coastline extending from Portland Bill to Berry Head. Meanwhile, to the northeast of Sidbury lies one of east Devon's hidden gems – **Sand House and Gardens**. Situated in a quiet valley, this historic house dates, principally, from the Elizabethan era and has been in the unbroken ownership of the same family since 1561. Members of the family lead guided tours of the house where a wealth of period interior features can be seen whilst the gardens, which extend for six acres, incorporate a sunny terrace, shady woodland, manicured lawns and colourful borders. The house is open on a limited basis between June and September whilst the gardens are open every Sunday to Tuesday from April to September.

Branscombe Church

Salcombe Regis

1½ miles E of Sidmouth off the A3052

Found set back from the coast in a tiny valley, this unspoilt and secluded village takes on an altogether different atmosphere at the time of its annual Country Fair. The village's ancient church stands over the combe that slopes gently down to the sea and there are red sandstone cliffs on the shore.

Branscombe

4 miles E of Sidmouth off the A3052

The coastal scenery around Branscombe is some of the finest in the southwest, with great towers of chalk rising from overgrown landslips, whilst legend has it that this ancient village takes its name from its position at the foot of two branching combes. A scattering of farmhouses and cottages, this is believed to be one of England's longest villages and, along with the 12th century Church of St Winifred, it has within its boundaries **Branscombe Manor Mill, the Old Bakery and Forge** (National Trust). Recently restored to working order, this water-powered mill provided flour for the adjacent bakery that was, until 1987, the last traditional bakery still operating in Devon. Here the old baking equipment has been preserved whilst the rest of the building is now a tea room with information displays in the outbuildings. Meanwhile, the Forge is still working on a regular basis and the blacksmith sells the ironwork produced here.

Beer

7 miles E of Sidmouth on the B3174

Set between the high white chalk cliffs of Beer Head and Seaton Hole, this picturesque fishing village, where the local fishing fleet can still be seen in the sheltered cove, has a long history of smuggling, lace-making and quarrying. Beer stone has been excavated here since Roman times and, much prized for carving, the results can be seen in countless Devon churches as well as further afield as it has been used in the construction of the cathedrals at Exeter and Winchester, at St Paul's and Westminster Abbey and at the Tower of London and Windsor Castle. Meanwhile, in 1839, it was Beer lace-makers who supplied the trimmings for Queen Victoria's wedding dress.

Beer

The Beach, Beer

The underground caverns of **Beer Quarry Caves** date back to Roman times and, throughout their working history, the caves were always quarried by hand, never by heavy machinery. Although the quarry closed nearly 100 years ago, visitors can now explore the caves during a one hour guided tour (when they are open between the end of March and the end of October) and discover not only what life was like underground but also the other uses to which the caves were put. Along with the secret chapel used by Catholics during times of persecution, the caves were a favourite haunt of smugglers and, in particular, of Jack Rattenbury, the county's most notorious smuggler who, in 1837, published his *Memoirs*

The Bay Tree Guest House

11 Seafield Road, Seaton, Devon EX12 2QS
Tel: 01297 24611

The charming **Bay Tree Guest House** is found close to Seaton's town centre, the famous electric tramway and opposite Seafield Gardens, with their children's play area. Owned and personally run by Hazel Cartwright, this spacious Victorian terrace house offers superb guest accommodation in a choice of three large en-suite rooms – some of which have sea views.

A friendly and relaxed establishment, Hazel serves a fantastic full English breakfast (with vegetarian options) that is ideal for anyone wishing to explore the delights of the surrounding area. Children are welcome.

of a Smuggler after he had become a law abiding fisherman. On the outskirts of Beer lies **Pecorama**, an attraction that the whole family can enjoy.

Seaton

7½ miles E of Sidmouth on the B3172

Situated at the mouth of the River Axe and sheltered by the white cliffs of Beer Head and the red sandstone of Haven Cliff, this pleasant seaside town of mainly Victorian and Edwardian buildings was once quite a significant port. However, by the 16th century the estuary had silted up with stones and pebbles and it was not until the wealthy Victorians came here and built their villas (and, in 1877, one of the first concrete bridges in the world) that Seaton was granted a new lease of life. The self-confident architecture of those times gives the little town an attractive appearance that is enhanced by its well-maintained public parks and gardens, manicured bowling greens, extensive walled promenade, pretty harbour and vast pebbled beach.

Found on the top floor of the Town Hall, the **Axe Valley Heritage Museum** has a large collection of photographs and other documents that illustrate the town's past whilst there are also displays detailing the natural history, archaeology and geology of the Axe Valley. The museum is open weekdays from May until the end of October. From Seaton there is a particularly attractive method of travelling along the Axe Valley – the **Seaton Tramway**. Linking the coastal resort with the ancient town of Colyton, three miles inland, the electric tram follows the course of the river and passengers in the open top double decker tramcars have an excellent view of the valley and also the new **Nature Reserve** along the way that is home to numerous ducks and waterfowl as well as herons, cormorants and kingfishers.

Colyton

8½ miles NE of Sidmouth on the B3161

An ancient village, and a former market town, Colyton dates back to around 700 and it featured as 'Culitone' in the *Domesday Book*. Throughout its long history, Colyton has been an important agricultural and commercial centre and, at one time, had its own corn mill, tannery, saw mill and iron foundry – it remains the home of the country's last oak bark tannery. The village's part-Norman **St Andrew's Church** is, undoubtedly, the most prominent feature and, along with having an unusual 14th century octagonal lantern tower, fragments of a Saxon cross were also found in the building. Nearby are the Vicarage of 1529 and the Old Church House, a part-medieval building that was enlarged in 1612 and that was used as a Grammar School until 1928.

Just to the north of Colyton are the exceptional remains of **Colcombe Castle**, which dates from the 16th and 17th centuries, whilst, to the south, lies **Great House**, which was built on the road to Colyford by a wealthy Elizabethan merchant. Meanwhile, to the west lies **Countryside Park Farway** that offers breathtaking views, woodland nature trails, both traditional and rare breed farm animals and a children's indoor play area. There is also a licensed restaurant and the park is open daily from the end of March to the beginning of November.

To the south of Colyton lies its pretty sister village, **Colyford**, whose main street is lined with ancient thatched cottages and characterful houses. Here, too, is an old filling station that was used by Lawrence of Arabia on his late and fateful journey. Colyford lies on the Seaton Tramway route as it travels up the valley to Colyton.

Otterton

3 miles SW of Sidmouth off the B3178

This delightful village has a charming mix of traditional cob and thatch cottages, along with other buildings constructed from the distinctive local red sandstone, and, amongst these is the tower of St Michael's parish church. Nearby, stands a manor house that was built in the 11th century as a small priory belonging to Mont St Michel, Normandy, and that is now divided into private residences.

The *Domesday Book* recorded a mill here on the banks of the River Otter and it almost certainly stood on the site of the present **Otterton Mill**. The last working mill on the river and one of the largest in Devon in the Middle Ages, this is a handsome, part-medieval building that was restored in the 1970s. The Mill Museum explains the history of the building and, also, the machinery whilst the mill continues to produce organic wholemeal flour that can be purchased here.

Another interesting feature of this village is the little stream that runs down Fore Street and, at the bottom of the hill, this beck joins the River Otter that is only a couple of miles from its estuary near Budleigh Salterton. There is a delightful riverside walk downstream whilst, upstream, the path stretches further to Ottery St Mary, some ten miles away.

Budleigh Salterton

5 miles SW of Sidmouth on the B3178

With its trim Victorian villas, broad promenade and a spotlessly clean beach flanked by 500-foot-high red sandstone cliffs, Budleigh Salterton retains its genteel 19th century resort atmosphere. Victorian tourists 'of the better sort' noted, with approval, that the two-mile long beach was of pink shingle rather than sand – sand, apparently, attracted a rowdier kind of holidaymaker – whilst the steeply-shelving beach was another

Bicton Park Botanical Gardens

East Budleigh, near Budleigh Salterton, Devon EX9 7BJ
Tel: 01395 568465 Fax: 01395 568374
e-mail: info@bictongardens.co.uk
website: www.bictongardens.co.uk

Spanning three centuries of horticultural history, **Bicton Park Botanical Gardens** are set in the picturesque Otter Valley. The 63-acre park's oldest ornamental area is the Italian Garden, created in the axial style of Versailles landscaper André le Nôtre in around 1735. By that time, formal designs were becoming unfashionable in England, which may explain why the garden was located out of view of the manor house. Today, the full grandeur of the Italian Garden can be seen from the spacious restaurant in the classically styled Orangery, built at the beginning of the 19th century.

Bicton's high-domed Palm House, one of the world's most beautiful garden buildings, was the first of many developments between 1820 and 1850. Others included an important collection of conifers in the Pinetum, now the subject of a rare species conservation project, and St Mary's Church, where Queen Victoria once worshipped.

A large museum reflects changes in agriculture and rural life generally over the past 200 years. The Grade I listed gardens, which are open all year, also feature a narrow-gauge railway, a gift shop, garden centre and children's indoor and outdoor play areas.

deterrent. The sea here is still a place better suited to paddling than swimming as, on some days, there is a strong undertow. One famous Victorian visitor to Budleigh Salterton was the celebrated artist Sir John Everett Millais, who stayed here during the summer of 1870 in the curiously-shaped house called **The Octagon**. It was beside the beach that he painted his most famous work, *The Boyhood of Raleigh*, using his two sons and a local ferryman as models.

However, the town goes back much further than the days of strolling along the promenade and sea bathing. Its name is derived from the salt pans at the mouth of the River Otter that brought great prosperity to the town during the Middle Ages and the little port was, then, busy with ships loading salt and wool. Unfortunately, by 1450, the Otter estuary had silted up and the salt pans had flooded and Budleigh's days as a bustling port were over.

For an insight into the history of the town and surrounding area there is the **Fairlynch Museum**, which can be found on the seafront.

Covering the whole of the river estuary, the **Otter Estuary Nature Reserve** includes areas of salt marsh, tidal mudflats, grazing marsh and redbuds that provide an interesting and varied habitat as well as it being an important area of over-wintering birds. There are footpaths on both sides of the estuary with viewing platforms (on the western side) and a hide (on the eastern).

Yettington

4½ miles W of Sidmouth off the A3178

Just to the south of the village lies **Hayes Barton**, a fine E-shaped Tudor house that is famous as being the birthplace, in 1552, of Sir Walter Raleigh and the family's pew can still be seen in All Saints' Church (dated 1537) and carved with their now sadly defaced coat of arms. The church also contains a series of more than fifty 16th century bench-ends that were carved by local artisans into weird and imaginative depictions of their various trades.

Meanwhile, to the northeast lies **Bicton Park Botanical Gardens**, one of the county's most magnificent historic gardens (see panel opposite).

Harpford

2½ miles NW of Sidmouth off the A3052

Occupying a particularly attractive location on the east bank of the River Otter and with wooded hills behind, Harpford has a 13th century church with an impressive tower and, in the churchyard, is a memorial to a former vicar of Harpford, Rev Augustus Toplayd who, in 1775, wrote the enduring hymn *Rock of Ages*.

A couple of miles further west across the river lies **Aylesbeare Common**, an RSPB sanctuary that covers one of the best stretches of heathland in the area. It is home to numerous species of birds including the Dartford Warbler, Stonechats, Tree Pipits and the Nightjar.

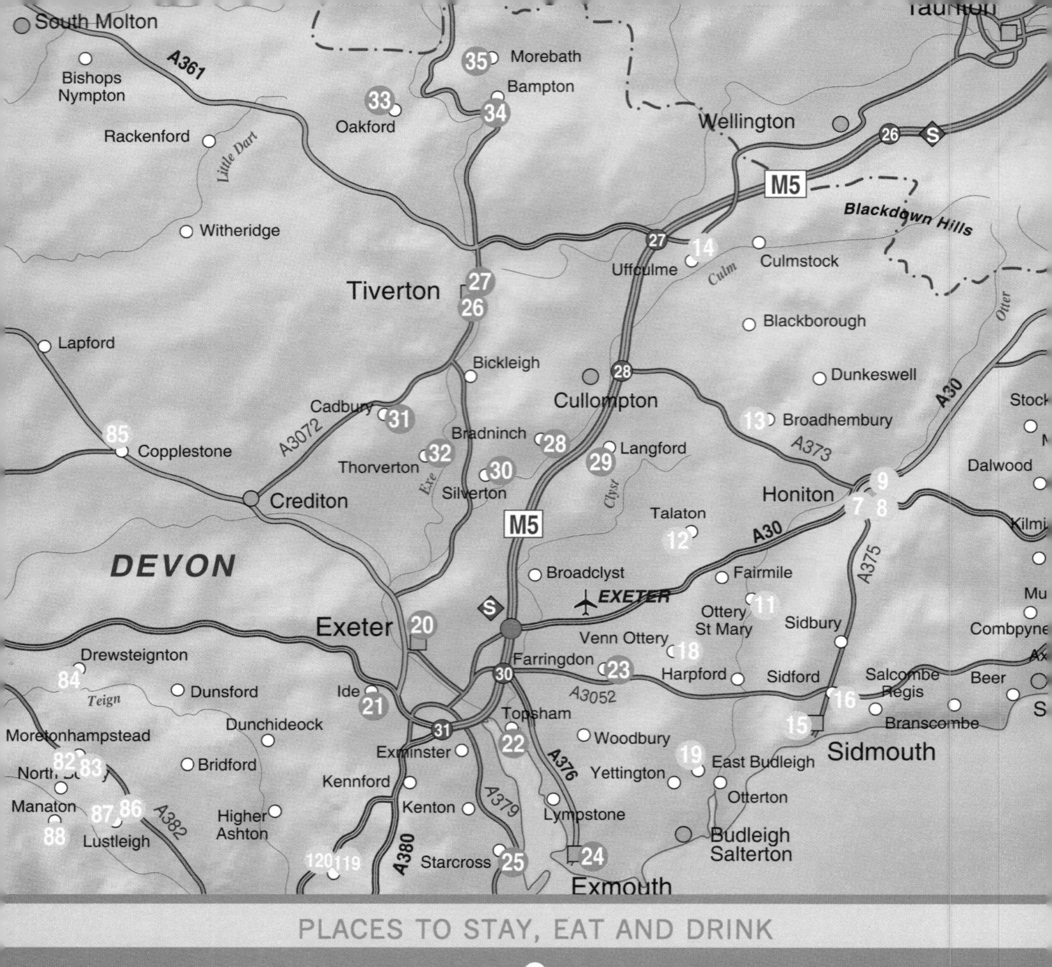

PLACES TO STAY, EAT AND DRINK

Exeter's Underground Passages, Exeter	20	Historic Attraction	p35
The Poachers Inn, Ide, Exeter	21	Pub, Food and Accommodation	p36
La Petite Maison, Topsham	22	Restaurant	p37
Home Farm, Farringdon, Exeter	23	Bed and Breakfast	p37
Quentance Farm, Exmouth	24	B&B and Self Catering	p38
The Galleon Inn, Starcross, Exeter	25	Pub, Food and Accommodation	p40
Tiverton Castle, Tiverton	26	Historic Attraction	p42
Grand Western Horse Boat Co., Tiverton	27	Canal Trips	p43
Diggerland, Bradninch, Tiverton	28	Family Attraction	p44
Newcourt Barton, Langford, Cullompton	29	Bed and Breakfast	p45
The Lamb Inn, Silverton	30	Pub and Restaurant	p46
Fursdon, Cadbury, Exeter	31	Self Catering	p47
The Thorverton Arms, Thorverton, Exeter	32	Pub, Restaurant and Accommodation	p48
The Red Lion Inn, Oakford	33	Pub, Restaurant and Accommodation	p49
The Exeter Inn, Bampton	34	Pub, Restaurant and Accommodation	p50
Lodfin Farm, Morebath, Bampton	35	Bed and Breakfast	p51

● Denotes entries in other chapters

2 Exeter and the Exe Valley

The valley of the River Exe is dominated by Devon's county town – the city of Exeter. The home of the Celtic Dumnonii tribe, it became the Roman's southwest stronghold and, although Isca as they called Exeter, was a substantial settlement there are few Roman remains to be seen today save for the Bath House that was discovered as recently as 1971. An abbey was founded here in the 7th century that turned Exeter into a major ecclesiastical centre but it was the Normans who constructed the magnificent St Peter's Cathedral that still dominates the city and that remains one of the best examples of the Decorated style of church architecture in the country. The city, too, was an important port and the area around the historic quayside, which reached its peak of activity in the 18th century, is a fascinating place where the old warehouses and port buildings have been given a new lease of life as speciality shops, cafés, restaurants and visitor attractions.

Quayside, Exeter

The Exe estuary stretches for six miles from Exeter to the sea and this is a place of international importance that supports an amazing diversity of bird life. The Exeter Ship Canal, one of the first to be constructed in England since Roman times, flows along the western bank of the estuary and, now the preserve of pleasure craft, the canal and its towpaths provide another opportunity to discover the wealth of wildlife along the estuary.

Exmouth, literally, stands at the mouth of the River Exe and this was, until the 18th century, little more than a small fishing village. However, its superb position, mild climate and the newly found craze for sea bathing saw Exmouth become one of the earliest seaside resorts in the country. Dubbed the 'Bath of the West', it remains a popular resort that is noted for its elegant buildings although its harbour and docks are still commercially active.

Travelling up the Exe Valley from Exeter there are quaint scattered villages set out in this glorious countryside and the only town of any size along the riverbanks is Tiverton. Built on the prosperity that it gained from the woollen trade, this ancient town developed around its castle that was constructed on the orders of Henry I. Along with several splendid stately homes, such as Fursdon, Knightshayes Court, Powderham Castle and Killerton House, the land around the Exe Valley is littered with prehistoric remains. In particular, there is Killerton Clump, an Iron Age earthwork, Cadbury Castle, a hill fort set some 700 feet above sea level and from where there are excellent views, and Woodbury Castle, another Iron Age hill fort where the numerous ditches and ramparts of this local chieftains stronghold can still be seen.

Exeter

The regional capital of the southwest, Exeter is a lively and thriving city and county town, with a majestic Norman cathedral, many fine old buildings, a wealth of excellent museums and a history that stretches back over 2,000 years. The present High Street was already in place some 200 years before the Romans arrived here and it was part of an ancient ridge way that crossed the West Country. The inhabitants then were the Celtic tribe of the Dumnonii and it was they who named the River Eisca meaning 'a river abounding in fish'.

The Romans made Isca their southwestern stronghold and surrounded the settlement with a massive defensive wall but, although most of this wall has now disappeared, a spectacular **Roman Bath House** (or Caldarium) was discovered in the Cathedral Close in 1971. During the Dark Ages that followed the Roman withdrawal from Britain, the city became a major ecclesiastical centre and, in 670, King Cenwealh founded an abbey on the site that is now occupied by the

Cathedral Close

Exeter Cathedral

cathedral. The abbey, along with the rest of Exeter, was ransacked by the Vikings in the 9th century and these invaders occupied the city twice before King Alfred finally expelled them.

The Normans were the next to arrive in the city although it was not until 20 years after the Battle of Hastings that William the Conqueror finally took possession of Exeter after a siege that lasted 18 days. Following this, William ordered the construction of **Rougemont Castle**, the gatehouse and tower of which are still standing at the top of Castle Street. Here, planted in and around the original moat of the castle, and with a section of the Roman walls as a backdrop, are **Rougemont Gardens** – a tranquil haven in the heart of this bustling city. In the 12th century the Normans began building **St Peter's Cathedral** and this was not completed until 1206 but, just 50 years later, all except the unique Norman twin towers, which still dominate the skyline today, were demolished and the present cathedral begun. These years saw the development of the Decorated Gothic style and Exeter cathedral is a sublime example of this appealing form of church architecture: the 300-foot-long nave contains the longest unbroken stretch of Gothic vaulting in the world whilst the west front is equally impressive with its staggering display of more than 60 sculptures, carved between 1327-69, which depict a curious mix of Biblical characters, soldiers, priests and Saxon and Norman kings. Other treasures within the cathedral include an intricately carved choir screen from about 1320, a 15th century astronomical clock that is reputed to be the inspiration for the children's nursery rhyme *Hickory, Dickory Dock*, a monumental organ and the tallest bishop's throne in England, with a 59-foot high canopy that was carved for Bishop Stapledon in 1316.

Whilst the cathedral certainly dominates the city there are other ecclesiastical buildings that are well worth seeking out. **St Nicholas' Priory**, founded in 1087, is the only remaining former monastic building to survive in the city centre and it is also an exceptional example of a small Norman priory. A house of the Benedictine order, visitors can see the Norman undercroft and kitchen whilst the guest

Quayside and Maritime Museum

wing of the priory went on to became an Elizabethan merchant's home and here there is some superb, elaborate Tudor plasterwork. The priory is also home to a display of the Devonshire and Dorset Regiment. Meanwhile, the **Church of St Mary Steps** has not only a beautifully preserved Norman font but also an ancient 'Matthew the Miller' tower clock that is named after a medieval miller who was noted for his undeviating punctuality. The church stands in Stepcote Hill, a narrow cobbled and steeped thoroughfare that, until as late as 1778, was the main road into Exeter from the west.

There are, of course, other interesting buildings in the city and those worthy of note include the remarkable **Guildhall**, in the High Street, and **The Tucker's Hall**, in Fore Street. Built in 1330 and used as the Town Hall ever since, the Guildhall is, now, one of the oldest municipal buildings in the country and, whilst the interior is still redolent of the Middle Ages, the great hall was remodelled in the mid 15th century and the Elizabethans added a striking, though rather fussy, portico. Meanwhile, Tucker's Hall was built in 1471 for the Company of Weavers, Fullers and Shearmen and it is the only surviving trades guild in the city. Its imposing architecture, along with its exceptional carved panelling and collection of rare silver, make this a place well worth visiting and it is open every Thursday morning throughout the year with additional days during between June and September.

Both the Church and trade has played an important part in the prosperity of Exeter but it was, too, once an important port and this is reflected in the **Historic Quayside**, from which the export trade in woollen cloth reached its peak in the 18th century. A fascinating complex of old warehouses, craft shops and cafés, at the centre of the quayside is the dignified **Custom House**, which dates from 1681. This is also the earliest substantial brick building in the city and it was used by HM Customs and Excise right up until 1989. Today, the Custom House can be visited on one of the city's Red Coat Guided Tours and visitors will be able to see the wonderfully ornate plaster ceilings of the first floor rooms. The development of the quayside can be discovered at the **Quay House Visitor**

Custom House

the cinema, the centre also looks at other forms of visual entertainment from prehistoric shadow plays, through 18th century peep shows to Victorian optical toys and magic lanterns. The hundreds of items on display were collected by the film-maker Bill Douglas and his friend Peter Jewell and, after Bill's death in 1991, the collection was donated to the University of Exeter. The centre can be found on the university's main campus.

Centre, which also shows a presentation of the city from Roman times to the present day. The centre is open daily from the end of March to the end of October and at weekends in the winter.

There are some other excellent museums in the city and they include the **Royal Albert Memorial Museum**, open Monday to Saturday, which has a series of displays and exhibitions that are of local, regional and national importance. Meanwhile, the **Bill Douglas Centre** concentrates very much on optical entertainments and, in particular, films. Whilst the stars of over a century of movies are well represented, along with the history of

The university campus is set on a hill overlooking Exeter and the **University of Exeter Gardens** not only have a special botanical garden and arboretum but they also offer superb views of the tors of Dartmoor beyond the campus. Here, too, can be found **Exeter University Sculpture Walk** where some 23 sculptures, including works by Barbara Hepworth and Henry Moore, are set out in both the grounds and within the university buildings. Meanwhile, back in the centre of Exeter is one of the city's most unusual

Exeter's Underground Passages

Tel: 01392 665887

Dating from the 14th century, **Exeter's Underground Passages** are a unique attraction – the only one of its kind open to the public in Britain. On guided tours beneath the streets of Exeter and through displays and a video, visitors can discover how water was brought into Exeter. During school holidays, throughout the year, there are special activities from quizzes to treasure hunts. Information about opening times can be obtained from Exeter Tourist Information Centre.

The Poachers Inn

High Street, Ide, near Exeter, Devon EX2 9RW
Tel: 01392 273847 Fax: 01392 273847
e-mail: chris@cistephens.freeserve.co.uk

Tucked away in this quiet village, yet just minutes from Exeter, **The Poachers Inn** is a wonderful, traditional village inn that provides both locals and visitors with outstanding hospitality. Along with offers of five real ales from the bar, landlords, Kelvin Burnett and Christopher Stephens have three superior en-suite guest rooms. However, it is for its food, prepared by chef John Hadley, that this inn is particularly popular. Specialising in fish dishes, there is always an extensive choice and it is essential to book at weekends.

attractions, **Exeter's Underground Passages**. (see panel on page 35)

Flowing between Exeter quay and the docks at Exmouth is the **Exeter Ship Canal**. The first canal to be built in Britain since Roman times, it was this waterway that enabled the city to grow into the important port it once was. Construction started on the canal in the 16th century when ships attempting to navigate up the River Exe had their journey obstructed by shoals, tidal restrictions and fishing weirs that were purposely enlarged by Countess Isabella de Fortibus who was concerned about trade being diverted from Topsham. Over the next century or so the canal was extended and enlarged as the size of ships increased and, today, it remains very much as it was when it was redesigned again in 1827. Still used by commercial traffic until the 1960s, the canal is now the preserve of pleasure craft and, during the summer, there are cruises along its full length whilst canoes can be hired from Exeter quay. A unique feature of the canal are the towpaths on each bank that enabled two horses to tow larger vessels and it was also against local byelaws to set sails along the canal. Those travelling the length of the canal, either by boat or on foot, will not only see a wealth of wildlife but also pass the **Paper Mill** at Countess Weir that dates from 1816 although there has been a corn mill on this site since 1284.

Around Exeter

Topsham

4 miles SE of Exeter off the A376

Once famous for its shipbuilding industry, surprisingly Topsham was once a larger port than Exeter and, today, its rich maritime history is reflected in the wealth of fine 17th and 18th century merchants' houses, many built in the Dutch style, which are such a feature of the town. Much of the town is now a conservation area and, housed in one of its finest late 17th century buildings, is **Topsham Museum**, which also has a courtyard and estuary garden with fine views out over the River Exe. Along

The River Exe, Topsham

with the furnished period rooms, the museum holds an excellent local history collection that portrays Topsham's maritime, commercial and shipbuilding past. Open several afternoons between April and October, the museum has a café and home-made teas are served in its riverside gardens.

Woodbury

6½ miles SE of Exeter off the B3179

The parish Church of St Swithin, in this large village, has achieved a rather sad kind of fame as its vicar, Rev J Loveband Fulford, when he arrived here in 1846, cut great chunks out of its medieval rood screen so that his parishioners could see him more clearly. Fortunately he left untouched the fine 15th century Beer stone font, the Jacobean pulpit and the interesting memorials.

La Petite Maison

35 Fore Street, Topsham, Devon EX3 0HR
Tel: 01392 873660
e-mail: user@lapetitemaison.fsnet.co.uk
website: www.lapetitemaison.co.uk

In the elegant surroundings of **La Petite Maison**, found in the heart of Topsham, customers can enjoy some of the best cuisine to be found in Devon. Owners Douglas and Elizabeth Pestell, along with their daughter Naomi, offer a superb range of dishes on the constantly changing menus that include such delights as Breast of guinea

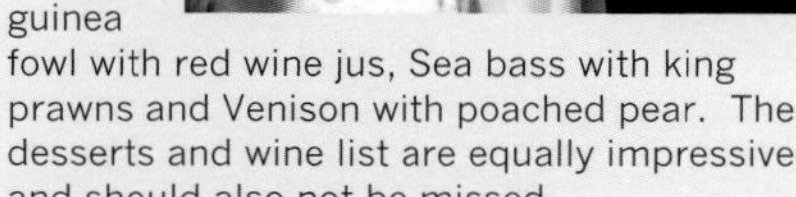

fowl with red wine jus, Sea bass with king prawns and Venison with poached pear. The desserts and wine list are equally impressive and should also not be missed.

Home Farm

Farringdon, near Exeter, Devon EX5 2HY
Tel: 01395 232293 Fax: 01395 233298

Despite being just a short drive from Exeter, **Home Farm** occupies a wonderfully scenic position, surrounded by acres of glorious farmland. The home of Alex and Rupert Thompson, this wonderful house was, surprisingly, only built in 1989 but it has an elegance that goes back to an earlier age. Beautifully decorated and furnished, Alex and Rupert offer exceptional bed and breakfast accommodation in a choice of three guest rooms. Children are very welcome here and, along with breakfast, a home-cooked dinner is available by arrangement.

To the east of the village lies the famous **Woodbury Common**, an expanse of unspoilt moorland that, at more than 560 feet above sea level, provides some spectacular views and, at several points, the English Channel can be seen on one side and the Exe estuary on the other. Also commanding extensive views is **Woodbury Castle**, the remains of an Iron Age hill fort that comprise numerous ditches and ramparts and the castle was probably a stronghold of a local chieftain.

Just to the north of Woodbury lies **Crealy Adventure Park**, a magnificent and award-winning all-weather entertainment centre that includes the largest indoor play area for children in the country. There are also numerous other amusements and the park is open daily all year round (except Christmas).

Lympstone

6½ miles SE of Exeter off the A376

Set beside the Exe estuary, Lympstone looks out across the water to the impressive outline of Powderham Castle on the other bank. The old part of the village is a delight, with its narrow streets, little courts, ancient cottages and tiny harbour whilst, on the beach, is a rather elaborate Italianate clock tower that was erected in 1885 by WH Peter. Set facing the sea, **Peter's Tower** commemorates his wife, Mary Jane, who was noted for her good works amongst the poor of the village.

Exmouth

9 miles SE of Exeter on the A376

Up until the early 18th century Exmouth was nothing more than a small fishing village that lay, as its name suggests, at the mouth of the River Exe. However, it was its superb position, with a splendid beach and glorious coastal scenery, and its mild climate that led to the village becoming one of the earliest seaside resorts in Devon and it is the county's oldest. Dubbed the 'Bath of the West', Exmouth was a place that welcomed the very highest echelons of fashionable society and both Lady Byron

and Lady Nelson came to stay in lodgings in **The Beacon**, an elegant Georgian terrace overlooking the Madeira Walk and the Esplanade. This terrace lay at the heart of life in Regency Exmouth and here can be found the **Assembly Rooms**, where most of the social events were held in the late 18th and early 19th centuries, and also **Nelson House**, the home of Lady Nelson in her latter years.

However, despite this early success the resort suffered a setback in the mid 19th century when Isambard Kingdom Brunel routed his Great Western Railway line along the other side of the Exe estuary (incidentally creating one of the most scenic railway journeys still possible in England) and it was not until a branch line reached Exmouth in 1861 that business picked up again. Today, Exmouth remains a popular and bustling seaside resort, with wonderful views westward from the promenade, but its harbour and docks are still commercially active and along with the fishing boats and coasters, there is a summer passenger service to Starcross. Meanwhile, from the marina there are cruises along the River Exe to Topsham.

Whilst in the town it is well worth finding time to visit the **Exmouth Museum** that not only holds an interesting collection of artefacts relating to the old village but that also has a 1930s living room and a Victorian kitchen. Naturally the maritime and natural history of the estuary is also explored along with local industries. The museum, which is housed in the old town council stables and an adjoining cottage, is open from the beginning of April to the end of October every morning except Sundays and on Tuesday and Thursday afternoons.

Meanwhile, on the outskirts of the town lies **A La Ronde** (National Trust) that has been described as "the most unusual house in Britain." Built in 1796 by the cousins Jane and Mary Parminter, who modelled their dwelling on the Church of San Vitale in Ravenna, this unique 16-sided building has some fantastic interior decoration that includes a shell encrusted gallery, a feather frieze and many 18th century object that the spinsters brought back from their European Grand Tour. The two ladies lived here in magnificent feminist seclusion, forbidding the presence of any man in their house or its 15 acres of grounds.

To the northeast of the town lies **Bystock Nature Reserve**, a place of heath, grassland, woods and boggy areas that is part of the East Devon Heaths Site of Special Scientific Interest. Despite being occupied by the military during World War II, the reserve is now returning to the heathland that, for centuries, was rough grazing for cattle. The network of paths crossing the reserve can be quite rough in places and the paths often follow the tops of narrow, raised banks to avoid boggy ground.

Just along the coast to the east of Exmouth lies **The World of Country**

Life, a wonderful place for all the family that provides a fun and informative introduction to the ways of the countryside. Children will love the Pets' Corner, with the goats, hens, ducks, rabbits, donkeys and miniature Shetland ponies, whilst there is also a Deer Park with both red deer and llamas to feed. Other exhibitions here include vintage agricultural machinery, steam engines and Victorian shops and there is also a restaurant serving delicious home-made dishes.

Exminster

3½ miles SE of Exeter off the A379

Now more a suburb of Exeter, to the north of this old village along the River Exe is **The Old Sludge Beds Nature Reserve**, which was, until 1969, a sewage treatment works but that has, since the works closed, become a wetland area and is now part of the Exe Estuary Site of Special Scientific Interest. There are paths through the reserve and they allow visitors to view a wide variety of wetland birds making their homes in the reed beds.

Kennford

3½ miles S of Exeter off the A38

Set on the slopes of Great Haldon Hill and beside the River Kenn, Kennford is a good example of the 'street village' as almost all its houses stand on either side of the one road through the village. This was once the main route to the far southwest until, thankfully, the main A38 was constructed and took the heavy traffic away from the village.

Just south of the village lies the Haldon ridge that climbs to a height of some 800 feet above sea level and, in the 1920s, the Forestry Commission established **Haldon Forest** here to produce timber. This work continues today but the forest has also become an important habitat for many species of wildlife and, in 1992, the forest was designated a Site of Special Scientific Interest by English Nature. Visitors can wander along a network of waymarked footpaths through the forest and

discover for themselves the wealth of birds, insects and animals here.

Kenton

6 miles SE of Exeter on the A379

Founded in Saxon times and recorded as 'Chentone' in the *Domesday Book*, this picturesque village is famous for its glorious late 14th century church whose tower stands over 100 feet tall and is decorated with a wonderful assortment of ornate carvings. Inside, there is more rich carving in the south porch and in the Beer stone arcades of the nave. The pulpit is a 15th century original that was rescued and restored after it was found in pieces in 1866 and the massive rood screen, one of the finest in Devon, is a further magnificent testimony to the 15th century wood carver's art.

To the east of the village, and set in a deer park beside the River Exe, is **Powderham Castle**, the historic family home of the Earls of Devon since the late 14th century. Originally built by Sir Philip Courtenay in 1391, most of the present building dates from the 18th century and, along with the magnificent State Rooms, there is a breathtaking Grand Staircase and numerous historic family portraits – some of them by Sir Joshua Reynolds, a Devon man himself. Meanwhile, outside there are the extensive grounds to explore that include the beautiful 18th century woodland walk, the tranquil Rose Garden and, at the Secret Garden, children can pat and chat to a variety of pet animals. A tractor and trailer ride takes visitors around the grounds and to see the working blacksmith and wheelwright. Open most days from April to the end of October, there is also a restaurant and tea rooms here along with a Country Store selling all manner of locally produced goods and foods.

Tiverton

Apart, of course, from Exeter, Tiverton is the only town of any size in the Exe Valley and its original name, 'Twyfyrde', means two fords, and it is here that the River Exe is joined by the River Lowman. The town developed around what is now its oldest building, **Tiverton Castle**, which was originally built in 1106 by Richard de Redvers on the orders of Henry I. (see panel on page 42)

During the Middle Ages, the people of Tiverton seem to have had a very highly developed sense of civic and social responsibility and throughout the town's golden age as a wool town, from the late 1400s to the 18th century, prosperous wool merchants put their wealth to good use. In the early 17th century, George Slee built himself the superb Jacobean mansion in St Peter Street, the **Great House**, and in his will he bequeathed the vast sum of £500 to establish the **Slee Almshouses** that were duly built adjacent to his old residence. Other almshouses, founded by John Waldron and John Greenway are still in use. Along with funding the almshouses, John Greenway also devoted another

Tiverton Castle

Park Hill, Tiverton, Devon EX16 6RP
Tel: 01884 253200 Fax: 01884 254200
e-mail: tiverton.castle@ukf.net
website: www.tivertoncastle.com

Few buildings evoke such an immediate feeling of history as **Tiverton Castle**, which was originally built in the early 12th century by Richard de Redvers, the first Earls of Devon. When this family line died out, in 1293, the Courtenays, who rebuilt and enlarged the castle and regarded it as their "head and chief mansion", succeeded them as Earls. In 1495 Princess Katherine Plantagenet married William Courtenay, who became Earl of Devon, but this royal marriage led to the family's eventual downfall and the senior line died out in 1556. Since then the castle has had various owners down the ages.

Now a peaceful and private house, the buildings, furnishings and exhibits on show here reflect the colourful history of the building and its development. In particular there is a fine collection of Civil War arms and armour, some pieces of which can be tried on. A fascinating place to visit that is set in three acres of private gardens, Tiverton Castle also has self-contained, self-catering apartments for hire and it is licensed for civil weddings.

sizeable portion of his fortune to the restoration of **St Peter's Church** in 1517 when he added a sumptuous porch and chapel, the walls of which are richly decorated with carvings depicting sailing ships of the time. However, Peter Blundell chose a different method of demonstrating his beneficence by endowing Tiverton with a school and it was in the **Old Blundell's School** building of 1604 that the author RD Blackmore received his education. He later used the school as a setting for the first chapter of his novel, *Lorna Doone*. Now a highly regarded public school, Blundell's moved to its present site on the edge of the town in 1880.

Like so many other towns in the country during the mid 18th century, Tiverton suffered a devastating fire in 1731 but one happy outcome of the disaster was the building of **St George's Church** that is, by common consent, the finest Georgian church in Devon. Of particular interest are its elegant period ceilings and galleries.

Open daily, except Sundays, between February and Christmas, the **Tiverton Museum of Mid Devon Life** concentrates on the social history of Tiverton and has a wealth of displays exhibited in its 15 galleries. From a steam locomotive, Devon farm wagons and carts and lace making to a wheelwright's shop, cider making equipment and local archaeology, every aspect of Devon life is explored here. There is also a museum shop.

On the southeastern edge of the town lies a quay that marks the western end of the **Grand Western Canal**, a beautiful, historic canal that was built in 1814 to carry limestone from the quarries at Lowdwells to Tiverton for firing and the production of lime for farming and house building. The original idea was to link the River Exe to Bridgwater and hence the Bristol Channel but this was never achieved and the canal, finally, closed to water traffic in the 1920s.

A couple of miles north of Tiverton lies **Knightshayes Court and Garden** (National Trust), a striking Victorian Gothic mansion that was designed by William Burgess and that was the home of the Heathcoat-Amory family. A rare survivor of the architect's work in Devon, the rich interior displays an opulent combination of medieval romanticism and lavish decoration whilst the contents give a fascinating insight into grand Victorian life. The surrounding gardens are some of the finest in the county and they are renowned for their rare plants and trees along with the formal terraces and the unusual topiary. Beyond there is extensive park and woodland and Knightshayes is open most days between Easter and October.

Topiary Garden at Knightshays Court

Around Tiverton

Bradninch

6½ miles SE of Tiverton off the B3191

This pleasant little village stands on what used to be the main Exeter to Taunton road but, today, it is now, thankfully, bypassed. Of particular note here is the striking parish church, with its crenellated tower spouting gargoyles, and, inside, there is a magnificent 16th century rood screen that is beautifully coloured in gleaming red, blue and gold.

Just to the northeast of the village lies **Diggerland** (see panel below), an exciting adventure park whose rides and activities are based around construction machinery, which is set in the glorious Devon countryside.

Broadclyst

11 miles SE of Tiverton off the B3191

This ancient settlement, which featured in the *Domesday Book*, is a largely unspoilt and well-preserved village and, to the north, lies **Killerton House and Gardens** (National Trust). The elegant 18th century house still retains a family home atmosphere and, inside the former home of the Acland family, there is not only the renowned Killerton costume collection but also a fascinating exhibition on lace. Meanwhile, the 19th century landscaped grounds include a wealth of rare trees, a Victorian rock garden, colourful herbaceous borders and wonderful woodland walks. The grounds, too, are home to **Killerton Clump**, an Iron Age earthwork.

Also part of the Killerton Estate is **Newhall Equestrian**, a working thoroughbred stud breeding National Hunt horses that provides visitors with a unique opportunity to look behind the scenes at the work involved in producing horses ready for the races. Along with the horses, the centre, which is housed in restored listed buildings, includes a coach house with Royal horse drawn vehicles, an equestrian art gallery, saddlers, children's pets corner and a tea rooms.

Diggerland

Tel: 08700 344437
e-mail: mail@diggerland.com
website: www.diggerland.com

Diggerland is an exciting new adventure park, based on the world of construction machinery, which is set in the beautiful Devon countryside at Verbeer Manor and that is within easy reach of the motorway. Suitable for children of all ages, from 1 to 90, Diggerland gives everyone the opportunity of driving real JCBs and dumpers (under fives sitting on an adults lap). There are numerous rides and activities here that are sure to keep the whole family amused for the whole day.

Newcourt Barton

Langford, Cullompton, Devon EX15 1SE
Tel: 01884 277326 Fax: 01884 277326
e-mail: newcourtbarton@btinternet.com
web: www.smoothhound.co.uk/hotels/newcourtbarton

Found in the peaceful hamlet of Langford, yet close to the M5, **Newcourt Barton** is an ideal place for those looking for a relaxing bed and breakfast establishment as either a convenient stopping point or for an extended stay. The traditional farm-house, the home of Helen Hitt and her young family, offers its guests a choice of comfortable colour co-ordinated en-suite bedrooms, a tasty breakfast, a separate cosy guest lounge and, in the substantial garden, there is a tennis court. Children are welcome and coarse fishing is available.

Bickleigh

3½ miles S of Tiverton on the A396

One of the most charming villages in the Exe Valley, Bickleigh is a traditional Devonshire village with a delightful riverside setting, picturesque thatched cottages and pretty gardens. Close to the river lies **Bickleigh Castle**, a fortified and moated medieval manor house that is the former home of the heirs of the Earls of Devon. Still a family home, this once Royalist stronghold has a wealth of treasures within including Tudor furniture and pictures, Civil War arms and armour, 18th and 19th century domestic objects and toys and an exhibition showing the castle's maritime connection. The 17th century farmhouse on the estate is equally atmospheric with its inglenook fireplace, oak beams and ancient bread ovens. However, even older is the 11th century thatched chapel that is the oldest complete building in Devon.

The village's old mill has been restored and is now at the centre of mid Devon's largest rural shopping, eating and recreation complex – **Bickleigh Mill**. Along with the numerous shops, there is a working pottery studio, a licensed restaurant, waterside tea garden and mill streams and trout ponds to explore. Meanwhile, the village's Victorian railway station is now the

Bickleigh Mill

The Lamb Inn

47 Fore Street, Silverton, Devon EX5 4HZ
Tel: 01392 860272 Fax: 01392 860235
e-mail: lamb-inn@easiness.com
website: www.lamb-inn.com

Found in this quiet and pleasant village, that is so well placed for many of east Devon's attractions and both Dartmoor and Exmoor National Parks, is the charming **Lamb Inn**. Dating back over 300 years, the inn was purchased by Alan and Jane Isaac in early 1999 and they completely refurbished the interior before opening their doors. However, despite the extensive work they undertook, none of this delightful building's original character has been lost and, along with the superb inglenook fireplace that adds warmth on a cold night, there are slate floors throughout the main bar area and the separate dining room. The addition of photographs of the local bowling team hanging on the walls indicate that this is very much a village inn but both locals and visitors alike are made welcome here. Now settled here, Jane and Alan have opened a function room that, whilst new, has the same rustic charm as the rest of the inn and, along with being hired out for meetings and dinners, this extension also includes a skittle alley.

Well known for their excellent range of real ales, including local brewery ale direct from the cask, The Lamb Inn has an enviable reputation for the high standard of its food. Served in the small and intimate restaurant or in the bar the menu and the daily specials board offer a mouth-watering array of dishes that also include imaginative vegetarian options. Such is the popularity of the food served here that it is essential to book at the weekend.

Whilst the hospitality found here is second to none what makes The Lamb Inn special is the friendly and welcoming atmosphere generated by Jane and Alan. Before opening the inn they had farmed locally for over 20 years and they still maintain their interest in this area. Meanwhile, the couple's two daughters help out at the inn that further adds to the family atmosphere whilst their son is following the family tradition and has been to agricultural college. Very much a village inn and a meeting place for locals the bell ringers retire to the pub to quench their thirst after bell ringing practice and the bowling club make regular visits.

Devon Railway Centre where not only are there several model railway layouts but also a narrow gauge railway that takes visitors on a train ride to a picturesque riverside picnic area. Here, too, is a museum of railway memorabilia. The centre is opened on a limited basis outside main holiday times.

Bickleigh

Finally, the unique five-arched Bickleigh Bridge that has spanned the River Exe here since 1630 is reputed to have been the inspiration for the famous Simon and Garfunkel song *Bridge over Troubled Water*.

Cadbury

6 miles SW of Tiverton off the A3072

To the north of this delightful hamlet is **Cadbury Castle** that is, in fact, an Iron

FURSDON

Cadbury, Exeter Ex5 5JS
Tel: 01392 860860 Fax: 01392 860126
e-mail: holidays@fursdon.co.uk
website: www.fursdon.co.uk

Few get the chance to stay on an estate as historic as **Fursdon** but David and Catriona, whose family have lived here since the 14th century, offer superb self-catering holiday accommodation in two apartments that are within their elegant manor house.

Surrounded by an estate of over 700 acres, that includes not only the well-kept gardens but also woodland and thatched cottages and farmhouses, the apartments provide the very best in comfortable country house living.

The larger, Park Wing, sleeps six and, as its name suggests, it has magnificent views out over the Park that was landscaped in the 18th century. The apartment's splendid sitting room, complete with open fire, was created out of part of the medieval Great Hall in the 18th century and it has lost nothing of the elegance of that era. Meanwhile, the Garden Wing, which sleeps three, overlooks Fox Garden and this too has an open fire in the sitting room that was once the family schoolroom.

Full of character, both apartments occupy the first floor of the house and each has a modern fitted kitchen. Children are welcome here and guests can use the family tennis court.

The Thorverton Arms

Thorverton, near Exeter, Devon EX5 5NS
Tel: 01392 860205 Fax: 01392 860511
e-mail: thorverton.arms@virgin.net

An ideal touring base for both the north and south coasts of Devon and for Dartmoor, yet found in the centre of a quiet and peaceful village, **The Thorverton Arms** is a quintessential English country inn that offers exceptional hospitality to both locals and visitors alike. Dating back to the 16th century and formerly a coaching inn, this charming old establishment has retained many of its age-old features whilst also being decorated in a stylish and sophisticated manner to provide a light and spacious environment for its patron. Although partners David Ough and Colin Lipscombe have only been here since February 2002, they have quickly put The Thorverton Arms on the map and it now has an enviable reputation for the high standard of its food, drink and accommodation.

Along with always keeping an excellent selection of real ales, as well as a good wine list and all the usual drinks, the inn is a particularly popular place for both lunch and dinner. Austin, the chef, is David's son and, daily, he creates a wonderful array of dishes that are sure to tempt even the most jaded palate. Formal dining in the restaurant is certainly an experience not to be missed and the impressive and imaginative à la carte menu is a sheer delight. Taking the very best of local produce, the dishes here vary from breasts of pigeon with celeriac mash and local venison stroganoff to fillet of trout on a bed of watercress and grilled monkfish tail. Meanwhile, those looking to dine more sparingly can choose from the snack menu that, whilst the dishes are lighter, they exhibit the same creative flair shown in the more formal menu. From salads of tomato, anchovy and capers and lamb hotpot to fishcakes and quail and bacon pasties, there is certainly no compromising on taste here. Children, too, are well catered for as they have their own menu.

Those looking to stay here will find there is choice of four luxury en-suite guest rooms that have all been carefully and individually designed and furnished and are sure to provide the right atmosphere for a restful night's sleep. There is interest, too, at the rear of the inn where, in the patioed beer garden, there is Devon's oldest wisteria tree that has been expertly dated as over 250 years old.

Age hill fort found some 700 feet above sea level and, it is claimed, from here the views are some of the most extensive in Devon. On a clear day both Dartmoor and Exmoor are in full view whilst, beyond, both the Quantocks and Bodmin Moor can be seen. Little more than a mile away stands **Fursdon House**, the 13th century home of one of Devon's oldest families.

Witheridge

9 miles W of Tiverton on the B3137

This ancient village, whose name comes from the Old English for 'ridge of the wethers', has a history that goes back to beyond Saxon times. Evidence, in the form of Bronze Age burial mounds, on the nearby moors suggests that this area was occupied some 3,000 years ago and, although the Romans made little impact here, by the 10th century Witheridge was important enough to give its name to one of the largest Hundreds in Devon. Eleven of the village's farms appeared in the *Domesday Book* and, once a thriving market town, Witheridge today continues to prosper.

Rackenford

7 miles NW of Tiverton off the A361

Set on the hillside above the Little Dart River, Rackenford has posed something of a problem for historians who cannot work out the origins of its name. What is, however, certain is that there was a

The Red Lion Inn

Rookery Hill, Oakford, Devon EX16 9ES
Tel: 01398 351219

Located in the beautiful Exe valley, **The Red Lion Inn**, in the heart of this attractive village dates back to the 17th century and it has, over the years, retained many of its original features – including its inglenook fireplace – whilst the brasses and copperware further take customers back to that era. Owners, Gloria and Geoff Howells welcome both locals and visitors alike to this warm and friendly inn where there is always an excellent choice of drinks at the bar including two real ales and hand pulled Scrumpy cider.

The food served here too is well known and, all freshly prepared by Geoff, the delicious home-made dishes can be taken in either the bar or the separate, elegant restaurant. Along with an attractive beer garden and patio, there are three comfortable en-suite guest rooms on the inn's first floor, one of which has a four poster bed. A hearty traditional breakfast is included in the tariff and both children and dogs are welcome. Finally, there is a monthly quiz held at the Red Lion to which all are invited to join in the fun.

The Exeter Inn

Tiverton Road, Bampton, Devon EX16 9DY
Tel: 01398 331345 Fax: 01398 331460
e-mail: innbampton@msn.com
website: www.exeterinn.co.uk

A typical 15th century Devon longhouse set in the beautiful Exe valley, **The Exeter Inn** is a superb country house inn that, over the years, has expanded to incorporate adjacent cottages. Many of the original features of these ancient buildings can still be seen in the inn's many rooms but perhaps the most interesting is the original water pump which brought spring water up to the inn and is still working today. The slate floor and impressive fireplace in the bar give the inn a traditional feel and, whilst the ceiling beams remain exposed throughout, the simple décor also creates a light and airy feel.

Personally run by owners Barry and Liz Clarke, this inn has everything both locals and visitors to the area could wish for – good food, drink and a warm and friendly atmosphere. There are always six real ales available from the bar, including the local brews Exmoor and Tawny Ales, whilst the local cider and apple juice is equally popular. Food too is an important aspect of life at The Exeter Inn and Barry and Liz's son Andrew, along with fellow chefs Jane and Lorna, create a superb range of menus that are served both in the bar and in the separate restaurant. Many of the traditional dishes on the various menus are given an imaginative twist so, along with steak sandwiches, there is a Italian tomato sandwich served on ciabatta bread and as well as steak and kidney pie customers can sample the spicy Cajun chicken or the Roasted red pepper lasagne. However, whatever the choice, the aim here is to provide customers with a taste of Devon by using only the very best of local produce.

As well as food and drink, The Exeter Inn has eight superior en-suite guest rooms and children are welcome here. The family dog too can join in the fun as there is kennelling available in what was once the old stable block. Although Barry and Liz already have a great success on their hands they are not standing still and there are plans for refurbishing an adjacent cottage into a self-catering family apartment whilst a new conservatory will enable many more people to enjoy the delights of the inn's cuisine.

settlement here at the time of the *Domesday Book* and that, in the 15th century, it was prosperous enough to build an impressive church. Like many other churches in this area, it has a striking black and white wagon roof, embossed with leaves and flowers and with 13 angels of carved oak perched on the corbels.

Close by is the **Rackenford and Knowstone Moors Nature Reserve** that encompasses a unique and threatened habitat that is a rich mix of wet grassland, heath, bog and scrub. This large reserve, much of which is registered common land and cattle graze here, also includes some of the largest remaining area of Culm grassland in the world. Not surprisingly, the nature reserve supports a wealth of wildlife and, particularly, it is a haven for butterflies.

Bampton

5½ miles N of Tiverton on the B3190

In medieval times Bampton was, like so many other West Country towns, an important centre of the wool trade but it is now best known for its annual **Exmoor Pony Sale**, which is held in late October. Throughout the rest of the year, though, this is a wonderfully peaceful place with some handsome Georgian cottages and houses set beside the River Batherm, a tributary of the River Exe. Bampton's parish Church of St Michael and All Angels is popular with collectors of unusual memorials and a stone on the west side of the tower replicated a memorial of 1776 that records the strange death of the parish clerk's son who was apparently killed by a falling icicle. The inscription is remarkably insensitive and reads:

"Bless my I I I I I I (eyes),
Here he lies,
In a sad pickle,
Killed by an icicle."

Meanwhile, to the north of the village lies a tree-covered mound that marks the site of Bampton Castle.

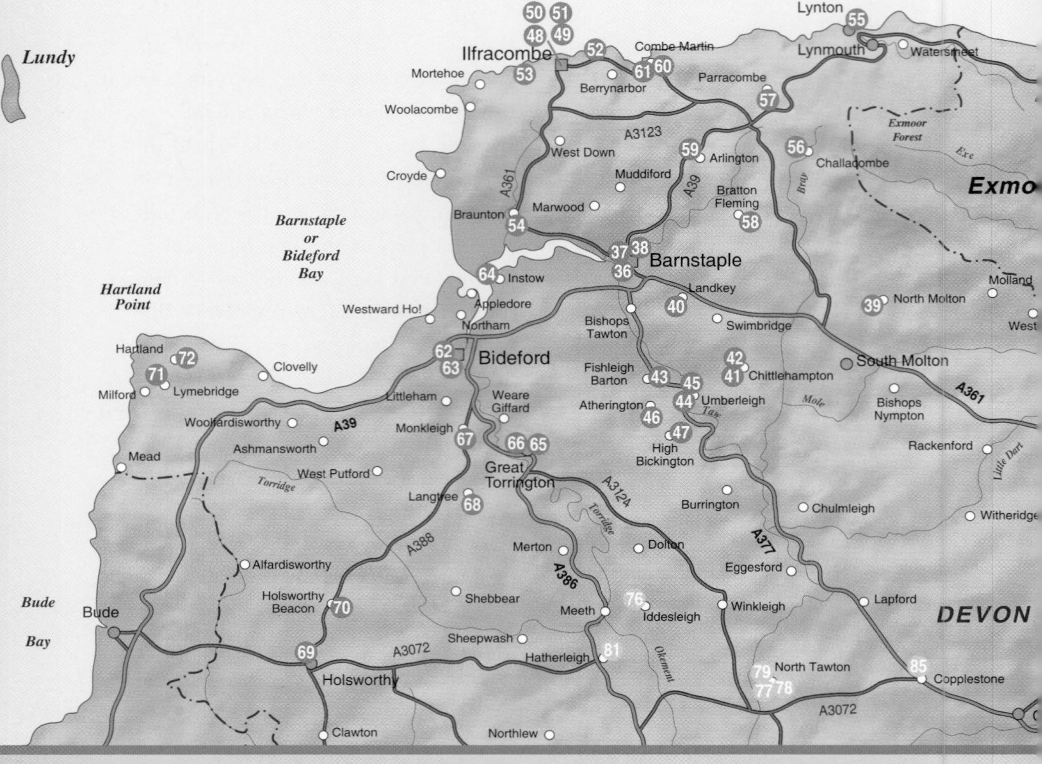

PLACES TO STAY, EAT AND DRINK

Pannier Market Café, Barnstaple 36 Café p56
The Three Tuns Tavern, Barnstaple 37 Pub with Food p57
Barnstaple Heritage Centre, Barnstaple 38 Historic Attraction p58
The Poltimore Inn, North Molton 39 Pub, Food and Accommodation p59
Ring O' Bells, Landkey, Barnstaple 40 Pub and Restaurant p61
Higher Biddacott Farm, Chittlehampton, Umberleigh 41 Bed and Breakfast p62
Cobbaton Combat Collection, Chittlehampton 42 Historic Attraction p63
Fishleigh Farmhouse Foods, Fishleigh Barton 43 Farm Shop with Restaurant and Tea Room p65
The Gables On The Bridge, Umberleigh 44 Tea Rooms and B&B p66
The Rising Sun Inn, Umberleigh 45 Pub, Restaurant and Accommodation p66
The Village Shoppe, Tearoom and B&B, Atherington 46 Shop, Tea Room and B&B p67
Barnfield House, High Bickington, Umberleigh 47 Bed and Breakfast p67
Seven Hills Hotel, Ilfracombe 48 Hotel p68
Ilfracombe Aquarium, Ilfracombe 49 Aquarium p69
Chambercombe Manor, Ilfracombe 50 Historic House and Gardens p70
Ilfracombe Museum, Ilfracombe 51 Museum p71
Old Corn Mill and Pottery, Hele Bay, Ilfracombe 52 Mill and Pottery p71
Watermouth Castle, Watermouth, Ilfracombe 53 Historic Attraction p72
Braunton Museum, Braunton 54 Museum p75

Denotes entries in other chapters

3 North Devon

The north of Devon is dominated by its glorious stretch of coastline that reaches from Hartland Point to Exmoor. It not only offers spectacular scenery but also fine sandy beaches and, in particular, there is the beach at Woolacombe that has awards for the cleanliness of its beach and seawater. Several of the popular holiday resorts along the coast were developed during the great interest in sea bathing and sea water therapies that were made fashionable by George III and the Prince Regent. However, another popular resort, Westward Ho!, was developed on the strength of the success of Charles Kingsley's famous novel of the same name that, inspired by the Devon countryside, is a tale of Elizabethan daring-do.

North Devon has another famous literary connection – that with novelist Henry Williamsom. Returning to Devon after active service in World War I, Williamson rescued an orphan otter cub and, naming it Tarka, the animal stayed

PLACES TO STAY, EAT AND DRINK

Lee House, Lynton	55	Hotel	p77
The Black Venus Inn, Challacombe, Barnstaple	56	Pub and Restaurant	p80
The Hunters Inn, Parracombe, Exmoor	57	Pub, Restaurant and Accommodation	p81
Exmoor Zoological Park, Bratton Fleming	58	Wildlife Attraction	p82
Arlington Court, Arlington, Barnstaple	59	Historic House and Gardens	p83
Wildlife & Dinosaur Park, Combe Martin	60	Wildlife Attraction	p84
Mellstock House, Combe Martin	61	Guest House	p84
Treats, Bideford	62	Café	p86
Orchard Hill Hotel, Bideford	63	Hotel	p88
Worlington House, Instow, Bideford	64	Bed and Breakfast	p90
Torrington 1646, Great Torrington	65	Museum	p91
RHS Garden Rosemoor, Great Torrington	66	Gardens	p92
The Bell Inn, Monkleigh, Bideford	67	Pub, Food and Accommodation	p94
Tor View Cottage, Langtree, Great Torrington	68	Bed and Breakfast	p95
Holsworthy Museum, Holsworthy	69	Museum	p97
Bramble Barn & Willow Barn, Holsworthy Beacon	70	Self Catering	p98
Docton Mill and Gardens, Lymebridge, Hartland	71	Gardens	p101
Yapham Cottages, Hartland, Bideford	72	Self Catering	p103

● Denotes entries in other chapters

Town and Sands, Woolacombe

with him until one day when it became caught in a rabbit trap. Williamson released the terrified creature but Tarka slipped through his grasp and was never seen again. This experience inspired Williamson to create his famous novel, *Tarka the Otter*, and the land between the Rivers Torridge and Taw have become known as Tarka Country as this was the land over which his mythical otter lived and roamed. Opened by the Prince of Wales in 1992, the Tarka Trail takes in many of the towns and villages that feature in the book.

Another long distance footpath through this region of Devon is the South West Coast Path, which follows the coastline around the whole of the southwest peninsula. The stretch of the footpath in Devon takes in the village of Clovelly, the unbelievably quaint community that tumbles down a steep hillside to the sea, and the towns of Bideford, Barnstaple and Ilfracombe.

To the east of Ilfracombe, and on the edge of Exmoor National Park, lie the twin villages of Lynton and Lynmouth that are linked by a unique water-powered cliff railway. Their particularly romantic setting led Victorians to refer to them as the 'English Switzerland' and their charm continues to draw people to this day. Meanwhile, the National Park, only one third of which lies in Devon, rises sharply to the south and east. From its highest point, Kinsford Gate, there are outstanding views over the surrounding uplands that are scattered with numerous prehistoric barrows and standing stones. Much less bleak than Dartmoor, Devon's other National Park, this is hill farming country with sheep, cattle and ponies roaming freely.

The Harbour, Clovelly

Ilfracombe

Inland, north Devon is characterised by small, unspoilt villages of thatched cottages and lonely farmsteads. Apart from the period during the Middle Ages, when the woollen trade flourished here, the economy of this beautiful area has never been particularly buoyant. However, there is the ancient market town of South Molton, close to the foothills of Exmoor, which has been officially designated as tranquil by the Council for the Protection of Rural England.

Barnstaple

Occupying a superb position at the head of the Taw estuary, at the furthest point downstream where it was possible to ford the river, Barnstaple was first settled by the Saxons nearly 1,000 years ago. The first bridge across the Taw was built here in the late 1200s but the present impressive 16-arched structure, which is known as the **Long Bridge**, dates from about 1450 although it has been much altered and widened over the years. The administrative and commercial capital of the region, Barnstaple has enjoyed this pre-eminence for around 1,000 years and, in the *Domesday Book*, it was recorded that, along with being one of only four boroughs in Devon, it had its own mint and a regular market that still continues today.

The produce market takes place twice a week whilst the **Pannier Market** is open every day and it takes its name from the baskets (two wicker baskets connected by a leather strap draped across the back of a donkey, pony or horse) in which country people would carry their fruit and vegetables to market. This huge, glass-roofed building was constructed in 1855 and its grandiose architecture resembles that of a major railway station. Each day of the

Bridge and Shore, Barnstaple

The Square, Barnstaple

week the market has a different emphasis that includes crafts and antiques.

Opposite the Pannier Market is **Butcher's Row**, a quaint line of booth-like Victorian shops built mostly of wood and with brightly painted canopies that were, 150 years ago, exclusively occupied by butchers. Now the site for speciality shops this is the place to come and try seaweed that is served as a breakfast dish with bacon and an egg on top. Meanwhile, in the High Street stands the rather austere **Guildhall** that was built in the Grecian style in the 1820s and that now houses some interesting civic memorabilia including portraits, municipal regalia and silverware. However, many of the town's buildings date from an earlier age and, in particular, there is the early 14th century **Church of St Peter and St Paul**. After having its spire twisted by a lightning strike in 1810, the church suffered again at the heavy hands of the Victorian restorers. Much more appealing are the charming 17th century **Horwood's Almshouses** nearby and the 15th century **St Anne's Chapel** that served for many years as the town's grammar school although it was originally a bone house. During the late 17th century John Gay, the author of *The Beggar's Opera*, was a pupil here and the town has several other literary connections: William Shakespeare visited in 1605 and it was the sight of its

PANNIER MARKET CAFÉ

Market Street, Barnstaple, Devon EX31 1BX
Tel: 01271 327227

Situated within the town's market area, the **Pannier Market Café** is a charming and popular place that has been owned and personally run by Sharon and Martin since mid 2000.

Open from Monday to Saturday (and Sundays in December), the menu here covers everything from a cup of tea to the house speciality – the Market Monster Munch breakfast – and each dish is carefully

prepared by Sharon. Always busy, the café has a strong following locally and is ideal for those looking to rest their weary feet.

The Three Tuns Tavern

80 High Street, Barnstaple, Devon EX31 1HX
Tel: 01271 371308

Found right in the heart of Barnstaple, **The Three Tuns Tavern** is recorded as being the oldest inn, in the oldest high street, in the oldest borough in England. First mention of there being a building here came in 1408 and the wonderful medieval exterior has changed little over the centuries and it would certainly be recognised by Charles I who is believed to have stayed here during the Civil War. He would also be familiar with the inn's interior as it has retained its olde worlde atmosphere and the exposed oak beams were, originally, ships timbers.

A busy and traditional inn, landlords, Andrew and Sharon Davies, believe in offering excellent and reasonably priced food and drink as well as providing a warm and friendly environment for both new and regular customers. Along with Bass real ale, there are keg bitters, lagers and draught ciders served from the bar whilst, throughout the day, delicious home-cooked food is served. All the usual favourites appear on the menu, which is supplemented by daily specials. It is necessary to book for Sunday lunch.

narrow streets bustling with traders that inspired him to write *The Merchant of Venice*. Another man of letters, the diarist Samuel Pepys, married a 15-year-old Barnstaple girl in 1655.

As elsewhere in Devon, the 17th century well-to-do residents of Barnstaple were given to charitable endowments and, as well as Thomas Horwood's almshouses, Messrs Paige and Penrose both bequeathed substantial funds for almshouses and, in 1659, Thomas Horwood's wife, Alice, paid for the building, in Church Lane, of a school for "20 poor maids." A slightly later building of distinction is **Queen Anne's Walk**, a colonnaded arcade with some lavish ornamentation that is surmounted by a statue of the Queen herself. Opened in 1708, it was used by the Barnstaple wool merchants who accepted that any verbal bargain they agreed over the Tome Stone was legally binding. The building stands in the old town quay from which, in 1588, five ships set sail to join Drake's fleet against the Spanish Armada. Today, the building is home to the **Barnstaple Heritage Centre**, where hands-on attractions tell over 1,000 years of Barnstaple history (see panel on page 58). The centre is open daily in the summer (except Sundays) and from Tuesday to Saturday in winter. Meanwhile, housed in a grand Victorian residence found at the end of the Long Bridge is the **Museum of Barnstaple and North Devon** where visitors can

St Peters Church, Barnstaple

wander through the galleries and discover not only more on the town's history but also see displays on the geology, natural history and archaeology of north Devon. The museum is open from Tuesdays to Saturdays.

Barnstaple is also home to one of the country's most traditional terracotta potteries, **Brannam's**, which was established in 1879. Local Fremington red clay is still used to create these impressive pots and, in particular, the pottery is famous for its range of kitchenware that has been successfully combining style, quality and functionality for many years. Here, too, visitors can not only try their hand at creating their own pot but also tour the Museum that illustrates the wide range of products that have been made here for more than 100 years. Tours of the pottery and pot throwing take place from Monday to Friday whilst the museum, shop and restaurant are open from Monday to Saturday and on Sundays between May and October.

However, for many visitors it is Barnstaple's links with Tarka, the otter created by Henry Williamson, which prove the greatest draw to the town. The northern terminus of the **Tarka Line**, a scenic 39-mile route that follows the gentle river valleys of the Yeo and the Taw, the railway is actually the main line route to Exeter but it was renamed in honour of one of the area's major visitor attractions. Meanwhile, walkers

Barnstaple Heritage Centre

Queen Anne's Walk, The Strand, Barnstaple, Devon EX31 1EU
Tel: 01271 373003 Fax: 01271 373003
website: www.devonmuseum.net/barnstapleheritage

Situated in the fine Grade I and II listed Queen Anne's Walk building, **Barnstaple Heritage Centre** is the place to discover the town's rich and vibrant past. A quality heritage attraction, the centre takes visitors on a fascinating journey through the major periods of Barnstaple's mercantile history from medieval times to the late 18th century. An exciting combination of visual and audio effect, hands-on activities and touch-screen computers bring the heritage of this important market town to life. Open all year, the centre has a gift shop, activity sheets and wheelchair access.

The Poltimore Inn

East Street, North Molton, Devon EX36 3HR
Tel: 01598 740338

Close to the edge of Exmoor **The Poltimore Inn** is a lovely traditional English hostelry that dates back over 300 years and it is an ideal place to call before or after a walk in the National Park. Landlords, Sue and Martin Jones offer their customers an excellent selection of real ales, including Flowers Original, along with a delicious menu of dishes (served all day in summer) that are all freshly prepared by Martin. A children friendly inn, there is a beer garden and four comfortable guest bedrooms.

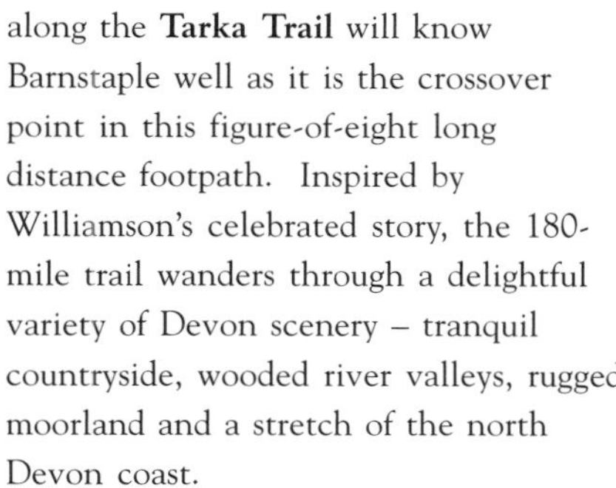

along the **Tarka Trail** will know Barnstaple well as it is the crossover point in this figure-of-eight long distance footpath. Inspired by Williamson's celebrated story, the 180-mile trail wanders through a delightful variety of Devon scenery – tranquil countryside, wooded river valleys, rugged moorland and a stretch of the north Devon coast.

Around Barnstaple

North Molton

11½ miles E of Barnstaple off the A361

Tucked away in the foothills of Exmoor, this village was once a busy wool and mining town and, at intervals from Elizabethan times until the late 1800s, copper and iron were extracted from the hills above North Molton and transported down the River Mole valley and on to the sea at Barnstaple. Evidence of the now abandoned mine workings can still be seen around the village along with the remains of the old Mole Valley tramway.

North Molton's former industrial importance is reflected in the grandeur of its 15th century parish **Church of All Saints** that is a particularly striking building with a high clerestory and a 100-foot pinnacled tower that now seems rather out of place in this remote community. Several other notable features have survived the centuries including a part-medieval 'wine-glass' pulpit complete with sounding board and trumpeting angel, a rood screen, some fine Jacobean panelling and an extraordinary 17th century alabaster monument to Sir Amyas Bampfylde. The memorial depicts the reclining knight with his wife Elizabeth reading a book and their 12 sons and five daughters kneeling nearby. Each figure is delightfully well executed, especially the small girl with plump cheeks holding an apple and gazing wide-eyed at her eldest sister. Also of interest is the church clock that was purchased in 1564 for the then exorbitant sum of £16 14s 4d. However, this proved to be a sound investment as the clock remained in working order for 370 years before its bells chimed for the last time in 1934.

Just to the west of the church is a fine 16th century house, Court Barton (private) and it was here that the iconoclastic biographer and critic Lytton Stracey stayed with a reading party in 1908. It seems that the eminent writer enjoyed his stay greatly, reporting enthusiastically on the area's "mild tranquillities", and a way of life that encompassed both beef and Devonshire cream.

Molland

15½ miles E of Barnstaple off the B3227

Found tucked away in the maze of lanes that skitter across the foothills of Exmoor, Molland is one of Devon's 'must visit' villages for anyone interested in wonderfully unspoilt churches. Following the sale of the village in the early 17th century, **St Mary's Church** stood within the estates of the Courtenay family and, during and following the Commonwealth years, the staunchly Catholic Courtenays showed no interest in restoring or modernising the Protestant parish church. As a result, today, the church has white-washed walls, an elaborate three-decker pulpit crowned by a trumpeting angel and a colourful Royal Arms blazoned with the name of its painter, Rowlands. However, despite their Catholic principles, three late 17th and early 18th century members of the family are commemorated here by some typically flamboyant monuments of the time.

Also within Molland parish lies Great Champson, the farm where, in the 18th century, the Quartly family introduced and developed their celebrated breed of red North Devon cattle.

West Anstey

18½ miles E of Barnstaple off the B3227

This tiny hamlet lies just a mile or so from the Somerset border and on the edge of Exmoor yet, despite its size, West Anstey has its own church that boasts a fine Norman font and an arcade from the 1200s although the building itself dates mostly from the 14th century. The area around West Anstey is one of the emptiest corners of Devon and the grand, open countryside is dotted with just the occasional farm or a tiny cluster of cottages. The **Two Moors Way** footpath passes just to the east of the hamlet and the slopes on which West Anstey stands continue to rise up into the wilds of Exmoor.

Landkey

2 miles SE of Barnstaple off the A361

Landkey boasts a fine church, with some impressive memorials, and also the distinction of being the only village bearing this name in Britain. Historians believe that its name is derived from 'Lan', the Celtic word for church, and the saint to which it was dedicated, Kea. An enduring legend claims that St Kea rowed over from Wales with his personal cow on board determined to convert the

Ring O' Bells

Manor Road, Landkey, near Barnstaple,
Devon EX32 0JH
Tel: 01271 830364
e-mail: kevburgess@hotmail.com

Found next to the village church, **The Ring O' Bells** was probably originally built to house the stonemasons working on the church but, today, it is a warm and welcoming village inn that remains very much the centre of life in Landkey. Owners, Kathryn and Kevin Burgess, have certainly created a friendly, family atmosphere at this traditional country inn and, well known for their hospitality, they are gaining an enviable reputation for the delicious home-cooked food served here.

In the charming rustic surroundings of the bar and the restaurant area, customers can choose from the tasty lunchtime menu that offers all the usual pub favourites, such as sandwiches, filled jacket potatoes and ham and eggs, whilst, in the evening there is a separate à la carte menu. Displaying considerable flair and imagination, the dishes served in the evening are sure to tempt even the most jaded palette. Children too are well catered for here and they have their own, specially designed, menu. Along with excellent food and drink, The Ring O' Bells is also a place of fun and, in these relaxed surroundings, customers can enjoy a variety of old fashioned pub games.

pagans of north Devon to Christianity. Sadly, the inhabitants were not impressed with the saint's eloquence so they chopped off his head. Not many public speakers could cope with this kind of negative response but St Kea is said to have calmly retrieved his severed head and continued, head in hand, to preach the Gospel for many years.

Swimbridge

4½ miles SE of Barnstaple off the A361

Along with some elegant Georgian houses, this village is home to one of Devon's most outstanding churches, the mostly 15th century **Church of St James**, which is particularly distinctive from the outside as it has an unusual lead-covered spire. Inside, there is a wealth of ecclesiastical treasures: a richly carved rood screen spanning both the nave and the aisles, an extraordinary 18th century font cover in the shape of an elongated octagonal 'cupboard', a fine 15th century stone pulpit supported by a tall pedestal and carved with the figures of saints and angels, and a wonderful nave roof with protective angels gazing down.

For almost half a century, from 1833, this attractive village was the home of Rev John 'Jack' Russell, the celebrated hunting parson and breeder of the first Jack Russell terriers. A larger than life character, he was an enthusiastic master of foxhounds and, when his bishop censured him for pursuing such an unseemly sport for a man of the cloth, he transferred the pack into his wife's name and continued his frequent sorties. He was still riding to hounds in his late 70s and when he died in 1880, at the age of 87, hundreds of people attended his funeral. Russell was buried in the churchyard of St James', the church where he had been a diligent pastor for so many years and where he was gratefully remembered for his brief sermons, delivered as his groom waited by the porch with his horse saddled and ready to go. In 1962, Swimbridge's village pub was renamed after its most famous resident.

Just outside Swimbridge lies **North Devon Farm Park** that not only offers an exciting and interesting day out for all the family but that is also situated in beautiful and unspoilt countryside. Centred around a traditional 15th century Devonshire farmhouse, the park aims to offer a glimpse into the lifestyles of those living on the land in the past whilst also providing numerous activities for everyone that include an all-weather indoor play area, an outdoor assault course, tractor rides, dog handling and ferret racing. Open daily from Easter to October, there is a licensed restaurant in the farmhouse.

Chittlehampton

7 miles SE of Barnstaple off the B3227

Recorded in the *Domesday Book* as 'Curem'tone', this village of thatched cottages is home to a prominent, mostly 15th century church that is dedicated to St Hieritha, a local martyr who was cut to pieces by heathen locals using scythes in the 6th century. Inside, the church, which has one of the best tower's in Devon, still maintains a shrine to the saint.

Just to the northwest of the village lies **Cobbaton Combat Collection**, an informative and interesting museum of

Cobbaton Combat Collection

Chittlehampton, Umberleigh, Devon EX37 9RZ
Tel: 01769 540740 Fax: 01769 540141
e-mail: info@cobbatoncombat.co.uk
website: www.cobbatoncombat.co.uk

A private museum that was the result of one man's lifetime of collection anything relating to World War II, **Cobbaton Combat Collection** has two hangars that house over 50 mainly British vehicles, including fully equipped tanks, that are all displayed in combat condition. Along with hardware, from mortar shells and machine guns to ration books and gas masks, visitors too can find refreshment at the NAAFI canteen truck whilst, outside in the children's play area, there is a Sherman tank. Open daily from April to October and weekdays in the winter.

militaria that was begun by Preston Isaac some 40 years ago (see panel above).

South Molton

11 miles SE of Barnstaple on the B3227

This pleasant, small market town, now bypassed by the North Devon link road, has been a focus for the local agriculture based economy since Saxon times and it appeared in the *Domesday Book* as 'Sudmoltone' when it was recorded as belonging to the King. By the late Middle Ages, South Molton, like so many other towns throughout Devon and the West Country, had become a centre of the wool trade and much of its prosperity is directly linked to that business. In the heart of the old town lies Broad Street, which is so broad that it is almost a square, and here can be found many of the handsome Georgian and Victorian civic buildings. Among the noteworthy is the **Market Hall**, the **Assembly Rooms**, the eccentric **Medical Hall**, with its iron balcony and four Ionic columns, and the **Guildhall** of 1743 that overhangs the pavement in a series of arches.

Just on the outskirts of the town lies **Quince Honey Farm** where the world's largest and most famous living honeybee exhibition explains the mysterious process of honey making. Established in 1949 in a cottage garden with just three hives, this is now the largest honey farm in the country – there are over 1,500 hives spread over Devon and Exmoor. The bees can be seen working and living inside their hives and, after harvesting, visitors can watch the honey being extracted, filtered and bottled from a viewing gallery above the production area. Meanwhile, at the farm shop, there is a full range of honey and honey products for sale including Devonshire honey ice cream. The farm is open from April to the end of October whilst the shop is open all year.

Burrington

11½ miles SE of Barnstaple off the A377

This picture postcard village of thatched and white-washed cottages lies perched on top of a hill and there are some glorious views from here of the surrounding countryside. Equally unspoilt is the early 16th century church with its unusual granite arcade and an impressive wagon roof decorated with carvings of angels.

Bishop's Nympton

14 miles SE of Barnstaple off the A361

Bishop's Nympton, along with King's Nympton, George Nympton and several Nymets, takes the Nympton element of its name from the River Yeo that, in Saxon and earlier times, was known as the Nymet, meaning 'river at a holy place'. First granted to Aelfhane in AD 974, by the time of the *Domesday Book* Nimetone, as it was then called, was owned by the Bishop of Exeter, which explains the other part of this ancient village's name.

The village's long, sloping main street is lined with thatched cottages and here, too, is a 15th century church whose lofty, well-proportioned tower is considered one of the most beautiful in Devon. For many years the church had a stained glass window that was erected in Tudor times at the expense of Lady Pollard, wife of Sir Lewis, an eminent judge and leading resident of Bishop's Nympton. At that time Sir Lewis and his wife already had 21 children, 11 sons and 10 daughters, and he left the details of the design of the window to Lady Pollard as he was away in London on business. "But," as John Price, the author of *The Worthies of Devon*, wrote "his lady caused one more child than she then had to be set there: presuming that, usually conceiving at her husband's coming home, she should have another. Which, inserted in expectation, came to pass in reality." The oddest thing though about the story is that Lady Pollard not only correctly predicted the forthcoming child but she also predicted its gender!

Chulmleigh

14 miles SE of Barnstaple on the B3096

This ancient and attractive hilltop town, of cob and thatch cottages above the valley of the Little Dart river, is one of several in mid Devon that prospered from the wool trade in the Middle Ages and then declined into sleepy, unspoilt communities. However, Chulmleigh's prosperity lasted longer than most since it was on the old wagon route to Barnstaple but, in 1830, a turnpike road was constructed along the Taw Valley and this siphoned off most of the town's trade. Just 20 or so years later the Exeter to Barnstaple railway was built along the same route and it proved to be the final straw for Chulmleigh as a trading centre.

A charming place to visit, with the old part of the town clustered around a fine 15th century church, which is noted for its lofty pinnacled tower, Chulmleigh comes alive in the first week of the summer holidays when its annual fair, held since 1253, takes place. Meanwhile, there is the Chulmleigh link of the Tarka Trail, the Little Dart Ridge and Valley Walk and the Two Moors

Way are all within easy reach of the town.

Eggesford

15½ miles SE of Barnstaple on the A377

First settled by the Saxons and probably named after the ford here across the River Taw, a little further upstream lies the late 14th century **All Saints Church** that marks the place where the medieval settlement stood along with the original Eggesford House. Situated on the **Tarka Line**, trains continue to stop at the village's station and, in summer, they bring visitors who come here to enjoy the surrounding scenery. To the west lies **Heywood Wood** that was planted in 1930s and, along with the magnificent trees and impressive views, the wood includes the remains of a Norman motte and bailey castle that was built to protect the river crossing. Meanwhile, to the southeast lies **Eggesford Country Centre**, based in Eggesford Gardens, and where visitors can get information on the history of the village and surrounding area.

Bishops Tawton

2 miles S of Barnstaple on the A377

This ancient village takes its name from the River Taw and from the fact that it was, up until the time of the Dissolution of the Monasteries, owned by the Bishop of Exeter and the turreted farmhouse in the village is all that remains of the bishop's palace. Today, the village is not over endowed with listed buildings but it can boast a very unusual one, a sociable three-seater outside lavatory that has been accorded Grade II listed status. This amenity has not been used for 40 years or more (and the brambles that have invaded it would make it rather uncomfortable to do so) but it still looks perfectly serviceable.

Atherington

7 miles S of Barnstaple on the B3217

A well-known landmark for miles around, **St Mary's Church** stands in the picturesque square of this hilltop village and it is noted for a feature that is

The Gables on the Bridge

Umberleigh, Devon EX37 9AB
Tel: 01769 560461

Just 100 yards or so from Umberleigh station is **The Gables on the Bridge** that offers a wide range of refreshments throughout the day as well as charming overnight accommodation. The tearooms are located at the back of the house in an attractive conservatory where customers can enjoy anything from breakfast to tea whilst also looking out for the grape vine here that is more than 100 years old. All the food here is home-cooked and prepared to order by owners Tony and Myra Pring but it is their traditional cream teas for which they are best known as they use a home-baked traditional Devon split – a sweet, yeast bun – rather than a modern scone.

There are also three attractive en suite guest rooms at The Gables and guests have a choice of a TV lounge or a cosy, quiet lounge in which to relax. Both salmon and sea trout fishing can be arranged for guests if required whilst, as the area around Umberleigh is such grand walking country, Myra and Tony have prepared a useful sketch map with detailed directions to local places of interest.

The Rising Sun Inn

Umberleigh, near Barnstaple,
Devon EX37 9DU
Tel: 01769 560447 Fax: 01769 560764
e-mail: risingsuninn@btinternet.com
website: www.risingsuninn.com

Found in the centre of the village and overlooking the River Taw, the Rising Sun Inn dates back to the 13th century and, today, under the ownership of father and son, Malcolm and Andrew Hogg, it is still attracting customers to this beautiful location. An ideal base for holidaymakers, walkers and cyclists, the inn has a traditional olde worlde charm whilst also providing excellent hospitality and modern creature comforts. The lounge bar, with its beamed ceiling and wood-burning stove, is a cosy place to sit and enjoy a pint of local ale or cider and chat about the day whilst the inn's separate restaurant is perfect for dining.

Justly proud of their award winning cuisine, both the à la carte menu and the bar menus feature the very best of West Country produce and, in particular, both local game and fish are a house speciality. This is also a sporting pub and, along with attracting golfers, it is renowned among fishermen who come to try their luck on the river that is well known for its salmon and sea trout. The Rising Sun offers excellent accommodation in a choice of nine en suite guest rooms.

The Village Shoppe, Tea Room and Bed and Breakfast

Atherington, near Umberleigh,
Devon EX37 9HY
Tel: 01769 560248

Dating back to the 17th century and formerly a coaching inn, **The Village Shoppe, Tea Room and Bed and Breakfast** is a versatile establishment owned by Chris and Jo Hart. Along with the village shop and post office, the couple personally run this quaint tea rooms that offers a wonderful range of home-cooked dishes, including cream teas, throughout the day (except non Bank Holiday Mondays). So popular is the food here that it is advisable to book for Sunday lunch. Two guest rooms are available all year round.

unique in Devon – a lavishly carved and alarmingly top-heavy rood loft. Created by two carvers from nearby Chittlehampton in the 1530s, the loft is an exceptionally fine example of their craft. The church also contains striking effigies of Sir John Wilmington, who died in 1349, and his wife; a window of medieval glass; and well-preserved brasses of Sir John Basset (who died in 1529), his wives and 12 children.

High Bickington

8½ miles S of Barnstaple on the B3217

Standing some 600 feet above sea level, this village commands excellent panoramic views in all directions. High Bickington also boasts a fine 16th century inn, The George, that is set amongst a delightful group of thatched cottages, and a parish church dating back to the 12th century, which is renowned for its exceptional collection of carved bench and pew ends. There are around 70 within the church and, whilst some are Gothic (characterised by fine tracery), others, with more rounded figures, date from the Renaissance era. More recent carvings, which depict an appealing collection of animals and birds, can be seen in the choir stalls.

Barnfield House

High Bickington, near Umberleigh,
Devon EX37 9BU
Tel: 01769 560990 Fax: 01769 560990
e-mail: martin.page3@virgin.net
website: www.barnfield-house.com

Surrounded by two acres of gardens that are a haven for wildlife, **Barnfield House** is a delightful 17th century barn that has been beautifully converted into a stunning family home. Still retaining many of its ancient features, Barnfield is the home of Jenny and Martin Page who offer superb bed and breakfast accommodation in a choice of three charming guest rooms. A wonderful place to relax and unwind, yet close to many of Devon's favourite attractions, Barnfield is ideal for all the family.

Ilfracombe

The Harbour, Ilfracombe

Today, Ilfracombe is the largest seaside resort on the north Devon coast but, up until 1800, this was just a small fishing and market town that relied entirely on the sea both for its living and as its principal means of communication. The boundaries of the old town are marked by a sheltered natural harbour to the north and by a part-Norman church, boasting one of the finest medieval wagon roofs in the West Country, half a mile to the south. The entrance to Ilfracombe harbour is guarded by Lantern Hill, a steep-sided conical rock that is crowned by the restored medieval chapel **St Nicholas**. For centuries, this highly conspicuous former fishermen's chapel has doubled as a lighthouse and a light was placed in a lantern at the western end of the building. From the chapel's hilltop setting there are superb views of the town, its still busy harbour and the craggy north Devon coastline.

Like so many West Country resorts, Ilfracombe developed in response to the early 19th century craze for sea bathing and sea water therapies and the town is home to one of this stretch of coast's most historic gems – **Tunnel Beaches** that are still the perfect place for a

Ilfracombe Aquarium

Ilfracombe, Devon
Tel: 01271 864533
website: www.ilfracombeaquarium.co.uk

The Ilfracombe Aquarium is housed in the Old Lifeboat House, below St Nicholas' Chapel on Lantern Hill and next to Ilfracombe Harbour.The Aquarium which opened in July 2001 provides an all weather facility enabling visitors to share in the beauty. It houses an impressive species collection in carefully recreated natural habitats and displays both freshwater and marine fauna which are fascinating in both their appearance and behaviour. It is also essential that you visit the fun fish retail area and outdoor café where simple snacks and drinks are served. Open daily mid March to January. Disabled access.

family day out. Meanwhile, the **Tunnel Baths**, with their extravagant Doric façade, were opened in Bath Place in 1836, by which time a number of elegant residential terraces had been built on the hillside to the south of the old town. Much of the town's architecture dates from the Victorian era, when the arrival of the railway brought visitors in much greater numbers, and the new streets were built, spreading inland, in steeply undulating rows. Around the same time, in the mid 19th century, the harbour was enlarged to cope with the paddle steamers bringing in tourists from Bristol and South Wales. Today, visitors can take advantage of regular sailings from the harbour to Lundy Island, which lies 12 miles offshore. The **South West Coast Path** provides walkers with some spectacular scenery and from the town, westwards, much of this wonderful stretch of coast is now in the hands of the National Trust. The harbour, too, is home to **Ilfracombe Aquarium** (see panel above).

First opened in 1932, and housed in the disused laundry of the now long forgotten Ilfracombe Hotel, is **Ilfracombe Museum** (see panel on page 71) and, adjacent to this fascinating place, is the **Landmark Theatre**, a superb multi-purpose theatre and arts complex with a café and a spacious display area.

Just to the east of Ilfracombe, at **Hele Bay**, is the **Old Corn Mill and Pottery** (see panel on page 71), a 16th century watermill with an 18-foot overshot wheel that is unique in north Devon. Lovingly restored from near dereliction, the mill is now, once again, producing flour that can

The Harbour and Capstone Hill, Ilfracombe

CHAMBERCOMBE MANOR

Ilfracombe, Devon EX34 9RJ
Tel: 01271 862624

Although the manor here was mentioned in the *Domesday Book*, the present **Chambercombe Manor** is believed to date from the 12th century and the first record of it was when it was owned by Sir Henry Champernon. It remained in that family for some three centuries, until the Champernons died out, but when, exactly, it fell from being a manor house to a farmhouse is unknown.

At the centre of the house is the Great Hall and here visitors can marvel at the 400-year-old lime ash floor that now resembles polished granite as well as the wonderful open fireplace whose fireback dates from 1696. Upstairs there are a series of bedrooms and, in particular, the Coat of Arms bedroom where Lady Jane Grey, a descendant of the Champernons, stayed. Graced by a fine oak 'tester' bed and 17th and 18th century furniture, the room has the Grey family coat of arms over the fireplace and a fine barrel ceiling and plaster frieze. Naturally with a house of this age, Chambercombe Manor is said to be haunted and, in 1865, whilst making some repairs to the roof, the tenant discovered a hidden chamber, next to the Coat of Arms room. Inside the chamber, lying on a handsome bed, was the skeleton of the woman who, it is believed, was visiting relatives at the house but was wrecked in a storm off Hele. Brought to the house to recover, she died here and, after taking her jewellery, the occupants of the house sealed the room.

Reached through a Gothic doorway, the Champernons private chapel is tiny and, at the entrance, stands a Holy water stoop that was discovered only last century whilst, after passing through an early Tudor doorway and descending some stairs, visitors will find their way to the Old Kitchen. Above are the old servants' quarters and here can be seen the two ancient bread ovens either side of the open fireplace.

Interesting though the house and its contents are the extensive grounds should not be missed. Extending over some 20 acres in this delightful wooded valley, there is a charming paved courtyard, with ornamental ponds, and the main garden with lawns, herbaceous borders, a rose garden and shrubbery. Equally tranquil is the water gardens, home to numerous waterfowl, that are reached by some stone steps and a bridge.

Ilfracombe Museum

Wilder Road, Ilfracombe, Devon EX43 8AF
Tel: 01271 863541 website:
www.devonmuseums.net

First opened in the 1930s and enlarged over the years, **Ilfracombe Museum** displays a fascinating range of exhibits that tell the story of the town and the surrounding area.

Meanwhile, the Lundy Room gives visitors plenty of interesting background information on the island whilst, elsewhere, there are displays that cover all manner of subjects that highlight people's desire for collecting. Along with the memorabilia on display, the museum has, in its archive, back copies of the local newspaper from the 1860s to the mid 20th century.

be purchased here. Meanwhile, a mile or two to the south, and found in a secluded valley, is **Chambercombe Manor** (see panel opposite), an 11th century manor house that was mentioned in the *Domesday Book*. Visitors here can wander around the rooms that display period furniture from the Elizabethan era to Victorian times, see the claustrophobic Priest Hole and look for the ghost in the Haunted Room.

Around Ilfracombe

Berrynarbor

2½ miles E of Ilfracombe off the A399

Found at the end of the beautiful Sterridge valley, this picturesque coastal village has quaint cottages and narrow streets, a 15th century manor house that later became the village school, and a 12th century church with a 96-foot high tower. Well known for its well-kept gardens and floral displays, this ancient place featured in the *Domesday Book* as 'Hurstesberie' takes its present name from the Berry family who once owned the manor here.

At the coast here lies the pretty cove of **Watermouth**, a natural, sheltered harbour that provides moorings for pleasure craft and there is also a gently shelving shoreline littered with rock pools. Here, too, is **Watermouth Castle** (see panel on page 72), where

Old Corn Mill and Pottery

Watermouth Road, Hele Bay, near Ilfracombe, Devon EX34 9QY
Tel: 01271 863185 Fax: 01271 863185 e-mail: grays@oldmllandpottery.co.uk website: www.oldmillandpottery.co.uk

Dating back to 1525, the Old Corn Mill has been saved from dereliction and, after extensive restoration, is once again producing flour that can be purchased at the mill shop. A tour of the mill provides the opportunity to see the working machinery whilst there is also a display on the restoration programme. Owner, Robin Gray, is a potter and, along with giving demonstrations at his wheel, his unique pieces are for sale here.

Watermouth Castle

Near Ilfracombe, Devon EX34 9SL
Tel: 01271 863879 Fax: 01271 865864
e-mail: enquiries@watermouthcastle.com
website: watermouthcastle.com

Watermouth Castle is a Victorian folly that has been transformed into a family theme park with attractions to suit all ages. In the castle's great hall, home to a collection of suits of armour, visitors can enjoy mechanical music demonstrations whilst, elsewhere in the castle, there are displays on Victorian life, antique pier machines and even a room devoted to model railways. Down in the depths of the dungeon labyrinths animated fairy tales come to life, there are craft shops from a bygone age but beware as this is also a place of witches, ghouls and phantoms.

Meanwhile, the castle grounds, too, have been transformed into a wonderful playground and here can be found the mystical water gardens with jumping fountains and a floating marble ball. In gnomeland, visitors can wander around the village and see the little people going about their daily business whilst, in adventure land, there is crazy water golf and a water ride. Finally there is the castle courtyard, where a tempting range of meals and snacks are available, along with a gift shop and, throughout the grounds, there are picnic areas.

there are displays, exhibits and attractions for all the family.

Muddiford

6 miles SE of Ilfracombe on the B3230

Despite its rather unappealing name, Muddiford is an attractive village, situated in a pretty valley, and it really did get its name from the 'muddy ford' by which medieval travellers used to cross the river.

Surrounded by hundreds of acres of beautiful wooded grounds, lies **Broomhill Sculpture Garden** where contemporary sculptures from around Europe are displayed in the gardens of this small late Victorian hotel and restaurant. Along with the numerous sculptures outside, the hotel also has a gallery and that, too, like the sculpture garden, continues to evolve.

West Down

3 miles S of Ilfracombe off the A361

This village of white-washed houses beside the River Caen is noted for its tiny church whose nave is barely 15 feet wide. Mostly rebuilt in the 17th and 18th centuries, the church has, nevertheless, retained a fine oak roof that dates from the 14th century, a Norman font that was discovered beneath the floor, and a rare wooden figure of Sir John Stowforth, Justice of the Common Pleas in the 1300s. Here, he is shown wearing the robes of a

Serjeant-at-Law and, luckily, much of the original colouring has survived.

Marwood

6 miles S of Ilfracombe off the B3230

This ancient village is home to **Marwood Hill Gardens**, where, in under 30 years, 18 acres of pastureland have been transformed into a spectacular water garden with three lakes that are surrounded by herbaceous plants, trees and shrubs. Home to the National Collections of Astilbe, Iris and Tulbaghia, the gardens also feature the Folly and the Scented Arbour as well as the largest Bog Garden in the West Country that links the lakes. Throughout the year there is plenty of interest – from the spring magnolias to the brilliant autumnal colours. The gardens are open daily from dawn to dusk and there are plants for sale, including rare and unusual species.

Woolacombe

4 miles SW of Ilfracombe on the B3343

A popular resort that lies between two dramatic headlands, both of which are now in the care of the National Trust, the wonderful stretch of golden sands at Woolacombe is justifiably regarded as the finest beach in north Devon. The sands and rock pools found between the two outcrops are a delight for children, along with traditional seaside trappings of swing boats and a more modern bouncy castle, whilst surfers revel in the monster waves that roll in from the Atlantic Ocean.

Back in the early 19th century, Woolacombe was little more than a hamlet whose few inhabitants sustained a precarious livelihood by fishing. Then, suddenly, the leisured classes were seized by the craze of sea bathing that was initiated by George III at Weymouth and enthusiastically endorsed by his eldest son, George IV, at Brighton. Inspired by the economic success of such places, the two families who owned most of the land around Woolacombe, the Fortescues and the Chichesters, began constructing villas and hotels in the Regency style and these elegant buildings still endow the town with a very special charm and genteel atmosphere today.

Many friends of the Fortescue and the Chichester families regarded their initiative as a suicidally rash enterprise

Putsborough Sand, Woolacombe

as Woolacombe was so remote and, at that time, the roads through north Devon were still little more than cart tracks. During the first few years only a trickle of well-to-do visitors undertook the arduous journey to Woolacombe as they came in search of a novel and comparatively inexpensive resort. But the intrepid holidaymaker's word of mouth recommendations soon ensured a steady flow of tourists, a flow that swelled to a flood over subsequent years. Today, Woolacombe is still as beautiful as it was then and it also now basks in the bureaucratic glow of a European Commission 'Seaside Award' – the sea water here is clean, there are lifeguards on the beach and there are disabled facilities easily available.

Just to the south of Woolacombe lies **Potters Hill**, a conical hill that was named after the 14th century Thomas Pottere and it was given to the National Trust in 1935. The path cut up the hill to the summit, from where there are glorious views, was constructed to celebrate King George V's Silver Jubilee whilst the cairn on the hilltop was a Millennium project. To the southeast lies the higher and wider hill of **Woolacombe Down**, a former sea-cliff that now supports a wealth of wildlife including some rare species of beetles and moths.

Croyde

7 miles SW of Ilfracombe on the B3231

Renowned for its excellent beach with, just around the headland, another stretch at Saunton Sands, Croyde still retains some of its thatched cottages as well as having some of the trappings of the modern resort and it remains one of the best family friendly seaside town's in the county.

To the northwest of Croyde lies **Baggy Point**, the southern headland that, along with Morte Point, forms Morte Bay. The land around the headland is owned by the National Trust and here the path to the tip of the headland climbs up high until the end is reached and the near vertical cliffs fall steeply away to the sea below. These cliffs provide a wonderful habitat for seabirds, including herring gull, fulmar, shag and cormorant, whilst grey seals can often be seen from here. Running northwestwards from the cliffs is **Baggy Leap**, a shoal on to which, in 1799, the *HMS Weazle* was driven during a gale and all 106 souls on board were drowned.

Croyde Bay

Baggy Point has also revealed evidence of early human occupation in the form of numerous prehistoric flint artefacts that have been excavated from here over the years. During World War II, much of the north Devon coast was used for training prior to the D-Day landings due to its similarity to the coast of Normandy and the stretch from Braunton Burrows to Morte Point was assigned to the US Army as Assault Training Centre (ATC) Croyde.

Meanwhile, just to the northeast of Croyde lies the village of **Georgeham** where Henry Williamson settled after returning from World War I. It was here that he wrote his famous novel, *Tarka the Otter* – a tale of an otter that is hunted and finally killed by an otter hound. Tarka lived in the land between the Taw and the Torridge rivers and many of the little villages and settlements feature in the story. Although in later life Williamson moved to Norfolk, he lies buried in Georgeham churchyard and is remembered for his vivid descriptions of the atmosphere of this area in the first half of the 20th century.

Braunton

7 miles SW of Ilfracombe on the A361

This ancient village claims to be the largest in Devon and it is certainly a sizeable community spread along both sides of the River Caen with some handsome Georgian houses and a substantial church that reflects its importance in medieval times. The church is dedicated to St Brannock, a Welsh missionary who first founded a church here in the 6th century that was built in a wooded valley away from the main Celtic settlement. It is said that St Brannock's tomb lies beneath the altar of the present 13th century church, a story that may well be true since the building stands on the site of its Saxon predecessor. The church contains some of the finest 16th century carved pews to be found in England and many of the carvings depict pigs, a clear allusion to the ancient legend that St Brannock was instructed in a dream to build a church where he came across a sow and her litter of seven pigs.

There is further evidence of Saxon

Braunton Museum

The Bakehouse Centre, Braunton,
Devon EX33 1AA
Tel: 01271 816688
e-mail: braunton@devonmuseums.net
website: www.devonmuseums.net/braunton

Although the village can trace its history back to the 6th century, **Braunton Museum** was only established in the 1970s but this small museum has some excellent displays. All the latest technology has been used to preserve the history of the village and here visitors can explore Braunton's long associations with the sea, gain an understanding of the importance of local agriculture and also discover what life was like here when a contingent of American soldiers were stationed here during World War II.

occupation of this area to be found in **Braunton Great Field**, just to the southwest of the village. A famous archaeological site, this area is one of the few remaining in the country that displays the ancient medieval method of strip farming: the vast acreage was divided first into 16 sections known as furlongs and then divided again into narrow strips that were shared between the villagers. Each strip was separated by an unploughed 'landshare' about a foot wide and, although over time, many of the strips have changed hands and been combined, there are still around 200 individual ones remaining.

In the early 19th century a bank was built around the tidal salt marsh to the south and west of the village, drainage ditches were dug and the salt gradually cleared to leave fertile land for grazing. Beyond the drained land lies some 1,000 acres of dunes known as **Braunton Burrows**, the largest system of dunes in the country that stretch along the coast towards Croyde. Internationally famous for its plants, such as the Marsh Orchid and Evening Primrose, this Nature Reserve and Site of Special Scientific Interest is also the home of curlew, oyster-catcher and cormorants.

Back in the village and housed in the Bakehouse Centre is **Braunton Museum** (see panel on page 75) that concentrates its exhibits and displays on local agricultural and marine history as well as village life, from the 6th century through to the two World Wars. The village is also home to the **Elliott Gallery** that contains one of the largest and most comprehensive exhibitions of fine art in the region.

Mortehoe

4 miles W of Ilfracombe off the B3343

The most northwesterly village in Devon, Mortehoe's name, meaning 'raggy stump', reflects the rugged character of the Morte peninsula. A pretty stone-built village, Mortehoe's small, part Norman church has a 15th century open-timbered wagon roof, an interesting early 14th century table tomb, a wonderful series of grotesquely carved Tudor bench ends and a bell in the tower that is said to be the oldest in Devon. Also inside is a large mosaic of 1905, in the chancel arch, which was designed by Selwyn Image, the Slade Professor of Art at Oxford, and it was created by the same craftsmen who produced the mosaics in St Paul's Cathedral.

Found in a Grade II listed barn, **Mortehoe Heritage Centre** has a wealth of local history exhibits that, through clever displays, bring life from yesteryear on this wild stretch of coast to life. Along with a museum shop and various activities for children, there are also tractor and trailer rides in high summer. The centre is open from Easter to the end of October from Sunday to Thursday, bank holiday weekends and daily during the school summer holiday.

Just a short walk from the village is **Morte Point** (National Trust), a place that is renowned for its wild beauty as well as its treacherous sea conditions. Over the years numerous ships have come to grief here and, in the winter of 1852, five ships floundered on the rocks here alone. Today, Morte Point has been designated a Site of Special Scientific Interest and, along with the fulmar, herring gull and oyster-catcher who have found their homes here, there are rare insects, coastal heather and maritime grassland. Further north from Mortehoe lies **Bull Point Lighthouse**, another popular destination for walkers, whilst, to the south, there is another footpath that takes in the splendid natural viewpoint of Morte Hill.

Valley of Rocks, Lynton

Lynton

Lynton and Lynmouth, though often mentioned in the same breath, are very different in character: Lynton, the younger of the two settlements, sits on top of a great cliff some 600 feet high whilst Lynmouth, far below, clusters around the junction of the East and West Lyn rivers, just before they reach the sea. The Victorians developed these twin towns into holiday centres and their quiet charm, as well as their scenic location, led to them being named 'Little Switzerland of England'. Most of the buildings here date from the Victorian era onwards and, in particular, there is the fascinating **Town Hall** that is typically Victorian Gothic but in the style of the Swiss chalet. Meanwhile, the **Lyn and Exmoor Museum**, which traces the story of the twin towns and Exmoor National Park, is housed in a charming 18th century cottage. Lynton,

too, has its own cinema, next to the impressive Town Hall, that shows all the latest releases whilst the old Methodist Chapel is home to the work of **Lyn Arts and Crafts** – a must to be visited.

To the west of Lynton lies one of the most remarkable natural features in Devon, the famous **Valley of Rocks** and, when the poet Robert Southey visited the area in 1800, he was most impressed by this natural gorge "covered with huge stones... the very bones and skeletons of the earth; rock reeling upon rock, stone piled upon stone, a huge terrific mass." Meanwhile, in *Lorna Doone*, RD Blackmore transforms the gorge into the 'Devil's Cheesering', where Jan Ridd visits Mother Meldrun who is sheltering under "eaves of lichened rock." The valley is dominated by Castle Rock and there are other strangely weathered rock formations that bear such names as Ragged Jack. Meanwhile, the valley is also home to the only surviving wild mountain goats to be found south of the Scottish borders.

Around Lynton

Lynmouth

½ mile E of Lynton on the A39

Lynmouth is connected to its sister town, Lynton, by the ingenious **Lynton and Lynmouth Cliff Railway** that, when it opened on Easter Monday 1890, was the first of its kind in Britain. A gift from Sir George Newnes, the publisher and newspaper tycoon, the railway is powered by water and each car has a 700 gallon water tank that is filled at the top and emptied at the bottom. Operating at a gradient of 1:13/4 and covering a vertical height of 500 feet, this cliff railway remains not only a popular attraction but also an integral means of joining the two communities. A spectacular ride that offers fantastic views, at the top of the railway is a licensed French-style cliff top café.

Picturesque though Lynmouth undoubtedly is, this coastline is also dangerous, particularly to shipping, and here, at the National Park Visitor Centre, there is the **Lifeboat Museum** that contains a wealth of interesting information. Meanwhile, in August 1952, Lynmouth made world-wide news when, after days of torrential

Lynmouth

rain, the East Lyn River flooded, burst its banks and sent a deluge of flood water into the town. The great flood was devastating: 34 people lost their lives and many were left homeless. At the **Flood Memorial Hall**, there is an exhibition that recounts the events of that terrible night. An earlier exceptional storm, in 1899, involved the Lynmouth lifeboat in a tale of epic endurance. A full-rigged ship, the *Forest Hall*, was in difficulty off Porlock, but the storm was so violent that it was impossible for the lifeboat to be launched from Lynmouth. Instead, the crewmen dragged their three and a half ton boat, the *Louisa*, 13 miles across the moor, including negotiating Countisbury Hill, with a climb of 1,000 feet over just two miles, before dropping down to Porlock Weir, where the *Louisa* was successfully launched and every member of crew of the stricken ship was saved.

For centuries, the people of Lynmouth subsisted on agriculture and fishing, especially herring fishing and curing, and, by good fortune, just as the herring shoals were moving away to new water, the north Devon coast began to benefit from the two new enthusiasms of 'romantic' scenery and sea bathing. Coleridge and Wordsworth arrived here on a walking tour in the 1790s, Shelley wrote fondly of his visit in 1812 and it was Robert Southey, later the Poet Laureat, who first described the dramatic scenery as 'the English Switzerland'. Meanwhile, the painter Gainsborough had already described it as "the most delightful place for a landscape painter this country can boast."

Finally, and rather differently, at the **Exmoor Brass Rubbing and Hobbycraft Centre**, visitors can have a go at taking a rubbing from one of the 2,000 plus facsimiles of brasses they have here that date from as far back as 1277. The centre also sells ready made brass rubbings in various sizes and colours that make a unique and interesting gift and the centre is open daily from the end of February to November.

Watersmeet

2 miles SE of Lynton off the A39

This world famous beauty spot, where the East Lyn River and Hoar Oak Water

Watersmeet

The Black Venus Inn

Challacombe, near Barnstaple,
Devon EX31 4TT
Tel: 01598 763251/763607
Fax: 01598 763607

Believed to be the only inn in England bearing this name, The Black Venus Inn is a splendid old stone-built pub that enjoys a wonderful situation on the edge of Exmoor National Park. Inside, this historic 16th century building is full of Devon character and charm: the low ceilings still have the original beams intact, the stone fireplace in the restaurant has a hand carved wooden surround whilst the walls display various examples of the work of local craftspeople. There are some glorious photographs of the local area and particularly Exmoor along with locally made walking sticks and some beautiful hand carved oak objects.

Although this is landlady, Jenny Lidbury-Smith's first pub she has certainly settled in here well and over the last couple of years has put The Black Venus on the map of Devon. A warm and friendly place that is popular with both locals and visitors alike, the inn concentrates on local ales and cider. The bar is a cosy place in which to enjoy a drink or a snack whilst there is also a comprehensive menu on offer in the separate restaurant. The choice of dishes changes constantly and Jenny specialises in Devonshire recipes as well as game and fish dishes although the inn is fast growing a reputation for its curries. Those dining here should also ensure that they save themselves for the pudding menu and, in particular, the house speciality – home-cooked bread and butter pudding. A take away service for those unable to stay in these relaxing surroundings and eat, is also offered. Each dish is made on the premises from fresh local produce and, where possible, the vegetables are gathered from the inn's own kitchen garden.

Along with enjoying the very best in both home-cooked food and local drinks, visitors to The Black Venus can, when the weather permits, also enjoy the fresh country air by sitting out in the inn's well-maintained beer garden. A charming and delightful place that features a live willow woven archway and fencing, the garden has a well-designed children's play area where they can let off steam safely. However, everyone will find Jenny's friendly black Labrador, Mr Pickwick, particularly appealing and there is also an aviary that features breeding pairs of Senegal parrots.

meet, is a deep tree-lined gorge that is owned by the National Trust and the old Victorian fishing lodge here has been converted into a tea garden and shop that is open during the season. There are many footpaths from here and, whilst spring and autumn bring their own delights, Watersmeet is best visited after a spell of rain as the river and waterfalls are both full and fast running.

Parracombe Church

Challacombe

5½ miles S of Lynton on the B3358

Situated just inside Exmoor National Park, with the Edgerley stone marking the border with Somerset only a mile and a half away, this settlement has been here since the days of the ancient Britons and it was they who gave the village its name. Experts cannot agree whether the name means 'cold valley' or 'calves' valley' but as some point out both interpretations are valid "for the wind is never still here, and the moorland raises good beef cattle."

Parracombe

4 miles SW of Lynton off the A39

The redundant **Church of St Petrock** is notable for its marvellously unspoilt interior, complete with 15th century benches, 17th century box pews, a Georgian pulpit and a perfectly preserved musician's gallery. However, perhaps the most striking feature of all is

Exmoor Zoological Park

South Stowford, Bratton Fleming,
near Barnstaple, Devon EX31 4SG
Tel: 01598 763352

Situated on the western side of Exmoor, in a gentle valley, **Exmoor Zoological Park** has evolved from the original bird gardens opened in 1983 to this unique family orientated attraction. Covering some 12 acres, the zoo contains a varied collection of birds, mammals, insects and reptiles from all over the world and there are over 200 species on display. Specialising in people participation through encounter sessions, mini guided tours and animal contact, this zoo has a welcoming and friendly atmosphere that encourages people to return again.

the unique gated screen between the chancel and the nave that bears a huge tympanum painted with the Royal Arms, the Lord's Prayer, the Creed and the Ten Commandments. The survival of this church is due to John Ruskin who led the protests against its intended demolition in 1879 after another church was built lower down the hill.

Bratton Fleming

7 miles SW of Lynton off the A399

Although the official boundary of Exmoor National Park lies three miles to the east, Bratton Fleming definitely has a moorland feel and, when there is access to the church tower, there are glorious views out across the fields and valleys to the sea, some 12 miles away, as well as to the National Park.

To the north of Bratton Fleming is **Exmoor Zoological Park** (see panel above), home to more than 170 species of unusual and exotic animals and birds. The residents of the 12 acres of gardens here range from Pygmy marmosets and tarantulas to penguins and capybara.

A little further north again lies **Wistlandpound Reservoir** around part of which a Nature Reserve has been established. A tranquil place that is home to a variety of wildlife, there is a waymarked path around the lake where fly fishing for rainbow trout is available with a permit.

To the northwest of Bratton Fleming is **Arlington Court** (National Trust - see panel opposite), an imposing property that was home to the Chichester family

Arlington Court Garden

ARLINGTON COURT

Arlington, Nr Barnstaple, Devon EX31 4LP
Tel: 01271 850296 Fax: 01271 851108
website: www.nationaltrust.org.uk

Nestling in the thickly wooded valley of the River Yeo lies the 3500 acre **Arlington Court** estate. At its centre stands Arlington Court, the intimate and intruiging Victorian home of Miss Rosalie Chichester. Crowded with treasures amassed from her travels, her collections include model ships, tapestry, pewter and shells. Arlington's stable block houses one of the best collections of 19th century horse-drawn vehicles in the country, which ranges from a very grand State Chariot with highly ornamented harness, to the sombre plumed bier carrier, and offers carriage rides around the grounds.

The 30 acre gardens are largely informal, featuring a beautiful Victorian garden complete with conservatory and ornamental pond leading to a partially restored walled garden which is slowly coming back to a productive vegetable area.

Miss Chichester was a keen conservationist and encouraged wildlife. Today the estate is home to deer, otters, heron, badgers and countless birds. Draped from the trees and shrubs are lichen that thrive in the moist air. The parkland is especially important for bats, providing flight lines from the house to their feeding areas. In the basement, from May to September, visitors can view the comings and goings of Devon's largest colony of Lesser Horseshoe bats via the newly installed 'batcam'.

from 1534 until the last owner, Rosalie Chichester, died childless in 1949. The present house was built in 1822 to an unambitious design by the Barnstaple architect, Thomas Lee, and, some 40 years later, it was extended by Sir Bruce Chichester, who also added the handsome stable block. When Sir Bruce died in 1881, he left the house and its considerable estate to his daughter, Rosalie, along with a staggering amount of debt. Only 15 years old when she inherited, Rosalie managed to keep the house and estate intact and stayed on at Arlington Court until her death at the age of 83.

Sir Francis Chichester, famous as an aviation pioneer and as the first solo round-the-world sailor, was a member of the family and he was born just two miles away at Shirwell.

Combe Martin

8 miles SW of Lynton on the A399

Found in the beautiful and fertile valley of the River Umber, on the western edge of Exmoor, Combe Martin is a popular seaside resort, with a good sandy beach, which also lies at the centre of some of north Devon's most spectacular coastal scenery. For children there is the added attraction of a large number of rock pools along Combe Martin Bay. In the village itself, whose main street, at more than two miles long, is reputed to be the longest in the country, there is a wide selection of inns, cafés and shops. Here, too, can be found **Combe Martin**

Combe Martin Wildlife and Dinosaur Park

Combe Martin, Devon EX34 0NG
Tel: 01271 882486 Fax: 01271 882486
e-mail: combemartinpark@hotmail.com
website: www.dinosaur-park.com

Set in natural parkland **Combe Martin Wildlife and Dinosaur Park** is home to a wide variety of animals but it is, perhaps, the collection of life-size dinosaurs that draw most people to the park. Some of the models are animated including the UK's only full size animatronic T-Rex. A 'Spitting Dilophosaurus' will shortly be an added attraction. Set out in the parkland, this is a fantastic way to see these once great creatures. However, dinosaurs are just a small part of the park and there are 26 acres of sub-tropical gardens to explore with rare plants, cascading waterfalls and free flying exotic birds. The park is also home to Snow Leopards, Timber Wolves, Meerkats, Apes and Monkeys, Sealions, a Tropical Butterfly House and lots more.

Other attractions are the Spectacular Light Show, Destination Mars and Earthquake Canyon, the most unique ride in the UK - experience a giant earthquake and survive! A superb day out for all the family, Combe Martin Wildlife and Dinosaur Park is full of surprises. Open March to November.

Mellstock House

Woodlands, Combe Martin, Devon EX34 0AR
Tel: 01271 882592 Fax: 01271 889134
mobile: 07941 006734
e-mail: mary@mellstockhouse.co.uk
website: www.mellstockhouse.co.uk

Just a couple of minutes walk from the seafront of this quaint old village, **Mellstock House** is a delightful example of an Edwardian villa residence.

Owners, Mary and Roy Burbidge have only been here since the summer of 2002 and, in a short space of time, they have not only settled in but also created a relaxed and friendly atmosphere at this comfortable guest house.

Throughout the house is decorated and furnished in such a way as to highlight the lovely architectural features of this exceptional property and, in particular, there are six excellent en-suite guest rooms, on two floors – those with children will be especially interested in the two bedroomed family suite. The property enjoys superb views over the sea and the countryside.

Both breakfast and dinner are served in the stylish dining room and the speciality here is old-fashioned home-cooked meals that use the very best of Devon's ample produce. Guests, too, can relax in the quiet of the residents' lounge and bar where not only can they enjoy a pre-dinner aperitif but also unwind reading a good book or play one of the many board games that are here for their amusement.

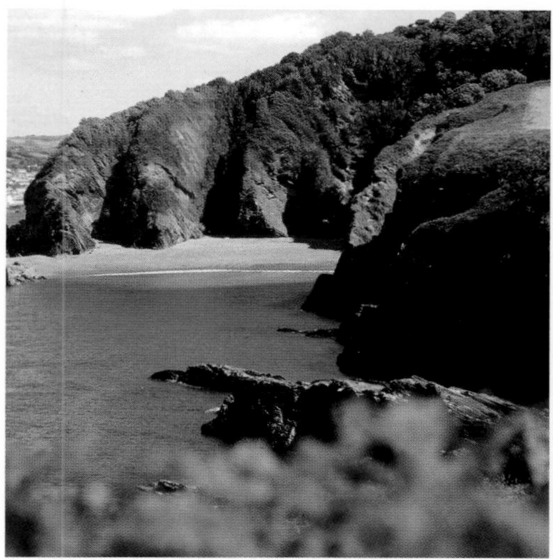
Combe Martin Bay

(see panel opposite).

Each Spring Bank Holiday the village holds the Hunting of the Earl of Rone Festival, a re-enactment of an ancient legend, when locals dress up and follow a Hobby Horse through Combe Martin in search of the Earl who rides, backwards, on a donkey. Later in the summer, at the end of June, there is the Strawberry Fair, which celebrates the wonderfully English fruit that has been grown in this area for centuries.

Museum, where the history of this village, whose harbour prospered from exporting locally grown strawberries and hemp, can be explored.

Another attraction in the town is the remarkable architectural curiosity, **The Pack o' Cards Inn** that was built by Squire George Ley in the early 18th century using the proceeds of a highly successful evening at the card table. A Grade II listed building, it represents a pack of cards with four floors, thirteen rooms and a total of 52 windows. Inside there are many features representing the cards in each suit. Meanwhile, on the outskirts of the village is **Combe Martin Wildlife and Dinosaur Park** where life-sized animated dinosaurs can be found living in the woods

Bideford

Described as the "Little White Town which slopes upward from its broad river tide" by the Victorian novelist Charles Kingsley, this attractive town, set beside the River Torridge, was once the third busiest port in Britain. Although little changed from the days when Charles

Bideford

Kingsley lived here nearly 150 years ago, Bideford was first mentioned as a crossing point of the River Torridge and, in the 1280s, the first bridge was built here by Sir Theobald Grenville. Known as the **Long Bridge**, it has 24 arches and is a permanent reminder of the early prosperity of the town. Some 670 feet long and built of massive oak lintels of varying length, which create a series of irregular arches between 12 and 15 feet apart, legend has it that the reason for the varying arch sizes is down to the local parishes who contributed to the funding of the bridge in varying amounts and the size of the arches reflects their contributions. These erratic dimensions were preserved when the bridge was rebuilt in stone in around 1460 (the old bridge was used as scaffolding) and, despite widening in the 1920s, they persist to this day. Bideford bridge is managed by an ancient corporation of trustees, known as feoffees, whose income, derived from property in the town, not only pays for the upkeep of the bridge but also supports local charities and good causes. A new, high level bridge a mile or so downstream, opened in 1987, has relieved some of the traffic congestion and also provides panoramic views of the town and the Torridge estuary.

Tantons Hotel, Bideford

The town received its Market Charter from Henry III in 1272 and markets still take place every Tuesday and Saturday and, since 1883, they have been held in the splendid **Pannier Market** building, which is reckoned to be one of the best surviving examples of a Victorian covered market.

The port of Bideford came to prominence in the Middle Ages and, like other Devon ports, it too specialised in particular commodities. At Bideford, it was tobacco from the North American colonies that brought almost two centuries of prosperity until the American War of Independence shut off supplies. It is widely believed that it was here that Sir Walter Raleigh landed his first cargo of tobacco – a pointer to its later specialisation. Evidence of this golden age can still be seen in the opulent merchants' residences in Bridgeland Street, and most strikingly in the Royal Hotel in East-the-Water, a former merchant's house of 1688 that has a pair of little seen plaster ceilings that are some of the finest and most extravagant of their kind in Devon. It was whilst staying at the Royal Hotel that Charles Kingsley penned most of *Westward Ho!* A quarter of a million words long, the novel was completed in just seven months. There is a statue of the novelist on Bideford Quay, which stands at the foot of the narrow maze of lanes that formed the old seaport.

Just around the corner from the quay, on the edge of Victoria Park, is the **Burton Art Gallery and Museum** where a great variety of arts and crafts by both local and national artists past and present are on display. Meanwhile, the museum contains many interesting curios relating to Bideford's past including a model of the Long Bridge around which the history of the town is displayed, north Devon slipware, carved ships' decorations and Napoleonic model ships carved by prisoners-of-war from bone. The art gallery and museum, which has a gift and coffee shop, is open daily all year round except for Mondays and Sunday mornings.

The town's strong maritime connection is represented by the *Kathleen & May*, which is moored on the River Torridge next to the old bridge. This historic three-masted schooner has been restored and the guided tours of the ship take in the cosy captain's cabin, the cramped crew's quarters and the vast hold that carried coal, bricks, slate and even gunpowder. There is also an information centre, with early prints and documents along with a collection of interesting artefacts, and a gift shop selling souvenirs.

St Helens Church, Lundy Island

Another form of transport is explored at the former **Bideford Railway Station**, now a museum, which displays many fascinating artefacts of local railway interest. Meanwhile, outside, there are a number of railway vehicles to be seen on a length of re-laid track. Found at the east end of the Long Bridge, the museum is open Sunday, Thursday and Bank Holiday afternoons from Easter to the end of October and on Sunday afternoons for the rest of the year and there are also brake van rides available as well as a gift shop.

Lundy Island

One further travelling experience in Bideford that certainly should not be missed is a day trip to **Lundy Island** on the supply boat MS *Oldenburg*. The natural and historic island, owned by the National Trust, is some three miles long and just half a mile wide and, as well as being a place of peace and tranquillity, it

Orchard Hill Hotel

Orchard Hill, Bideford, Devon EX39 2QY
Tel: 01237 472872 Fax: 01237 423803
e-mail: info@orchardhillhotel.co.uk
website: www.orchardhillhotel.co.uk

Found just outside the centre of Bideford and commanding excellent views down over the "Little White Town" and the River Torridge, Orchard Hill Hotel is a charming and friendly establishment that is sure to please the most discerning guest.

After coming here in early 2002, new owners Roger and Rachel Pavitt undertook a short, but extensive, period of refurbishment and, today, this spacious Victorian family house can offer guests a choice of nine en-suite guest rooms, two of which lie on the ground floor.

Both breakfast and dinner are served in the delightful dining room whilst there is also a licensed bar and a private lounge at guests' disposal. The building, once called Rosekerry House, is surrounded by a well-maintained and established garden that provides children, who are welcome here, with an opportunity to let off steam.

Along with ensuring that all guests have an enjoyable and comfortable stay here, Roger and Rachel offer a series of short breaks for sporting and leisure activities and, in particular, golfing packages that include discounted green fees at some of the nearby excellent courses.

is also home to three lighthouses, a medieval castle and a pub, the Marisco Tavern, where the island's own brew is served. Self-catering accommodation is available, and visitors can send back postcards to the main land stamped with the island's famous own stamps. Lundy, too, has a wealth of wildlife and its name is derived from the Norse 'lunde ey', meaning puffin island, and these attractive birds, with their multi-coloured beaks, are still in residence along with many other species of bird, black rabbits and Lundy ponies. The MS *Oldenburg*, which can carry 267 passengers, makes the 12 mile sea journey to the island all year round from Bideford and there are other sailings, between Easter and October, from Ilfracombe.

Around Bideford

Northam

1½ miles N of Bideford on the A386

It was here, three years after William the Conqueror's triumph at Hastings, that the slain King Harold's three illegitimate sons landed, from Ireland, with a force of more than 60 ships. Their attempt to regain the English throne from William was mercilessly put down at a site to the south of this small town that, today, is still known as Bloody Corner. A busy place, with some elegant Georgian houses on Orchard Hill, and a fine church tower that has acted as a landmark for sailors for generations, the extensive sand dunes and salt marshes to the north of the town are now the **Northam Burrows Country Park** that is also home to the oldest 18-hole links golf course in England. The **Royal North Devon Golf Course** was laid out in 1864 by 'Old Tom Morris' and it is considered to represent a true test of the game although, from some vantage points, it can look benign. The park is home to a wide variety of wildlife along with grazing animals and the Visitor Centre contains information about the area and, from here, rangers lead regular walks and hold talks.

Appledore

3½ miles N of Bideford on the A386

Overlooking the Taw and Torridge estuaries, where both rivers meet the Atlantic Ocean, this attractive little town, much of which is a conservation area, has been a thriving port since it was settled by the Cistercian monks in the 14th century, although, earlier, the Saxons fished from here. The town's oldest building is **Docton House** that was built by the monks as a rest house for pilgrims making the journey to Hartland Abbey and it remained in their hands until 1540. Given 'free port' status in 1588 by Elizabeth I for the vital role it played in the Armada, the port grew rapidly in the 18th century when it became the largest port in the country trading in tobacco. A delightful place of narrow winding lanes and sturdy 18th

and 19th century fishermen's cottages, Appledore was a 'strand' village, where the houses on the west side of Market Street were built with gardens that ran down to the river. The first quay here was built in the mid 19th century by joining up the garden walls to create a single barrier and, later, sail lofts and warehouses were erected in the gardens. The quay was extended in the 1930s and, in 1997, the present quay was built.

With such a nautical history it is appropriate that Appledore is the home of the **North Devon Maritime Museum** that is housed in a former shipowner's residence and where there is a wealth of seafaring memorabilia as well as a reconstructed Victorian kitchen and an exhibition detailing the military exercises that took place around the estuary in preparation for the D-Day landings of World War II. Here, too, is a special display devoted to Prince Edward Island, Canada, as links were forged with the country when shipbuilders from the Appledore area emigrated to Canada because of the shortage of timber.

Also well worth a visit is the **Appledore Crafts Company**, a co-operative of 14 leading local craftspeople that was founded in 1991. Displaying work that ranges from fine furniture, paintings and ceramics to wood carving, metal work and contemporary crafts, the gallery, which is open daily in the summer and from Wednesdays to Sundays in the winter, is staffed by the members themselves and also holds a series of exhibitions.

Instow

3 miles NE of Bideford on the B3233

The older part of this village lies inland from the Torridge estuary whilst, closer to the shore there are some early 19th century villas. Here, too, is the **Instow Signal Box** that was built in 1873 to control the crossing gates and the passing loop at Instow Station. Restored and now the first Grade II listed signal box in the country, visitors can see its levers, gate wheel and instruments as well as 'pull off' a reinstated signal.

Just south of the village lie **Tapeley**

Park Gardens, some 35 acres of grounds situated on the eastern bank of the River Torridge and from here there are excellent views across the estuary and to Lundy Island. A national garden in the making, along with the lake reached by a woodland walk, the masses of hydrangeas, rhododendrons and camellias, the renovated Italian terraces and the restored walled kitchen garden, Tapeley has a new organic permaculture garden, where fruit, vegetables, nuts and herbs are mixed together using companion planting. There is also a children's play area and a variety of animals and pets to entertain the youngsters. Tapeley Park Gardens are open daily (except Saturdays) from mid March to the end of October. Here, too, is a plant shop and a tea room.

Weare Giffard

3 miles S of Bideford off the A386

This appealing village claims to be the longest riverside village in England and it straggles for almost two miles along the banks of the River Torridge. Weare Giffard (pronounced 'Jiffard') has a charm all its own and it seems to be suspended in time and to belong to the more peaceful days of half a century ago. The villagers have even refused to have full street lighting installed, so avoiding the 'street furniture' that blemishes so many attractive places. Another attraction in the village is a fine old 15th century manor house, **Weare Giffard Hall** and, although its outer walls were partially demolished during the Civil War, the splendid gatehouse, with its mighty doors and guardian lions, has survived. Inside, the main hall has a magnificent hammer-beam roof and several of the other rooms are lined with Tudor and Jacobean oak panelling. For centuries, the house was the home of the Fortescue family and, in the nearby church, there is an interesting 'family tree' with portraits of past family members carved in stone.

Great Torrington

5 miles S of Bideford on the A386

A good place from which to begin an exploration of Great Torrington is **Castle Hill**, which commands grand views along the valley of the River

Royal Horticultural Society Garden Rosemoor

Great Torrington, Devon Ex38 8PH
Tel: 01805 624067 Fax: 01805 624717
website: www.rhs.org.uk

The Royal Horticultural Society Garden Rosemoor is acclaimed by gardeners throughout the world, but visitors do not have to be keen gardeners to appreciate the beauty and diversity of Rosemoor. Whatever the season, the garden is a unique and enchanting place that people return to time and time again. Situated on the west-facing slopes of the beautiful Torridge Valley, Rosemoor has become one of the jewels in the West Country crown.

Generously donated to the Society by Lady Anne Palmer in 1988, Rosemoor is now established as a garden of national importance, famous for its variety and planting. To Lady Anne's collection of rare and interesting plants a wide range of varied features have been added. They include a formal garden, where the object is to show an enormous selection of plants and planting schemes, and a series of individual gardens such as the renowned Rose Gardens, Foliage Garden and the Cottage, Square and Spiral Gardens, and the Winter Garden with stunning effects in the colder months. All this, a lake, a bamboo and fern planted rock gully, an Arboretum and three new Model Gardens, as well as a marvellous Fruit and Vegetable Garden, make a visit to Rosemoor essential.

Torridge although the castle itself was demolished as long ago as 1228 and its site is now a bowling green. On the opposite bank of the river is the hamlet of Taddiport where the tiny 14th century church by the bridge was originally a chapel of a leper hospital.

During the Civil War, Great Torrington was host to two important, though small scale, clashes in the consecutive years and it was the site of the last major battle of the war when over 10,000 troops fought through the streets of the town. Great Torrington also has the dubious distinction of having had its church blown up by gunpowder when the original Church of St Michael and All Angels was destroyed, also during the Civil War. In 1645, General Fairfax bundled his Royalist prisoners into the church, which they had been using as an arsenal, and, in the darkness, the 80 barrels of gunpowder stored there were somehow set alight. The resultant massive explosion demolished the church, 200 men lost their lives and Fairfax himself narrowly escaped death. The present spacious church was built five years later, one of very few in the country to have been erected during the Commonwealth years. Local tradition suggests that the Black Horse Inn was the headquarters of Lord Hopton, the general of the Royalist soldiers defending the town.

An ancient country market town, Great Torrington continues to hold its May Fair as it has done since 1554 and, on the first Thursday of May, a Queen is crowned, there is traditional Maypole dancing and a banner proclaims the greeting "Us be plazed to see 'ee." The **Torrington Museum** is an ideal place to discover the history of this small Devon town through the centuries and the collections here cover agriculture, transport, domestic life and local industries. The museum also has a collection of artefacts on the life and work of William Keble-Martin, the author of the *Definitive Book on Wild Flowers* and a vicar in the town for nine years. Also worth a visit is **Dartington Crystal**, which is internationally famous for its clear, contemporary glassware, and here visitors can see the skilled craftsmen at work during the factory tour. An exhibition on the story of glass, from the ancient Egyptians to the present day, and a glass activity area add to the enjoyment and, along with the restaurant, Dartington has one of the largest glass shops in the country.

About a mile south of Great Torrington is the **Royal Horticultural Society Garden Rosemoor** (see panel opposite) that occupies a breathtaking setting in the Torridge Valley. Along with the masses of plants there are trails for children, a shop, a restaurant, a plant centre and an award-winning Visitor Centre.

Merton

10 miles SE of Bideford on the A386

This village is home to **Barometer World and Museum**, a remarkable collection that was begun by Edwin Banfield, a retired bank manager in the early 1970s. Along with housing the largest collection of English barometers on public display in the world, the museum is home to an exhibition that charts the development of domestic barometers from the 1680s to the present days as well as other unusual items that have been used, over the years, to predict the weather. Perhaps most extraordinary of all these bizarre devices is the Tempest Prognosticator that was designed by Dr George Merryweather and that he exhibited at the Great Exhibition of 1851. Styled on an Indian temple, the 'machine' uses live leeches to determine whether a storm is on its way! The museum and showroom, where barometers are still made and restored, are open from Tuesdays to Saturdays.

Dolton

11½ miles SE of Bideford on the B3217

Situated above the wooded Torridge Valley, this village clusters around its parish Church of St Edmund's that boasts a true treasure – a font that dates back more than 1,000 years. Made from two pieces of a Saxon cross, the intricate carvings on the font depict a fantastic menagerie of winged dragons and writhing serpents with yet more dragons emerging from the upturned head of a man. Their relevance to the Christian message may be a little obscure but there is no denying their powerful impact.

Just to the northwest lies the **Halsdon Nature Reserve** that encompasses an extremely pretty valley of deciduous trees and pasture along with a mile and a half stretch of the River Torridge. This river is particularly important for its otter population and they can be found in the reserve along with a wide variety of birds.

Meeth

13 miles SE of Bideford on the A386

This pleasant little village, whose Old English name means 'the meeting of the streams', lies close to the point where a small brook runs down a hillside into the River Torridge. From the early 1700s, Meeth and the surrounding area was noted for its 'pipe' and 'ball clay' products, which are generically known as pottery clay, and there are still extensive clay works to the be found to the northwest of the village.

However, Meeth is best known to cyclists and walkers as the southern terminus of the **Tarka Trail**, a cycle and walkway that runs northwards through Bideford and Barnstaple and around the Taw and Torrindge estuaries to Braunton.

Monkleigh

3½ miles S of Bideford on the A388

Set high in the Torridge family,

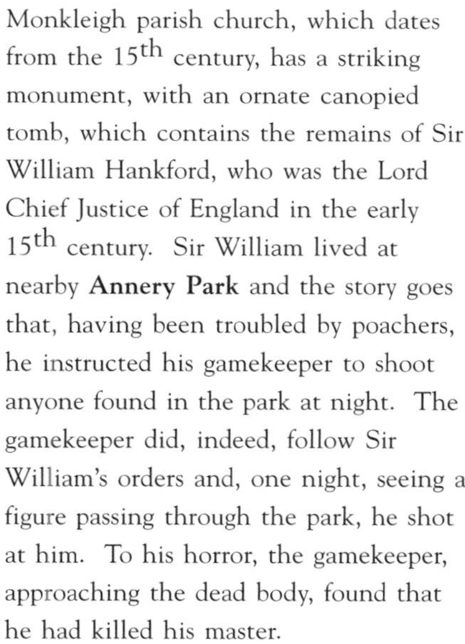

Monkleigh parish church, which dates from the 15th century, has a striking monument, with an ornate canopied tomb, which contains the remains of Sir William Hankford, who was the Lord Chief Justice of England in the early 15th century. Sir William lived at nearby **Annery Park** and the story goes that, having been troubled by poachers, he instructed his gamekeeper to shoot anyone found in the park at night. The gamekeeper did, indeed, follow Sir William's orders and, one night, seeing a figure passing through the park, he shot at him. To his horror, the gamekeeper, approaching the dead body, found that he had killed his master.

Found in the outbuildings of a small holding near the village is **Monkleigh Pottery**, where Richard Champion, a traditional craft potter who specialises in hand thrown stoneware pottery works. Visitors are welcome to come a see the pots being made, which include dinner services, vases and planters, and there is also a picnic and children's play area.

Shebbear

11 miles S of Bideford off the A388

This attractive and ancient village (it appeared as 'Sepesberie' in the *Domesday Book*) is set around a spacious square laid out in the Saxon manner with a church at one end and a hostelry at the other. Lying in a hollow just outside the churchyard is a huge lump of rock, weighing around a ton, which is known as the **Devil's Stone** and it marks an ancient sacred site. However, according to local legend, the huge boulder was placed here by the Devil who challenged the villagers to move it, threatening that disaster would strike if they could not do so. Every year since then, on November 5th (a date established long before the Gunpowder Plot of 1605), a curious ceremony has taken place. After sounding a peal of bells, the bell ringers come out of the church and set about the stone with sticks and crowbars. Once they have successfully turned the stone over, they returned in triumph to the bell tower to sound a second peal.

Sheepwash

12½ miles S of Bideford off the A3072

This village, like so many Devon communities, suffered a devastating fire that took place in 1742 and the destruction was so great that for more than 10 years the village remained completely deserted. However, slowly the villagers returned, building new houses in stone, and, today, it still has the essence of a Devon village distilled in one location with several thatched cottages situated around a village square. Here, along one side of the square, stands the famous Half Moon Inn that is renowned amongst fishermen whilst, on another side, the old church tower rises above the pink washed cottages and, in the centre of the square, cherry trees shelter the ancient village pump.

Just to the south of Sheepwash lies the River Torridge and, until well into the 17th century, the only way of crossing the river here was by means of stepping stones. One day, when the river was in full spate, a young man, attempting to return to the village, was swept away and drowned. His father, John Tusbury, was grief-stricken but responded to the tragedy by providing the funds to build a bridge. He also donated sufficient money for it to be maintained by establishing the Bridgeland Trust and stipulating that any surplus income should be used to help in the upkeep of the church and chapel. The trust is still in operation and nowadays also funds outings for village children and pensioners.

Littleham

2½ miles SW of Bideford off the A386

This tiny village, set on the hills above the River Yeo, comprises just a few houses, an ancient church and an excellent pub but, unusually for Devon, the church and pub stand at opposite ends of the village. They are, however, linked by the inn's name, the Crealock Arms, as the grandest monument inside St Swithin's Church is the impressive memorial to General Crealock, a distinguished Victorian soldier and local landowner whose tomb stands nearly six feet high.

Westward Ho!

2 miles NW of Bideford on the B3236

The only place in the country named after a novel, it was following the huge success, in 1855, of Charles Kingsley's tale of Elizabethan daring-do, that a company was formed to develop this spectacular site, with its rocky cliffs and sandy beach, into a holiday resort. However, the early years of the development were troubled when a powerful storm washed away the newly built pier and most of the houses. When, in 1874, Rudyard Kipling came here as a pupil at the United Services

College he described the village as "twelve bleak houses by the shore." Kipling later made reference to his four years at the college in his novel *Stalky & Co.* A popular family holiday resort today, there are over two miles of golden sands as well as all the usual traditional seaside attractions.

Each year Westward Ho! plays host to the rather unusual **Pot Walloping Festival**, a fabulous spring time event that dates back to the 1800s and where local people come down to the beach to throw back pebbles that have been dislodged from the pebble ridge by the winter storms . It is, today, a large and bustling occasion with fun and entertainment, as well as displays and local craft stalls, that all the family can enjoy.

Just a couple of miles southwest of Westward Ho! lies **The Big Sheep**, which has been described as "a working farm turned wacky tourist attraction." Along with 'one dog and his ducks', sheep racing and the horse whisperers, there is a huge indoor adventure play area for children and, more conventionally, cheese making, sheep shearing and sheepdog trailing demonstrations. The Big Sheep, which now has its own brewery, is open daily from April to the end of October.

Holsworthy

A well-established agricultural centre, this little town, which lies just a few miles from the Cornish border, comes alive each week when the traditional street market takes place. Holsworthy serves a large area of the surrounding countryside and, at the market, there is a wide range of locally-produced goods, including fresh cream, butter, cheese and vegetables. However, the town gets even livelier in early July when the three-day-long **St Peter's Fair** takes place and it begins with the rather curious old custom of the Pretty Maid Ceremony. Back in 1841, a Holsworthy merchant bequeathed a legacy to provide a small payment each year to a local spinster, under the age of 30 and noted for her good looks, demure manner and regular attendance at church. Rather surprisingly, in view of the last two requirements, the bequest

Holsworthy Museum

Manor Offices, Holsworthy, Devon EX22 6DJ
Tel: 01409 259337
e-mail: Holsworthy@devonmuseums.net
website: www.devonmuseums.net/holsworthy

Housed in an 18th century parsonage, this small museum gives you an insight into Holsworthy's heritage and traditions. Various themed displays cover the town, local railway, agriculture, trades, medical and the World Wars. Researchers into family and local history may view, by prior arrangement, a selection of local parish registers on microfiche, IGI fiche and Census data as well as information held in the Local History unit. The museum is run entirely by volunteers and is dependent on donations, a small entrance fee and support from local Councils. Open February to December. Groups can visit at other times by arrangement.

still finds a suitable recipient each year. Holsworthy, too, is one of the few remaining places in the country where the Court Leet, which dates from the 12th century, still meets and, here, the meeting takes place on the eve of the fair.

An interesting feature in the parish church is an organ built in 1688 by Renatus Hunt for All Saints Church, Chelsea, London. In 1723, the organ was declared worn out but was, nevertheless, purchased by a Bideford church and moved there where, for some 140 years, it gave excellent service. Once again written off, in the 1860s, the organ was moved to Holsworthy's church and it has been here ever since. **Holsworthy Museum**, which is open week day mornings and all day Wednesdays throughout the year as well as occasional Saturday mornings, is, itself, housed in a building that is something of a museum piece (see panel on page 97).

The countryside around Holsworthy is particularly popular with cyclists and there are three clearly designated routes starting and finishing in the town. It also lies on the **West Country Way**, a 250-mile long cycle route from Padstow to Bristol and Bath that opened in the spring of 1997.

Around Holsworthy

West Putford

7½ miles N of Holsworthy off the A388

Close to this rural village in the Torridge Valley lies the **Gnome Reserve and Wild Flower Garden**, where, amongst the beechwood, over 1,000 gnomes and pixies are on display whilst, in the wild flower garden, there are over 250 labelled species of wild flowers, herbs, grasses and ferns. Open daily from March to October, visitors here can also see the garden gnomes and pixies being made in the studio of Ann Atkin.

Ashmansworthy

9 miles N of Holsworthy off the A39

Just to the south of Ashmansworthy lies

the **Volehouse Moor Nature Reserve**, a diverse site that includes a stretch of the River Torridge, woodland and one of the finest Culm grassland areas in the West Country. The whole reserve is managed by cattle grazing and, although there are now formal footpaths, the reserve can be freely explored and there is also a crossing point over the river.

Woolfardisworthy

10½ miles N of Holsworthy off the A39

This large village is also known as Woolsery and both names appear on local road signs. The longer and more eccentric name, Woolfardisworthy, goes back to Saxon times when the land was owned by Wulfheard who established a 'worthig' or homestead here. Just to the north of the village lies the **Milkyway Adventure Park**, an extraordinary family entertainment complex that includes exhilarating rides, a vast indoor play area, a pets' corner, miniature railway, archery and laser target shooting and a bird of prey centre. Open daily during the season and at weekends in the winter, this is an amazing place that will enthral all the family.

Clovelly

13 miles N of Holsworthy off the A39

An unbelievably quaint and picturesque village, which tumbles down a steep hillside in terraced levels, Clovelly is many people's idea of the typical Devonshire coastal community. Almost every white-washed and flower-strewn cottage here is worthy of its own picture postcard and, from the sheltered little harbour, there is an enchanting view of this unique place. One reason why this village has remained so unspoilt is that it has belonged to the Rous family since 1738 and they have ensured that it has been spared such modern defacements as telegraph poles and 'street furniture'.

The only access to the beach and the beautifully restored 14th century quay is on foot although the donkeys that were once the method of transport

Clovelly

Clovelly Harbour

restored Victorian greenhouses, is open to visitors. Finally, the village's award-winning **Visitor Centre**, which is modelled on a traditional Devon long barn, has an audio-visual show narrating the development of Clovelly from around 2000 BC to the present day.

now no longer carry heavy loads and there is a Land Rover service from the Red Lion Hotel for those who cannot face the climb back up the hill. The only other forms of transport here are the sledges that are used to deliver the weekly supplies. During the summer months there are regular boat trips around the bay and the *Jessica Hettie* can be booked for a trip to Lundy Island with timings that allow passengers to spend some six hours there, watching the seals and abundant wildlife.

This captivating village has some strong literary links and it features as 'Steepway' in the novel *A Message from the Sea* by Wilkie Collins. Charles Kingsley, the author of *The Water Babies*, was at school here in the 1820s and the **Kingsley Museum** explores his links with the village and it was whilst staying here that he wrote *Westward Ho!* Close by is a **Fisherman's Cottage** that provides an insight into what life was like here in the 1930s whilst, the ancient manor house, **Clovelly Court**, with its walled kitchen gardens and

Clawton

3 miles S of Holsworthy on the A388

A good indication of the mildness of the Devon climate is the number of vineyards that have been established here over the last 30 years or so and, in the valley of the River Claw, lies **Clawford Vineyard**. Set in more than 78 acres of vines and orchards, the vineyard's owners welcome visitors to sample their home-produced wines and ciders and, in the autumn, to watch that year's vintage being produced.

Alfardisworthy

5 ½ miles NW of Holsworthy off the A39

Situated almost on top of the county border with Cornwall, to the north and south of the village lie the **Tamar Lakes**, two attractive lakes that are not only an important area for birds but also offer an excellent opportunity for a day out in the countryside. The interpretation centre provides information about the lakes and the activities in the area whilst the watersports centre offers sailing, windsurfing and canoeing tuition. Also here is a children's play area, picnic meadow and, open from Easter to autumn, a gift shop and tea room.

Mead

11½ miles NW of Holsworthy off the A39

Close to this small coastal village, which lies near to the county border with Cornwall, is the **Welcombe and Marsland Nature Reserve**, which incorporates two adjacent valleys and extends inland from this dramatic stretch of coastline. With wooded steep-sided valleys and maritime heath and grassland, there is a wide variety of bird, animal and plant life to discover by taking the footpaths through the reserve.

Milford

13½ miles NW of Holsworthy off the A39

Found in Speke valley, just north of the village, and only a short walk from the famous **Spekes Mill Mouth Coastal Waterfall**, lies **Docton Mill and Gardens** (see panel below). The mill dates back to Saxon times and it only ceased working in 1910 but, in 1980, these superb gardens were created around the existing river, leats and ponds. Docton Mill and Gardens is open daily from the beginning of March to the end of October.

Hartland

14½ miles NW of Holsworthy on the B3248

This pleasant village, with its narrow streets and small square, was once larger and more important that Bideford, further along the coast, and from the times of King Alfred to the Norman Conquest, it was a royal possession. Hartland continued to be a busy centre right up until the 19th century although it was at its most prosperous in the 1700s and some fine Georgian buildings survive from that period. However, the most striking building is the parish **Church of St Nectan** that stands a mile or so west of the village. Its exterior is impressive with its 128-foot tower but it is the glorious 15th century screen inside

Docton Mill and Gardens

Created in 1980 the gardens at **Docton Mill**, which can be traced back to Saxon times, were designed and planted by Iris Pugh and it is to her that the gardens' famous magnolia collection is dedicated.

However, there are many more plants, trees and shrubs to see at this sheltered site that makes the most of the ancient mill buildings as a backdrop. Visitors can also enjoy some light refreshment at the gardens whilst enjoying the peaceful and tranquil setting.

Hartland

the Royal wine cellars and it remains in the family today. The house was partly rebuilt in the mid 18th century in the Strawberry Hill Gothic style and, around 100 years later, Sir George Gilbert Scott was commissioned to add the front hall and entrance. The abbey's owner, Sir George Stucley, had recently visited the Alhambra Palace in Spain, which he much admired, and he asked Scott to design something in a similar style and the result was the elegant corridor with its blue vaulted ceiling and white stencilled patterns. The abbey is home to a wonderful collection of paintings, porcelain and

that makes this church one of the most visited in the county. A masterpiece of the medieval woodcarvers' art, its elegant arches are topped by four exquisitely fretted bands of intricate designs, whilst the arches are delicately painted – a reminder of how colourful English churches used to be before the vandalism of the Puritan years. In the churchyard is the grave of Allen Lane who, in 1935, revolutionised publishing by his introduction of Penguin Books – paperbacks that were sold at just sixpence each.

To the west of the village lies **Hartland Abbey** that was founded soon after 1157 and, although it survived longer than any other monastery in the country, it was finally dissolved in 1539. Henry VIII gave the building and its wide estates to William Abbott, Sergeant of

Lighthouse, Hartland Point

furniture, acquired by the family over the generations and there is also a unique collection of documents dating from 1160 along with Victorian and Edwardian photographs. The gardens are equally impressive and include an 18th century walled garden, a Victorian Fernery and the Baronet's Bog Garden designed by Gertrude Jekyll.

A mile further west is **Hartland Quay** that, despite being exposed to all the wrath of Atlantic storms, was a busy landing place until the sea finally overwhelmed the 16th century quay in 1893. Several of the old buildings have been converted into a comfortable hotel whilst another is now a **Museum** recording the many wrecks that have littered this jagged coastline.

Meanwhile, to the north of the quay and reached by winding country lanes, is **Hartland Point**. On Ptolemy's map of Britain, drawn up in Roman times, he names it the 'Promontory of Hercules', a fitting name for this fearsome stretch of upended rocks that rise at right angles to the sea. One local legend suggests that Hercules actually landed here, defeated the English giants and then successfully governed the region. Another story tells that the headland was the site of the cell of the 6th century Welsh hermit, St Nectan. Those making their way out here will be rewarded with breathtaking views that also take in the lighthouse built in 1874.

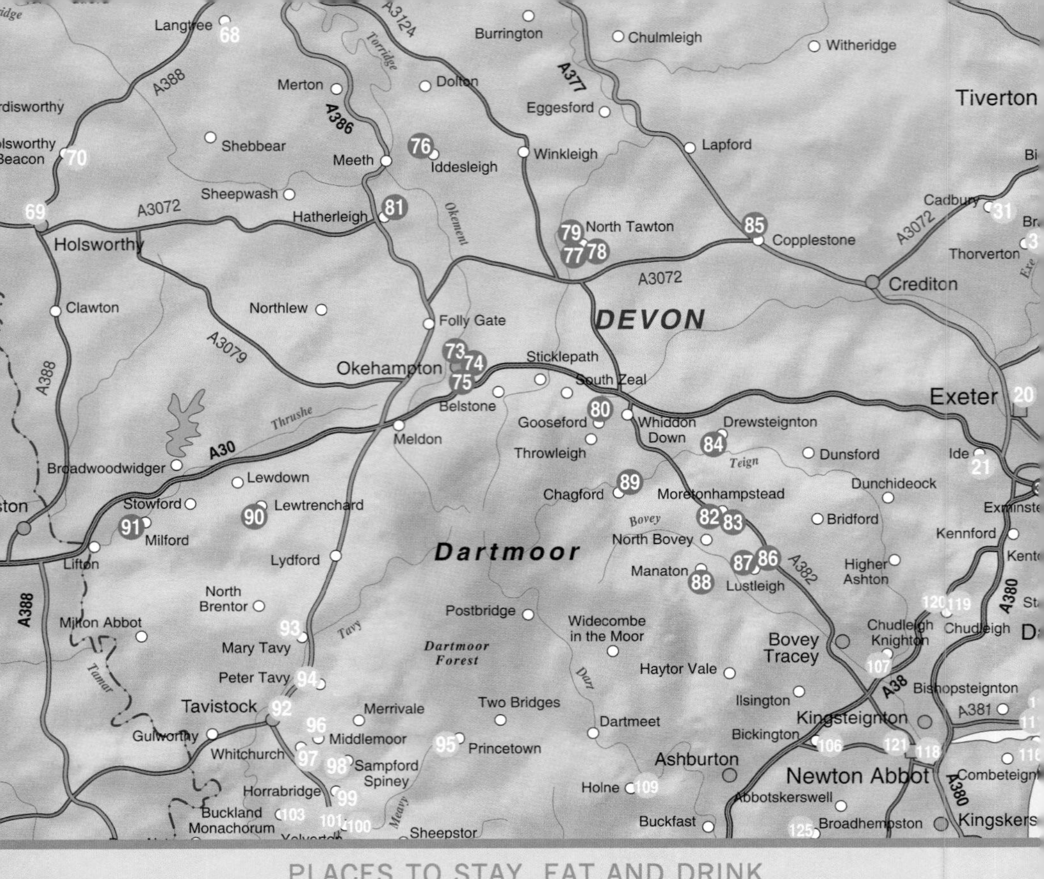

PLACES TO STAY, EAT AND DRINK

Victorian Pantry Tea Rooms, Okehampton	73	Tea Rooms	p106
Le Café Noir, Okehampton	74	Café and Restaurant	p107
Okehampton Castle, Okehampton	75	Historic Attraction	p107
Parsonage Farm, Iddesleigh, Winkleigh	76	Bed and Breakfast	p108
Kayden House Hotel, North Tawton	77	Hotel	p110
The Copper Key Inn, North Tawton	78	Pub and Restaurant	p110
Oaklands Farm, North Tawton	79	Bed and Breakfast	p111
Fairhaven Farm, Gooseford, Whiddon Down	80	Bed and Breakfast	p112
Acorns Café and Tea Rooms, Hatherleigh	81	Café and Tea Rooms	p114
Great Sloncombe Farm, Mortonhampstead	82	Bed and Breakfast	p115
Budleigh Farm, Mortonhampstead	83	Self Catering	p116
Castle Drogo, Drewsteignton	84	House and Gardens	p117
The Devonshire Dumpling, Copplestone	85	Pub, Food and Accommodation	p119
The Cleave at Lustleigh, Lustleigh	86	Pub with Food	p120
Lustleigh Mills, Lustleigh	87	Self Catering	p121
Becky Falls Woodland Park, Manaton	88	Scenic Attraction	p122
The Three Crowns Hotel, Chagford	89	Hotel	p123
Lewtrenchard Manor, Lewtrenchard	90	Hotel	p127
Dingles Steam Village, Milford, Lifton	91	Historic Attraction	p128

Denotes entries in other chapters

4 North Dartmoor

High, wild and bleak, Dartmoor is the south of England's only true wilderness and it is easy for walkers to lose their way in the rolling granite uplands, particularly when the mists descend unexpectedly and with great speed. Roughly 21 miles long and 15 miles wide, the Dartmoor National Park covers an area of some 365 square miles and it rises to a height of more than 2,000 feet. However, geologists believe that some 400 million years ago this volcanic tableland stood at over 15,000 feet above the Devonian Sea but millions of years of erosion have reduce the area to a plateau of whale-backed granite ridges. The highest and most dramatic area of the moor lies to the northwest, on Okehampton Common, where High Willhays and Yes Tor rise to a height of 2,038 feet and 2,029 feet respectively. Meanwhile, although not so high, Brent Tor is one of the moorland's most striking features as, on its 1,000-foot summit, is a 12th century church and, from here, on a clear day there are superb views across Dartmoor, westwards to Bodmin Moor and southwards to the sea at Plymouth Sound.

Several of Devon's rivers have their source on the moorland and some have given rise to another feature of the moorland – waterfalls. In particular there is Lydford Gorge, the suddenly narrowing valley of the River Lyd where not only is there some spectacular scenery but also the impressive 90-foot White Lady Waterfall and a series of whirlpools. On the eastern edge of the National Park and in the valley of the River Bovey is the Becky Falls Woodland Park whilst, close by, in the valley of the River Teign, there is England's highest waterfall, Canonteign Falls.

Dartmoor

However, Dartmoor is, perhaps, best associated with the Sir Arthur Conan Doyle who, in his spine-chilling novel *The Hound of the Baskervilles*, made the moorland bleaker and more sinister than it is in reality. This most famous of all the Sherlock Holmes tales, when his creator brought him back from death, was inspired by stories told to Conan Doyle by his Dartmoor guide, Harry Baskerville. Although he took the liberty of changing some of the geography of the moorland, the novel has brought many visitors to Dartmoor since it was first published. Anyone walking the moorland today cannot help but come across one of the hundreds of letterboxes that litter the landscape. These were first installed by the famous Dartmoor guide, James Perrot who installed the first letterbox at Cranmere Pool, near the heart of the moor, so that his Victorian clients could send postcards home especially stamped to prove where they had been.

New Bridge, River Dart

Okehampton

Although it is using a cliché to describe the landscape around Okehampton as one of contrasts, it cannot be avoided as, to the north and west there are the puckered green hills of north Devon rolling away to the coast whilst, to the south, lie the wildest stretches of Dartmoor with the great peaks of **High Willhays** and **Yes Tor** rising to more than 2,000 feet. At this height they are, officially, mountains but they are now quite tiny compared with their original height: geologists believe that, at one time, the surface of Dartmoor stood at 15,000 feet above sea level. Millions of

Le Café Noir

6 Red Lion Yard, Okehampton,
Devon Ex20 1AW
Tel: 01837 54234

Found right in the heart of Okehampton the traditional and olde worlde exterior of **Le Café Noir** does nothing to prepare customers for the chic and modern interior of this stylish and sophisticated café and restaurant.

Although owners Paul and Helen Ranger only took over Le Café Noir in June 2002, their many years of experience in the hotel and catering trade are evident in the highly professional manner in which the café is run.

Despite only being open during the day, though this is likely to change in the near future, Paul and Helen have quickly established their café as being one of the most popular places to eat in the town.

The extensive menu, which is supplemented by a daily specials board, ranges from traditional toasted teacakes, open sandwiches and omelettes through to intriguing salads and continental crostini. However, whatever is chosen customers can be sure that each dish is home-cooked and, wherever possible, the food, including meat, comes from local sources.

Le Café Noir is also licensed and along with bottled beers and spirits there is a select wine list that, like the dishes, are very reasonably priced.

years of erosion have reduced the area to a plateau of whale-backed granite ridges, with an average height of around 1,200 feet, and the moor has become strewn with fragments of surface granite, or moorstone. It was because of this ready to use stone that Dartmoor became one of the most populous areas of early Britain and the inhabitants used the easily quarried granite to create their stone rows, circles and burial chambers and along with their distinctive hut circles of which there are still more than 1,500 scattered across the moor.

An attractive town that can certainly claim to be a 'Gateway to Dartmoor', Okehampton was, from Celtic times, an important place as it stood on the main

Okehampton Castle

Okehampton, Devon
Tel: 01837 52844
website: www.english-heritage.org.uk

Once the largest castle in Devon and a potent symbol of the feudal power of its owners, after the Norman Conquest **Okehampton Castle** (English Heritage) provided an awe-inspiring reminder of the newly arrived nobility. Although now in ruins, the massive keep still stands tall and, surrounded by woodland, it is a tranquil and peaceful setting for a building that is steeped in history. Open from April to October, the castle is brought to life for visitors on the audio tour whilst a series of special events help to re-create life during the castle's heyday.

route into Cornwall. Mentioned in the *Domesday Book*, as Ochementone, this market town had, even then, a castle and today the ruins of **Okehampton Castle** (English Heritage) can be found romantically sited on a hilltop and dominating the surrounding valley of the West Okement River (see panel on page 107).

Amongst the town's other interesting buildings is the 15th century **Chapel of Ease** and the **Town Hall**, a striking three storey building that was erected in 1685 as a private house and converted to its current use in the 1820s. Another excellent place to visit is the **Museum of Dartmoor Life** that is housed in an early 19th century mill whose water wheel has been restored. Here, in the three galleries, the story of life on Dartmoor, down the ages, is told and, in particular, the museum displays illustrate how the moorland has shaped the lives of its inhabitants and vice versa. The museum is open daily in summer and weekdays only in winter. In the surrounding courtyard are gift shops, a tea rooms and the Okehampton Tourist Information Centre.

The beautifully restored Okehampton Station lies at the centre of the **Dartmoor Railway**, which runs trains from Crediton down to Plymouth and Cornwall but it also climbs into the National Park and terminates at Meldon Viaduct. At Okehampton there is not only a buffet but also a large shop that specialises in all manner of railway paraphernalia.

Around Okehampton

Iddesleigh

8 miles N of Okehampton on the B3217

Situated in the heartland of rural Devon, this pretty little village was once the home of the famous 'Sporting Parson', Rev Jack Russell who resided for six years at Iddesleigh, living at Parsonage Farm (The Rectory at that time). His son John Bury was buried, as an infant, in Iddesleigh churchyard in May 1928. The author Charles Noon wrote: "Revd Jack Russell was the epitome of the 19th century hunting parson. A true sportsman and

countryman he developed the strain of terrier with which he will ever be associated, and by the end of his life he was virtually MFH emeritis for the whole of fox-hunting land. No Devon sporting occasion was complete without him, and in time, his fame as the 'sporting parson' or as plain Jack Russell became celebrated nationally. But Russell was not just a good fox-hunter, he was also a good and popular clergyman, robust, life-enhancing, a man of peace and a good neighbour and friend to all classes and conditions from royalty to farm labourers".

Charles Noon describes the village as follows: "On a clear day from the parish church Dartmoor fills the southern horizon with its strong, round outlines, but in the other directions the farming patchwork of greens, browns and yellows stretches away unbroken by pylons or urban haze. One is in the heartland of rural Devon and its roots are Saxon deep - about 700AD Eadwig gave the parish its name".

Winkleigh

8½ miles N of Okehampton off the A3124

This attractive hilltop village, with its open views across Dartmoor, is believed to have been a beacon station in prehistoric times and, when the Normans arrived, they built two small castles, one at each end of the village. These were probably intended as bases for hunting in the nearby park – the only Devon park to be mentioned in the *Domesday Book.*

For centuries, Winkleigh was an important local trading centre, with its own market, fair and borough court, but, today, it is a peaceful little place with thatched cottages nestling up to the mainly 15th century church.

Found on the historic Inch's Site, where cider has been made at Western Barn since 1916, lies the **Winkleigh Cider Company**, who use only locally grown apples to produce their range of ciders. The apples are pressed in October and November, and visitors at this time can see the operation, before the cider is fermented in the 100 year old vats. The cider company is open from Monday to Saturday throughout the year and, at the site shop, not only can these be bought but there are also local crafts and personal gifts on sale.

North Tawton

6½ miles NE of Okehampton off the A3072

Well known today to walkers along the **Tarka Trail**, this small market town was once an important borough governed by a portreeve, an official who was elected each year, until the end of the 19th century. This scattered rural community prospered in medieval times but the decline of the local textile industry in the late 18th century dealt a blow from which it never really recovered – the population today is still less than it was in 1750. North Tawton also suffered badly from a series of fires that destroyed most of the older and more interesting buildings, however, a few survivors can

Kayden House Hotel

High Street, North Tawton, Devon EX20 2HF
Tel: 01837 82242 Fax: 01837 82242
e-mail: kaydenhouse@tisculi.com

Dating back to the 18th century and found in the heart of North Tawton, **Kayden House Hotel** is a charming and traditional property and, in summer, its front is ablaze with colourful hanging baskets and window boxes brimming over with flowers.

An ideal base from which to explore nearby Dartmoor, the hotel has six charming and individual guest rooms and owners, Elizabeth and Stephen Parker, have paid great attention to detail here to ensure that guests are comfortable.

The hotel also has a restaurant that is open to non-residents and, open from morning coffee through to dinner, this is a popular place that is well known throughout the town. Elizabeth and Stephen share the cooking and the menus here range from light meals and snacks through to à la carte. However, whatever the dish, customers at this small and intimate restaurant can be sure that only the freshest produce is used to create the traditional English meals.

Whether dining in the formal area or in the more relaxed surroundings of the bar, eating here is an enjoyable experience. Children are welcome at Kayden House Hotel.

The Copper Key Inn

Fore Street, North Tawton, Devon EX20 2ED
Tel: 01837 82357

Found on the edge of the smallest town in Devon, **The Copper Key Inn** is a wonderful and traditional country inn that dates back to the 16th century. Inside, it is full of olde worlde charm and has still retained many of its original features, including open fires in winter, but it also has a spacious feel.

Experienced owners Penny and Arthur Bath have been here since 2000 and they have certainly made this freehouse a friendly and popular meeting place for the locals whilst visitors are always made welcome. Along with an excellent range of beers, lagers and stouts, there is always a choice of real ales served from the bar.

Food, too, is an important aspect of life here and, served at both lunchtime and in the evening, the menu and the ever-changing specials board provides plenty of choice. Penny is the chef of the partnership and whether eating in the bar or in the more formal separate restaurant customers can be assured of being served freshly prepared dishes.

Children are welcome here and, to the rear of the inn, there is a pleasant beer garden complete with pets' corner.

Oaklands Farm

North Tawton, Devon EX20 2BQ
Tel: 01837 82340
e-mail: headon@oaklandsfarm02.fsnet.co.uk

Ideally situated for exploring both Devon's north and south coasts and Dartmoor, **Oaklands Farm** lies on the edge of the village and there are wonderful views from this working dairy farm out over the National Park. Owned by Win Headon, she has been offering superb bed and breakfast accommodation in a choice of three en-suite guest rooms since the late 1980s. Well known for her magnificent traditional farmhouse breakfasts, home-cooked evening meals are available by prior arrangement and children are very welcome at Oaklands Farm.

still be found and the most notable is the privately owned 15th century **Broad Hall**.

Lapford

12 ½ miles NE of Okehampton off the A377

Standing high above the River Yeo, Lapford's hilltop church has been a famous local landmark for generations and, inside, there is a 15th century rood screen that is regarded as one of the most exquisitely fashioned in the country. There are five bands of the most delicate carving at the top and, above them, rise modern figures of the Holy Family (Jesus, Mary and John) surmounted by the original ornamental ceiling with its carved angels gazing down from the nave roof. Dating back to the early 13th century the **Lapford Revel** is four days of family fun that began as a celebration of Thomas à Becket being proclaimed a saint.

Remarkably, this small community still has its own railway station and passenger numbers here have been much enlarged since the line through Lapford was re-christened the Tarka Line. The original name, the Exeter to Barnstaple route, may have been lacklustre but, whatever the name, the 39-mile journey has always been delightful as it winds slowly along the gentle river valleys of the Yeo and the Taw.

Belstone

2 miles SE of Okehampton off the A30

Surrounded by the magnificent scenery of north Dartmoor, this is a pretty village of thatched cottages with a church dating back to the 13th century and a triangular village green, complete with its stocks and a stone commemorating the coronation of George V. However, its Post Office is rather unusual as it is housed in a building that was once a chapel.

A path from the village leads up to the ancient standing stone circle that is known as the **Nine Maidens** although there are, actually, a dozen of them. Local legend suggests that these stones, under Belstone Tor, were formed when a group of maidens was discovered dancing on the Sabbath and were turned to stone. However, the problem with this story is that the stone circle was in place long before the arrival of Christianity in England and it also claimed that the mysterious stones changed position when the clock strikes noon. What is certain, though, is that the view from this prehistoric stone circle across mid Devon is quite breathtaking.

For lovers of solitude, the countryside to the south of Belstone is memorable and also unforgettable, as any readers of Sir Arthur Conan Doyle's novel, *The Hound of the Baskervilles*, will remember. Recalling the villain's fate in that story, walkers should beware of the notorious 'feather beds' – deep bogs signalled by a quaking cover of brilliant green moss.

Sticklepath

3½ miles E of Okehampton off the A30

A neat little village on the edge of Dartmoor, Sticklepath was, from the 17th century, a busy industrial place with seven water wheels powering machinery that was used to produce tools for both agriculture and mining. Today, the village is home to the **Finch Foundry Working Museum** (National Trust) that was, from 1814 to the 1960s, renowned for producing the finest sharp-edged agricultural tools in the West Country. Powered by three massive water wheels, which have now been restored, visitors can still see the massive tilt hammers, feel the heat from the furnace and hear the screech of the grinding stone during one of the regular demonstrations held here.

South Zeal

4 miles E of Okehampton off the A30

A thriving village since the Middle Ages, South Zeal stands on what was the main road from Exeter to Launceston and the Cornish coast but, today, it is thankfully bypassed. It was here, whilst snowbound, that Charles Dickens wrote *Pickwick Papers*. Isolated in the middle of the broad main street stands a simple medieval market cross and St Mary's

Fairhaven Farm

Gooseford, Whiddon Down, near Okehampton, Devon EX20 2QH
Tel: 01647 231261

Surrounded by glorious unspoilt countryside and within Dartmoor National Park, **Fairhaven Farm** has been in the Scott family for many years and, since 1982, April Scott has been offering comfortable and friendly bed and breakfast accommodation from their charming farmhouse. The two guest rooms, which both have their own bathroom, each have fabulous views from their windows and, for elder visitors, there is a stair lift. Along with a hearty breakfast each morning, guests here will delight in the peace and tranquillity of the location. Children are welcome.

Chapel that was rebuilt in 1713 whilst, to the south of the village, on Ramsley Common, are the remains of a copper mine that was worked for just a few years between 1901 and 1909.

Whiddon Down

6½ miles E of Okehampton on the A382

About a mile south of the village stands the **Spinster's Rock**, the best surviving chambered tomb in the whole of Devon. According to legend, three spinsters erected the dolmen one morning before breakfast, an impressive feat since the capstone, supported by just three uprights 7 feet high, weighs 16 tons!

Throwleigh

5½ miles SE of Okehampton off the A382

This interesting village is centred around a cross that bears an inscription commemorating Queen Victoria's Jubilee and not only are the medieval church and 16th century church house built of granite but all Throwleigh's thatched cottages are also constructed from the stone. Close by, on Throwleigh Common, are the remains of a number of prehistoric hut circles, whilst, to the south, are the remains of **Gidleigh Castle**, a late 13th century fortified manor house.

Meldon

2½ miles SW of Okehampton on the B3260

Situated on the Dartmoor Railway, **Meldon Viaduct Station** is the highest station in southern England and it can be reached by taking the Dartmoor Pony train that climbs up from Sampford Courtenay and Okehampton. Here, too, is **Meldon Visitor Centre** where the history of the railway and the impressive viaduct, as well as Meldon Quarry, is explained through a display of photographs and artefacts. There is also a buffet at the centre that offers not only food but superb moorland views.

Just to the south of the village and, surrounded by open moorland, is **Meldon Reservoir**, the ideal place for a walk and a picnic and where anglers can fish for natural brown trout.

Folly Gate

2 miles NW of Okehampton on the A386

To the east of this village lies **Abbeyford Woods**, a particularly pleasant place for a walk and that incorporates a lovely stretch of the River Okement.

Northlew

6 miles NW of Okehampton off the A3079

The thatched cottages and houses at Northlew stand around a large central square that is dominated by a charming 15th century church, which stands on a hilltop overlooking the River Lew. The church is noted for its Norman remains and the exceptional, mainly Tudor, woodwork in the roof, bench ends and screen. Also of interest in the church is one of the stained glass windows that features four saints: St Thomas, to whom the church is dedicated, is shown holding a model of the church; St Augustine, the first Archbishop of Canterbury, holds the priory gateway; and St Joseph carries the Holy Grail and the staff that grew into the famous Glastonbury thorn tree. The fourth figure, who is simply clad in a brown habit and carries a bishop's crosier and a spade, is St Brannock who is credited with being the first man to cultivate the wild lands of this area by clearing woodland and ploughing and he is, therefore, often regarded as the patron saint of farmers.

Hatherleigh

6½ miles NW of Okehampton off the A386

A medieval market town in the heart of rural Devon, the first record of Hatherleigh dates from AD 981 when it was noted as a Saxon settlement going by the name of 'Haegporn Leah', meaning the hawthorn glade. Then part of the estate of Tavistock Abbey, it remained in the abbey's ownership until the Dissolution of the Monasteries and the picturesquely thatched George Hotel is believed to have been built in around 1450 as the Abbot's court house. The London Inn also dates from around that time and the Old Church House is thought to be even older.

The town would have possessed an even finer stock of early buildings were it not for a devastating fire in 1840 that destroyed much of its ancient centre. Fortunately, the 15th century Church of St John the Baptist escaped the flames but, a century and half later, in 1990, hurricane winds blew over the spindly medieval wooden spire and it crashed through the roof of the nave. Thankfully, no one was in the church at the time but the damage was extensive. Now fully restored, the church, set high above the Lew Valley, continues to provide a striking focus for this pleasant rural community.

During medieval times, Hatherleigh was a borough and, in 1220, Henry III granted it a license to hold a weekly market. The current market day, Tuesday, dates from 1693 and it continues to be a traditional market day when farmers from the surrounding area

Acorns Café and Tea Rooms

12 Bridge Street, Hatherleigh,
Devon EX20 3HU
Tel: 01837 810479

Acorns Café and Tea Rooms is an attractive and quintessentially English tea rooms that proves to be popular with locals and visitors alike – particularly on Tuesdays (market day) and during the annual Carnival held in November. Owners, Joanne and Trevor Hobson, share the cooking and along with the standard menu of home-made dishes there are various different Cream Teas on offer as well as the Acorns' speciality – the 'Pig Out' Breakfast. Pigs feature largely here as this charming café houses Joanne's extensive collection of over 300 ornamental pigs!

come to buy and sell their livestock. This is also a popular place for fishermen who come to try their luck on the nearby River Torridge and its tributary, the River Lew, which runs alongside the town.

Until 1966, the Okehampton to Bude railway ran through the town but, in that year, it was closed as part of the notorious 'Beeching Cuts'. Dr Richard Beeching, a successful businessman who made his name with the multi-national company ICI, was appointed, in 1963, by the Prime Minister, Harold Macmillan, to sort out what the Conservative government regarded as the mess created by Labour's nationalisation of the railways in 1948. Naturally, Dr Beeching's solution was to close every mile of line that did not produce a paper profit and the last train on the Hatherleigh to Bude line, a prized local amenity, steamed its way into Cornwall in 1966. Long stretches of the old track bed of the railway now provide some attractive and reasonably level walking.

Established by Elizabeth Aylmer in 1984, **Hatherleigh Pottery and Stock in Trade Textiles** is a working pottery and textile studio, along with a gallery, which lies in the beautiful courtyard. Elizabeth grew up in Zimbabwe and her pottery contains strong African influences and, in particular, there is her Rukweza range of tableware (Rukweza is a Shona word meaning grain) that includes plates, bowls, jugs and dishes that are safe to use in the oven, microwave, dishwasher and freezer. Meanwhile, in the textile workshop there is an extensive range of hand-dyed and hand-printed soft furnishings. The gallery is open from Monday to Saturday.

Moretonhampstead

Known locally as Moreton, this attractive market town has long claimed the title of 'Gateway to east Dartmoor', a role in which it was greatly helped by the branch railway from Newton Abbot that operated between 1866 and 1964. The landscape around

Budleigh Farm

Moretonhampstead, Devon TQ13 8SB
Tel: 01647 440835 Fax: 01647 440436
e-mail: harvey@budleighfarm.co.uk
website: www.budleighfarm.co.uk

Tucked away in the picturesque Wray Valley is **Budleigh Farm** an ancient farmstead with some barns that are 150 years old. Owner Judith Harvey has seven self-catering holiday cottages that have been stylishly and imaginatively designed from the farm's original distinctive granite barns. An ideal place for children, dogs are allowed in several of the cottages, and along with the numerous walks straight from the farm, there is also an outdoor heated swimming pool in the summer, table tennis, facilities for archery and an expert on hand for target shooting.

Moretonhampstead is gentler than the rest of Dartmoor and this is an area of woods, plantations and steep-sided river valleys. Moreton is best approached from the southwest as visitors are then greeted with splendid views of this little hilltop town, surrounded by fields, and with the tower of **St Andrew's Church** piercing the skyline. Built of Dartmoor granite during the early 15th century, the church overlooks the Sentry, or Sanctuary Field, an attractive public park. In the church's south porch are the tomb stones of two French officers who died here as prisoners of war in 1807. At one point during the years of the Napoleonic Wars there were nearly 400 French officers living in Moreton on parole from the military prison at Princetown. One of them, General Rochambeau, must have sorely tested the patience of the local people as, whenever news arrived of a French success, he would put on his full dress uniform and parade through the streets of the town.

One of the most interesting buildings here is the row of unusual two-storey arcaded **Almshouses** (National Trust) in Cross Street that were built in 1637 and are still thatched. They are not open to the public. Once an industrial centre with wool, paper, tannery and tallow works, Moreton has, now, become home to a thriving community of craft workshops, several of which are open to the public. Around the town there are potteries, a forge and the **Lion House Gallery**, the town's former bank, which is a showcase for the work of local contemporary artists.

Just a couple of miles west of Moreton lies the **Miniature Pony and Animal Farm** where not only can visitors see the farm's famous ponies but also donkeys, pigs, goats, calves, lambs and birds. There are numerous country and farming activities for children and adults to enjoy whilst, in the courtyard, there are craft shops, a gallery and a café. The farm, which lies in some 20 acres of beautiful Dartmoor parkland, is open from Easter to the beginning of November.

Castle Drogo

Drewsteignton, near Exeter EX6 6PB
Tel: 01647 433306 Fax: 01647 433186

Castle Drogo (National Trust) is spectacularly sited on a rocky outcrop with commanding views out over Dartmoor and, surrounding this 20th century dream country home, lies an equally impressive garden – the highest in the Trust. The square shape of the castle and the large rotund croquet lawn exemplifies the simple ethos of the architect, Lutyens, of "circles and squares". From spring bulbs in the formal garden, the rhododendron garden, the stunning herbaceous borders, the rose garden and the winter garden there is colour and interest here all year round.

Around Moretonhampstead

Drewsteignton

3 miles N of Moretonhampstead off the A30

Found in a beautiful situation overlooking the valley of the River Teign, this appealing village of thatched cottages and a medieval church grouped around a village square is much visited and much photographed. The village also overlooks the well-known beauty spot **Fingle Bridge**, a 400-year-old structure over the River Teign and from where there are circular walks as well as footpaths up and down the river. One of the most scenic is the **Hunter's Path** that climbs up through an oak wood, to well above the tree line, and from where there are fabulous views out over northern Dartmoor.

To the south of the village lies the Iron Age hilltop fortresses of **Prestonbury Castle** and **Scrapbook Castle** whilst, close by, is **Castle Drogo** (National Trust) that looks every inch a medieval castle but was, in fact, built between 1911 and 1930 (see panel above). The last castle to be built in England, its owner, the India tea baron Julius Drew, commissioned Edwin Lutyens to create his dream country home and it remains one of the architect's most remarkable works.

Dunsford

4 miles NE of Moretonhampstead off the B3212

To the west of the village lies the **Dunsford Nature Reserve**, which supports a diverse range of plants and

Dunsford

animals in a mixture of habitats that include oak woodland, bracken-covered slopes and exposed rocky outcrops. Owned by the National Trust, the reserve lies within the National Park and is also part of the Teign Valley Site of Special Scientific Interest.

Crediton

10 miles NE of Moretonhampstead on the A377

Nestling between two hills and situated on the western bank of the River Creed, this ancient market town, which was originally called Citron, was once famous for its wool industry and cattle market. There were also tanneries here and this lead to the town becoming associated with the manufacture of shoes and boots. However, the town is best known as being the birthplace, in AD 680, of Winfred who went on to become one of only a few Britons to become saints. His name is derived from the Saxon words 'Wine' meaning friend, and 'Frith', meaning peace and, after being educated at the Saxon monastery in Exeter, Winfred became a monk and began his life as a missionary. Rising swiftly through the ranks of the Benedictine Order, he was sent by Pope Gregory II to the Netherlands and Germany to convert the heathens to Christianity and, such was his success, that the Pope gave him the name Boniface and created him a bishop. However, at the age of 71, Boniface and 53 members of his party were ambushed and murdered whilst they were on their way to the great monastery at Fulda in Hesse, which Boniface had founded and where he was then laid to rest.

Statue of St Boniface, Crediton

Despite his violent and untimely death, Boniface was greatly revered throughout Germany and, a few years later, the Pope formally pronounced his sanctification but it was almost 1,200 years before the town of his birth accorded him any recognition. Finally, in 1897, the people of Crediton installed an east window in the town's grand, cathedral-like **Church of the Holy Cross** that depicts events from his life. The interior of this early 15th century church is especially notable for its monuments that include one to Sir John Sully, who fought alongside the Black Prince and died at the ripe old age of

105, and another to Sir William Peryam, a commissioner at the trial of Mary, Queen of Scots. However, the most impressive monument here is the richly ornamented arch that was erected in memory of Sir Henry Redvers Buller, commander-in-chief during the Boer War and the hero of the Relief of Ladysmith. Born in the town in 1839, Redvers Buller was one of the leading military men of his day and, along with the town's memorial, there is a statue of him, mounted on horseback, in Exeter and his Victoria Cross medal is on display in the Royal Green Jackets Museum, Winchester.

Church of the Holy Cross, Crediton

Like so many towns, Crediton experienced a number of fires in the 18th century but the worst here, in 1743, consumed some 460 dwellings in just 10 hours. Said to have been started by two men attempting to spit-roast the family dinner after having had a little too much to drink the night before, the rebuilt western part of the town was once again gutted by fire just 26 years later.

To the south of the town lies Crediton Railway Station, which lies on the famous Tarka Line whilst, on the first Saturday in October, the town comes alive when the floats of the **Crediton Carnival** parade through the streets.

Bridford

4 miles E of Moretonhampstead off the B3212

This village nestles in the hill country on the edge of Dartmoor and, as well as the woodland walks along the banks of the River Teign, there are nature trails in the National Trust owned **Bridford Woods**. Back in the village there is a pretty 14th century church, dedicated to St Thomas à Becket, which contains some fine Tudor carvings, and an early 14th century farmhouse.

Dunchideock

7 miles E of Moretonhampstead off the B3212

This beautifully located village hugs the sides of a steeply-sloping combe and, at the northern end, stands the modest red sandstone Church of St Michael, which has a number of noteworthy features. Along with the medieval font and a set of carved pew ends, there is a richly carved rood screen that, at one point, makes a surprising diversion around three sides of an octagonal roof column. Amongst the monuments is one to Major-General Stringer Lawrence, the 'Father of the Indian Army', who, in 1775, left a legacy of £50,000 to his lifelong friend, Sir Robert Palk. Palk proceeded to build himself a mansion, Haldon House, half a mile to the south, along with a folly in memory of his benefactor. Known locally as **Haldon Belvedere**, or Lawrence Castle, this tall triangular structure stands on the summit of Haldon Bridge and can be seen for miles around.

Higher Ashton

6½ miles E of Moretonhampstead off the B3139

Like its neighbour, Lower Ashton, this village is situated in the Teign valley and here can be found England's highest waterfall – **Canonteign Falls**. Dropping some 200 feet and situated in an area of outstanding natural beauty, these breathtaking falls are complemented by the magnificent surrounding ancient woodland and spectacular rock formations.

Lustleigh

3½ miles SE of Moretonhampstead off the A382

One of Dartmoor's prettiest villages, Lustleigh is situated on a hillside and has an assortment of 15th and 16th century thatched, colour-washed

The Cleave at Lustleigh

Lustleigh, near Newton Abbot,
Devon TQ13 9TJ
Tel: 01647 277223 Fax: 01647 277223

In the heart of this pretty Dartmoor village, **The Cleave at Lustleigh** is a delightful old country inn whose front dates from the 16th century whilst the back is Victorian! Only an inn since the 1920s, owner Alison Perring has been offering exceptional hospitality to both locals and visitors alike for nearly 20 years and she has an enviable reputation for not only the fine ales served here but also the superb food that is all freshly prepared from local produce. Children welcome and there is a delightful beer garden.

Lustleigh

cottages picturesquely grouped around the 15th century church. Appropriately enough for such a genuinely olde worlde village, Lustleigh keeps alive some of the time-honoured traditions of country life and here May Day is enthusiastically celebrated with a procession through the village, dancing round the maypole and the coronation of a May Queen. From the village there are some delightful walks, especially one that passes through Lustleigh Cleave, a wooded section of the steep-sided Bovey Valley.

To the northeast of the village, and on the edge of Dartmoor, are the three beautiful reservoirs of **Kennick**, **Tottiford** and **Trenchford** that not only offer excellent facilities to fishermen but also there are a number of way marked trails through the surrounding woodland and farmland.

North Bovey

1½ miles S of Moretonhampstead off the B3212

Approached by steep, narrow lanes, this picturesque village, set beside the River Bovey, is quite unspoiled, with thatched cottages grouped around its village green, a 15th century church and a delightful old inn, the Ring of Bells, which like many Devon inns was originally built in the 13th century as lodgings for the stonemasons building the church.

Manaton

4 miles S of Moretonhampstead off the A382

From the porch of this attractive village's 15th century church can be

Becky Falls Woodland Park

Manaton, near Newton Abbot,
Devon TQ13 9UG
Tel: 01647 221259 Fax: 01647 221555
e-mail: beckyfalls@btconnect.com
website: www.beckyfalls-dartmoor.com

Set high on Dartmoor and lying in a tranquil, hidden valley that has been enjoyed by visitors since Victorian times, **Becky Falls Woodland Park**, with its huge oak canopy, rugged landscape, massive granite boulders and waterfalls provides some of the most scenic and enjoyable walks in the southwest as well as lots of fun for all the family. The trees and falls are timeless but a recently opened walk now takes in the Lower Falls and includes a stiff 200-foot climb back through pine trees to the new paddocks that are home to native Dartmoor ponies.

Meanwhile, there are birds of prey and owls, many of which have been rescued, pygmy goats, rabbits, sheep and lambs for visitors to experience and touch and also pony rides for small children. The licensed cafeteria and gift shop are supplemented by a craft shop where regular demonstrations are given by local Dartmoor craftspeople. The woodland park is open daily from March to October and, weather permitting, on winter weekends.

seen the granite stack of **Bowerman's Nose** whilst, to the west lies **Grimspound** that is, perhaps, the most impressive of all Dartmoor's surviving Bronze Age settlements. Occupied between 1800 BC and 500 BC and remarkably well preserved, Grimspound consists of 24 hut circles, some of them reconstructed, and it is still possible to make out the positions of door lintels and stone sleeping shelves. The area around Grimspound is bleak and moody, an atmosphere that recommended itself to Sir Arthur Conan Coyle who had Sherlock Holmes send Dr Watson into hiding here to help solve the case of *The Hound of the Baskervilles*.

Another novelist linked with Manaton is John Galsworthy who once lived at Wingstone Farm and his short novel, *The Apple Tree*, is based on the tragic story of Kitty Jay, a local girl, who committed suicide rather than face life as an unmarried mother. Her grave can be found to the northwest of Hound Tor, to the south of the village.

Just to the southeast of the village is the **Becky Falls Woodland Park** (see panel above), one the most beautiful places in the county that is also an area of outstanding natural beauty and that is home to a wide variety of wildlife.

Chagford

3½ miles NW of Moretonhampstead on the B3206

Beautifully situated between the pleasant wooded valley of the North Teign River and the stark expanses of the high moorland, this ancient and unspoilt settlement was one of Devon's four stannary towns. Nothing remains in the town from that era although in the 15th century Church of St Michael can be seen the tinners' symbol, three conjoint rabbits, whilst exploration of the surrounding countryside will reveal some scant evidence of former mining activity. In the centre of the town lies a square that is dominated by a charming octagonal building, formerly the **Market House**, which dates from 1862 and around which there are some old style family shops offering interesting shopping with plenty of atmosphere.

Also contributing greatly to the architectural heritage of this small town is the Three Crowns Hotel, which dates from the 13th century and that was once the home of the Whyddon family. One member of the family, Sir John Whyddon, was a justice of the King's Bench in the mid 16th century, but it is another family member, Mary Whyddon, who has become a local legend. In October 1641, Mary was shot by a jealous lover on her wedding day as she was returning from church to her family home and it is this incident that is thought to have inspired RD Blackmore to write *Lorna Doone*. Just a couple of years later, during the Civil

The Scorhill Stone Circle

A Clapper Bridge, Near Scorhill Stone Circle

War, the hotel was again the venue for a violent death when the young poet and Cavalier, Sydney Godolphin, was killed by musket fire in the porch way. Although he was buried at Okehampton, his ghost is still said to haunt the inn.

The famous Dartmoor guide, James Perrot, lived in the town between 1854 and 1895 and it was he who noted that some of the farms around Chagford had no wheeled vehicles as late as 1830. On the other hand, Perrot lived to see the town install electric street lighting in 1891 making Chagford one of the first communities west of London to possess this amenity. It was also Perrot who began the curious practice of letterbox stamp collecting. He installed the first letterbox at **Cranmere Pool** near the heart of the moor so his Victorian clients could send postcards home, stamped to prove they had been there. Today, there are hundreds of such letterboxes scattered all over Dartmoor. He lies buried in St Michael's churchyard.

To the west of Chagford, an exceptionally pleasant lane, which is joined for part of its length by the **Two Moors Way** long distance footpath, leads upstream from **Chagford Bridge** through the wooded valley of the North Teign River. A rock beside the river, known as the **Holed Stone**, has a large round cavity and it is locally believed that anyone climbing through the hole will be cured of a whole host of afflictions from rheumatism to infertility.

The land to the south of Chagford rises abruptly towards **Kestor Rock** and **Shovel Down**, the sites of impressive Bronze Age settlements and, a little further on, the imposing **Long Stone** stands at the point where the parishes of Gidleigh and Chagford end and Duchy of Cornwall land begins. Meanwhile, to the southwest of the town is **Fernworthy Reservoir** around which there are a number of way marked walks that also lead into the woodland. The various paths offer excellent views out over Bronze Age hut circles, the reservoir and its impressive dam whilst this is a good starting point for walks into the open moorland.

Lydford

White Lady Waterfall, Lydford

In Saxon times there were just four Royal boroughs in Devon: Exeter, Barnstaple, Totnes and Lydford, which may surprise visitors today as this is a quiet, secluded village but it still occupies the same strategic position on the River Lyd that made it such an important place in the past. A settlement was established here in the late 9th century and, in the 11th century, the Normans built a fortification at the river crossing that was, in 1195, superseded by the present **Lydford Castle** (English Heritage). An austere stone fortress that, for generations, served the independent tin miners of Dartmoor as both a court and a prison and the justice meted out here was said to be notoriously arbitrary. In the early 17th century, William Browne of Tavistock observed:

> *"I oft have heard of Lydford law,*
> *How in the morn they hang and draw*
> *And sit in judgement after."*

Encompassing the whole of the Forest of Dartmoor, Lydford parish is the largest in England and, for many centuries, the dead were brought down from the moor along the ancient **Lych Way** for burial at the village's St Petrock's Church. Inside the church there are ornamental bench ends that depict Dartmoor plants, animals and birds along with saints and martyrs whilst, out in the churchyard, is a tombstone that bears a rather lengthy and laboriously humorous epitaph to the local watchmaker, George Routleigh, who died in 1802. The inscription

Lydford

includes the statement that George's life had been "Wound up in hope of being taken in hand by his Maker and of being thoroughly cleansed and repaired and set going in the world to come."

To the southwest of the village, the valley of the River Lyd suddenly narrows to form the famous **Lydford Gorge** (National Trust), which is one of Devon's most spectacular natural features. The gorge runs for one and a half miles and there are walks along the top of this steep-sided oak raving to the impressive 90-foot **White Lady Waterfall** whilst an enchanting riverside path leads to a series of whirlpools that include the **Devil's Cauldron**. Back in the 17th century, this then remote gorge provided a secure refuge for a band of brigands who called themselves the Gubbinses. Their leader, Roger Rowle, became known as the 'Robin Hood of the West' and it is his exploits that are recounted in Charles Kingsley's novel *Westward Ho!*

Around Lydford

North Brentor

3 miles SW of Lydford off the A386

This pleasant village is overlooked by **Brent Tor**, which lies to the south, and, on its 1,000-foot summit lies a medieval **Church** dedicated to St Michael de Rupe. One of the most striking features of Dartmoor, this is the fourth smallest complete church in England – it measures just 15 feet wide and 37 feet long and, although its walls are just 10 feet high, they are three feet thick. Built in around 1140, with additions made in the 13th and 14th centuries, and constructed of stone quarried from the rock beneath it, the church is surrounded by a steep churchyard that contains a surprising number of graves. Though sometimes lost in cloud, the scramble up to the summit of this volcanic plug that rises dramatically from the surrounding farmland is rewarded, on a clear day, by magnificent views of Dartmoor, Bodmin Moor and the sea at Plymouth Sound. This is also a place well known to walkers and cyclists as both the **West Devon Way** and the **Coast-to-Coast Cycle Way** pass through North Brentor.

Lewtrenchard

3½ miles NW of Lydford off the A30

A pleasant village situated in a wooded valley, for some 43 years, between 1881 and 1924, the Rev Sabine Baring Gould was the rector of this rural parish. Best known as the author of the hymn *Onward, Christian Soldiers*, Baring Gould was also an extraordinarily prolific writer who regularly produced two or three books a year – including novels, books on Devon legend and folklore and historic works such as *Curious Myths of the Middle Ages*. He nevertheless found time to restore St Peter's Church, an undertaking that included the remarkably successful creation of a

Lewtrenchard Manor

Lewtrenchard, Lewdown, near Okehampton, Devon EX20 4PN
Tel: 01566 783256 Fax: 01566 783332
e-mail: stay@lewtenchard.co.uk
website: lewtrenchard.co.uk

Situated on the site of a dwelling that is recorded in the Domesday Book, **Lewtrenchard Manor** is a delightful house, dating from the early 17th century, that is the home of James and Sue Murray.

Along with being a large family home, the couple have opened the manor as a small and select hotel where guests can experience the special and relaxed atmosphere of a true English country house. Sumptuous furnishings and decoration add to the house's grand features, which include ornate plaster ceilings, stained glass windows and open fires, whilst historic family antiques give the rooms a personal and more intimate feel.

Guests here have a choice of nine individually and luxuriously styled en-suite guest rooms but, before retiring, dinner is served in the oak panelled dining room. The restaurant here has won many awards and is renowned for its imaginative use of fresh local produce and for the exquisite presentation. Eating here is an experience that non-residents too can enjoy although booking is essential. Guests can also enjoy the manor's fabulous gardens and grounds, with the help of the couple's two dogs, Ben and Meggie, as guides.

replica of a glorious medieval screen that his grandfather, also a rector here, had destroyed. The grandson had found enough pieces for the replica to be made and it is as impressive as the original, with an elaborate canopied loft decorated with paintings of some 23 saints.

Despite his good in restoring the church, Rev Baring Gould also managed to scandalise Victorian society by marrying a Lancashire mill girl but, much to the displeasure of his doubters, the union proved to be a happy and romantic one and they went on to have a huge family. The story goes that, "One day, emerging from his study, the rector saw a little girl coming down the stairs. 'You do look nice, my dear, in your pretty frock', he said, vaguely recalling that a children's party was taking place in the rectory. 'Whose little girl are you?' he asked. 'Yours, papa', she answered and burst into tears."

Lewdown

4 miles NW of Lydford off the A30

Visitors to this pleasant village today will find it hard to believe that Lewdown's main street was once part of the major route from Exeter to Launceston and on into Cornwall. However, now the village is by passed and the new found peace and quiet has made this, once again, a rural community. The village is also home to the **Tuit Centre** where visitors can

Dingles Steam Village

Milford, near Lifton, Devon PL16 0AT
Tel: 01566 783425
website: www.dinglesteam.co.uk

Opened in 1995 by steam enthusiast and former steeple-jack, Fred Dibnah, **Dingles Steam Village** makes Britain's industrial heritage come alive. This is one of the best working steam collections in the country and the exhibits are a celebration of the golden age of steam. In this beautiful rural setting, the steam village is home to a wide range of working traction engines, steam rollers, fairground attractions and vintage machinery and they can be viewed in a massive undercover exhibition area. Fascinating even when 'resting', these giant machines are totally absorbing to watch when they are all steamed up and working.

The village also has an excellent café, Mrs Dingles Kitchen, which serves a wide range of dishes, from home-made soups and pasties to home-baked cakes and traditional Devon cream teas. Add to this the play areas for children, a gift shop, riverside walks along the banks of the Rivers Thrushel and Wolf and a collection of vintage road signs and Dingles Steam Village really does have something for all the family. The village is open from Easter to the end of October daily except Fridays.

browse, and buy, from an extensive range of fresh meats and other food items, gifts, plants and fine art. Virtually everything found here has been produced or sourced from within the West Country and, along with a fantastic range of dairy products, meats, smoked fish and organic vegetables, there is a full range of craft and gift items – from terracotta pots and painted glassware to books, toys and greeting cards. The Tuit Centre also has a café serving light meals and snacks throughout the year.

Stowford

5 miles NW of Lydford off the A30

An unusual feature in the churchyard of St John's Church is a stone by the gate that is carved in the Ogham script with the word 'Gunglei' and this is believed to be the name of a Roman soldier who was buried here some 1,600 years ago. Inside the church are two monuments to the Harris family: John who died in 1767 and Christopher who departed this life in 1718. The latter is curious not only for showing Christopher in the costume of a Roman centurion but also because "the figures are life-size down to the waist and then stunted as if the sculptor had grown weary of them."

Broadwoodwidger

7 miles NW of Lydford off the A30

Just to the northeast of this village lies **Roadford Lake**, a reservoir that was completed in 1990 and that has, among its many visitor attractions, a Victorian steam launch, the *SL Elegance*, which takes passengers on a trip around the lake between April and October. There is a network of footpaths around most of the lake, although the northern area has been designated a Special Protection Zone to allow wildlife a safe haven, and close to the Peninsula Gifts and Tea Shop there is a children's play area. Those interested in both water sports and angling will find that the centre here has some excellent facilities.

Also close to Broadwoodwidger is **Dingles Steam Village**, which provides a unique opportunity to see the area's industrial heritage set out in a beautiful rural setting (see panel opposite).

Lifton

8 miles NW of Lydford off the A30

Standing on the banks of the River Lyd, Lifton was an important centre of the wool trade in medieval times, like so many other Devon towns and villages, but the Dartmoor sheep tended to have rather coarse fleeces due to the cold pastureland on which they lived. So the good weavers of Lifton petitioned Henry VII "by reason of the grossness and stubbornness of their district" to allow them to mix as much lambs' wool and flock with their wool "as may be required to work it."

PLACES TO STAY, EAT AND DRINK

The Cornish Arms, Tavistock	92	Pub and Restaurant	p133
Mary Tavy Inn, Mary Tavy, Tavistock	93	Pub, Food and Accommodation	p134
Sowtontown Farmhouse, Peter Tavy, Tavistock	94	Bed and Breakfast	p135
The Prince of Wales, Princetown	95	Pub, Food and Accommodation	p136
Edgemoor Cottage, Middlemoor, Tavistock	96	Self Catering	p137
The Whitchurch Inn, Whitchurch, Tavistock	97	Pub with Food	p138
Sampford Manor, Sampford Spiney, Yelverton	98	Bed and Breakfast	p138
Overcombe Hotel, Horrabridge, Yelverton	99	Hotel	p138
Harrabeer Country House Hotel, Yelverton	100	Hotel	p139
The Rock Inn, Yelverton	101	Pub with Food	p140
The Royal Oak Inn, Meavy, Yelverton	102	Pub with Food	p141
The Garden House, Buckland Monochorum	103	Gardens	p142
Venn Farm, Ugborough, Ivybridge	104	Guest House	p145
The Dartmoor Wildlife Park, Sparkwell	105	Wildlife Attraction	p146
Chipley Mill Cottages, Bickington	106	Self Catering	p148
The Anchor Inn, Chudleigh Knighton	107	Pub with Food	p150
Buckfast Butterflies & Otters, Buckfastleigh	108	Wildlife Attraction	p153
River Dart Adventures, Holne Park	109	Outdoor Family Attraction	p154

● Denotes entries in other chapters

5 South Dartmoor

Despite its bleak and wild landscape Dartmoor has been inhabited for centuries: the moorland was dotted with settlements and, along with Neolithic tombs, there is a wealth of Bronze Age remains to be discovered. In particular, at Merrivale, there is a series of remains, including stone circles, burial chambers, standing stones and a group of stone huts that, though hard to distinguish from the natural rocks, are the some of the largest and most interesting Bronze Age remains on Dartmoor. Meanwhile, the row of 150 stones on Stall Moor, near Cornwood, is believed to be the longest prehistoric stone row in the world.

Along with prehistoric remains, the moorland is littered with the remains of commercial activity as tin has been mined here since at least the 12th century and this has left the moor pitted with the scars of disused mine working, ruined pump and smelting houses, although most of them are now softened by a cloak of bracken and heather. Tin and, later copper, lead, iron and even arsenic mining, brought wealth to the area and Devon had four Stannary towns –Tavistock, Chagford, Ashburton and Plympton – which were the only places licensed to weigh and stamp the metal. It was near the centre of the moor, at Crockern Tor, between 1474 and 1703 that the Stannary Court, the administrative body of the Dartmoor miners, met. Of the industrial remains to be seen in Dartmoor one of the most impressive is Wheal Betsey, a restored pumping station dating from the 18th century that cleared water from a lead,

Bowermans Nose, Dartmoor

zinc and silver mine whilst, on the outskirts of Dartmoor, on the border with Cornwall, is Morwellham Quay. An historic village, copper mine and port, this is now an open-air museum that brings vividly to life a busy 19th century community.

However, the most famous inhabitants of Dartmoor are, undoubtedly, the prisoners that were incarcerated at Dartmoor's prison at Princetown. Originally built to house prisoners of war from the Napoleonic Wars in the early 19th century and later taking in soldiers captured during the American War of Independence, the prison closed for a while before being reopened when the practice of deportation ceased in the mid 19th century. Now one of the country's best known and most isolated prisons, visitors to Princetown will understand why it was built here as it lies at the centre of this inhospitable moorland.

By contrast, Widecombe in the Moor, the village made famous by Uncle Tom Cobleigh, is an altogether more inviting place and, whilst it comes alive each September when its fair is held, it is an attractive and picturesque village, sheltered in the valley of the East Webburn river, that is worth a visit at any time of year.

Chinkwell Tor, Dartmoor

Tavistock

This charming and handsome market town, on the River Tavy, became one of Devon's four Stannary towns after tin was discovered here in the 13th century. The name comes from the Latin for tin, 'Stannum', and these four towns (the others are Ashburton, Chagford and Plympton) were the only places licensed to weigh and stamp the metal mined on the moor. First settled in prehistoric times, Tavistock was recorded as having a Saxon abbey, dating from AD 974, in the *Domesday Book*, and from then, until 1539, it was owned by Tavistock Abbey. After Henry VIII closed the abbey and he sold the building, along with its vast estates, to John Russell whose family, as Earls and Dukes of Bedford, owned most of the town until 1911. The present town centre is, essentially, the creation of the Russell family, who after virtually obliterating the once-glorious abbey, created a completely new town plan. Later, in the 1840s, Francis, the 7th

The Cornish Arms

15 West Street, Tavistock, Devon PL19 8AN
Tel: 01822 612145 Fax: 01822 617196 e-mail: cornishtavy@aol.com

Found in the heart of this stannary town, **The Cornish Arms** is so called as it was the last coaching inn in Devon before the county of Cornwall. A wonderfully atmospheric inn that has retained many of its original 18th century features, landlords Alan and Sandra have been here since the mid 1980s and they have, in that time, gained an enviable reputation not only for their superb hospitality but also for the inn's excellent food and drink.

Along with three real ales, including Courage Best, there are all the usual drinks and the comfortable bar area is just the place to relax and enjoy a glass or two. The inn is equally popular for its cuisine that is served daily although booking is essential on Friday and Saturday evenings. Served in the separate wooden floored restaurant, there is plenty to choose from here but the house specialities are American and Mexican dishes that are all freshly prepared here. Children too are welcome at this interesting and friendly inn.

Duke, diverted some of the profits from his copper mines to building the imposing **Guildhall**, along with several other civic buildings. He was also responsible for remodelling the Bedford Hotel and for the construction of a model estate of artisans' cottages on the western side of the town. A statue of the duke stands in Bedford Square whilst, at the western entrance to Tavistock, there is a statue of Sir Francis Drake, who is believed to have been born at nearby Crowndale. The statue may look familiar as it is identical to the one standing on Plymouth Hoe – Tavistock's is the original whilst the one in Plymouth is a copy.

Although little of the abbey remains today, the town's medieval parish church, which was built to serve Tavistock's common folk, still stands. An especially good monument to Sir John Glanville can be found in the Lady Chapel whilst there is some superb William Morris glass in the northeast window. However, one of the abbey's legacies is the annual three day fair, granted in 1105, which has now evolved into the **Goose Fair**, a wonderful, traditional street fair held in October. Tavistock was also permitted to hold a weekly market that, 900 years later, still takes place every Friday in the **Pannier Market**, a building that was purpose-built in the 1850s by the 7th Duke of Bedford, the then holder of the market charter. Virtually unaltered today, the market building is considered to be one of the finest in the southwest.

Beside Drake's statue is the **Fitzford Gate**, the original gatehouse of a private residence that no longer exists. According to local stories, several times a year the ghost of Lady Howard rides through the gates in a coach of bones, drawn by headless horses and preceded by a fierce hound with only one, central eye. This gruesome procession travels to Okehampton church where Lady Howard gets down from the coach, picks a blade of grass from the churchyard and, clutching it to her chest, returns to Fitzford Gate. Born in 1536, Lady Howard was twice widowed before she was 16 years old and is said to have murdered all her four husbands – despite her fourth husband, in fact, outliving her.

Also on the western side of Tavistock can be found the beginning of the **Tavistock-Morwellham Canal**, which was built in the early 19th century at a time when the town and surrounding area was experiencing a copper boom. The force behind the construction of the canal, which began in 1803, was John Taylor, a young engineer and the manager of the Wheal Friendship mine, and it was designed to follow the countryside's contours as far as Morwell Down, through which a tunnel over a mile long carried the canal on to Morwellham, Cornwall. This tunnel took over 14 years to complete, long after the rest of the canal, but, by 1872, this waterway had closed as it could no longer compete with the railway that arrived in Tavistock in the late 1850s.

Around Tavistock

Mary Tavy

3½ miles NE of Tavistock off the A386

Named after its church and the nearby river, this old industrial village is situated in the heart of Dartmoor's former lead, tin and copper mining country and the most evocative survivor of those days lies just a mile or so to the north of Mary Tavy. Standing lonely on the hillside and a conspicuous feature of the landscape, **Wheal Betsy** (National Trust) is a restored pumping engine house dating from the 18th century that was part of the Prince Arthur Consols mine that produced lead, zinc and silver.

For lovers of Dartmoor and its history, St Mary's Church is a place of pilgrimage as, in the churchyard, lies the grave of William Crossing, the historian of the moor whose magisterial guide, published in the early 20th century, is still in print.

Peter Tavy

3 miles NE of Tavistock off the A386

The twin village of Mary Tavy, Peter Tavy stands on the opposite bank of the River Tavy and it is linked to its twin by a bridle path and this village, too, takes part of its name from the patron saint of its parish church. The smaller of the two, Peter Tavy has changed little since William Crossing, the historian of Dartmoor, came here in 1909 and described "a quiet little place, with a church embosomed in trees, a chapel, a school and a small inn." Inside the impressive medieval church, with its octagonal tower and four pinnacles, is a poignant memorial to the five daughters of a 17th century rector – the oldest of whom was less than a year old when she died.

Merrivale

4½ miles E of Tavistock on the B3357

An excellent starting point for exploring the southwest section of Dartmoor, Merrivale is home to the last of the area's granite quarries that closed in 1997 and that, at one time, produced a record 1,500 tons of stone in a single firing.

To the east of Merrivale can be found the **Merrivale Antiquities**, a series of Bronze age remains that are some of the largest and most interesting on Dartmoor. Sometimes hard to distinguish from the natural rocks that litter the landscape, here can be found stone circles, burial chambers, standing stones and groups of circular huts.

Princetown

6½ miles E of Tavistock on the B3212

Found in the heart of Dartmoor, some 1,400 feet above sea level, Princetown is an isolated and desolate settlement that is surrounded by spectacular scenery. It is also notorious for its atrocious weather: the annual rainfall here is between 80 and 100 inches a year and this is more than three times that of Exeter just 20 miles away. Princetown is, of course, home to the country's best known and most forbidding prison – **Dartmoor Prison**. That a settlement should be located here at all was the brainchild of Sir Thomas Tyrwhitt, the owner of the local granite quarry, who proposed that a special prison be built here to house the thousands of troops captured during the Napoleonic Wars who were becoming too numerous and unruly for the prison ships moored in Plymouth Sound.

Construction of the prison was completed in 1809 by the prisoners themselves, using granite from Sir Thomas' quarry, and, paid at a rate of sixpence a day, they also built the main east-west road across the moor and the famous Devonport leat, which supplied water to the dockyard. Another building constructed by the prisoners is the nearby Church of St Mary, a charmless building in whose churchyard stands a tall granite cross in memory of all those prisoners whose bodies lie in unmarked graves. In the early 19th century the mortality rate of the inmates was around fifty per cent. Since the beginning of the 20th century, prisoners' graves have been marked with just their initials and date of death and the lines of small stones are a particularly gloomy sight.

Holding some 9,000 French prisoners when it first opened the prison population was swelled later when American prisoners from the War of Independence were held here too. However, by 1816, with the cessation of hostilities, the prison became redundant and closed. Princetown virtually collapsed as a result and it was not until 1823, when the quarries were reopened to supply granite for the construction of the Dartmoor Railway, another of

Tyrwhitt's initiatives, that it was saved from becoming a ghost town. In 1850, the prison was reopened to hold long-serving convicts, who up until then were deported, and since it has been considerably enlarged and upgraded. The history of this famous prison is revealed in the **Dartmoor Prison Museum**, which is housed in the old prison stables, and visitors can not only learn about the harsh conditions in which the prisoners lived but also purchase garden features and other items that have been made by today's inmates. The museum is open from Tuesday to Saturday.

In the centre of the town is the National Park's **High Moorland Visitor Centre** that contains some excellent and informative displays about the surrounding moorland and also stocks a wide range of books, maps and leaflets of local interest. The centre is housed in the former Duchy Hotel where Sir Arthur Conan Doyle stayed whilst writing some of the chapters of *The Hound of the Baskervilles* that was published in 1902. Having 'killed off' his pipe-smoking detective in his previous novel, Sir Arthur was touring the county when he stumbled on local stories of a spectral hound that haunted the moorland. These local tales were based on Squire Cabell of Brook, near Buckfastleigh, a man so evil that, when he died in 1677, a pack of fire-breathing hounds were said to have emerged from the moor to carry his soul to Hell. Having first revived his hero, Sir Arthur then took considerable liberties with the landscape of Dartmoor: he made the area larger and wilder, Grimspound became Grimpen Mire and he moved Princetown to another location.

There are many walks into the moorland from Princetown including the **Tyrwhitt Trails**, named after the town's founder, and also the **Princetown Railway Path**, which follows the disused railway to King's Tor.

Two Bridges

8 ½ miles E of Tavistock on the B3212

this scattered hamlet is well named as it lies at a point where the two main roads

The Whitchurch Inn

Church Hill, Whitchurch, near Tavistock,
Devon PL19 9ED
Tel: 01822 612181

Found in this quiet village, beside the beautiful St Andrew's Church, **The Whitchurch Inn** dates back to the 16th century and it has been extensively and sympathetically renovated by landlord Paul Langton. Attractive from the outside, the interior has retained its cosy and traditional English pub feel. There are low beamed ceilings, exposed stone walls, wood burning stoves in stone inglenook fireplaces and gleaming copperware. However, what makes this inn so popular is the warm welcome that all customers, both old and new, receive along with the superb hospitality on offer.

The vast selection of drinks available from the bar includes a good range of real ales and a wide choice of wines. Meanwhile the mouth-watering menu of home-cooked food here is sure to satisfy all the family and along with the traditional bar snacks, such as scampi and chips and omelettes, there are a wide range of seafood, vegetarian and chicken dishes whilst the steaks here all come from local beef stock, from the foothills of Dartmoor. A charming and delightful family run inn, The Whitchurch Inn is owned by the same family as the nearby Rock Inn, Yelverton (see page 140).

Sampford Manor

Sampford Spiney, near Yelverton,
Devon PL20 6LH
Tel: 01822 853442 Fax: 01822 855691
e-mail: manor@sampford-spiney.fsnet.co.uk
website: www.sampford-spiney.fsnet.co.uk

Close to some of Dartmoor's wilder areas, **Sampford Manor** dates back to the 11th century and once belonged to the estate of Sir Frances Drake. Now the home of Rosalind Spedding, this excellent Devonshire manor

farmhouse with beamed ceilings and slate floors, offers superb bed and breakfast accommodation in attractive guest rooms with private bathroom or shower. Home-cooked evening meals are also available. A peaceful place to relax or enjoy the coutryside. Children and dogs welcome.

Overcombe Hotel

Old Station Road, off Plymouth Road,
Horrabridge, near Yelverton, Devon PL20 7RN
Tel: 01822 853501 Fax: 01822 853501
e-mail: enquiries@overcombehotel.co.uk
website: www.overcombehotel.co.uk

An attractive family run establishment, **Overcombe Hotel**, on the edge of Dartmoor, offers its guests excellent accommodation in a comfortable and relaxed atmosphere. Each of the stylish en suite guest rooms has its own individual appeal and owners, John and Gillian Wright, provide a substantial breakfast each morning to set guests up for exploring

the local area. Superb walking country lies just beyond the hotel's front door whilst there are numerous other activities, including golf and fishing, nearby.

that traverse the moor cross and also at the convergence of the Rivers West Dart and Coswick and there have been bridges here since ancient times.

Whitchurch

1½ miles SE of Tavistock off the A386

Although close to Tavistock, Whitchurch has managed to retain its village atmosphere and, standing beside the village pub, is the beautiful St Andrew's church. A footpath leads up Church Hill and out onto Whitchurch Down from where there are excellent views of the spectacular tors of Dartmoor.

Sampford Spiney

3½ miles SE of Tavistock off the B3357

This secluded hamlet lies between Pew Tor and the Walkham Valley and its 14th century church along with a 17th century manor house, which is now a farm, can be found hidden in a remote hollow. Just to the north can be found some remarkable interconnecting rock basins.

Horrabridge

3½ miles SE of Tavistock off the A386

This picturesque village, with some old slate hung cottages still standing, lies on the River Walkham that is famous for its salmon and trout. Spanning the river is a medieval bridge that has an arched recess for pedestrians.

Yelverton

4½ miles SE of Tavistock on the B3212

This attractive large village stands on the very edge of Dartmoor and it enjoys grand views out across the Walkham Valley to the north with Brent Tor church, perched on its 1,100 foot summit some ten miles away, clearly visible on a good day. Yelverton itself is 'as flat as a pancake' and, with its broad street lined with wide verges, has been described as looking "rather like a thriving racecourse!" In prehistoric times, the area around the town was relatively heavily populated and there are numerous remains, such as stone circles, hut circles and burial chambers,

Harrabeer Country House Hotel

Harrowbeer Lane, Yelverton, Devon PL20 6EA
Tel: 01822 853302 Fax: 01822 853302
e-mail: reception@harrabeer.co.uk
website: www.harrabeer.co.uk

Originally thought to be a Devonshire longhouse, the **Harrabeer Country House Hotel**, surrounded by secluded gardens, is a small and friendly hotel, personally run by owners Michael and Amanda Willats. Such is the high standard of personal service offered here, along with its comfortable accommodation,

relaxed atmosphere and superb food, that Amanda was a finalist for the prestigious AA Landlady of the Year (2002) award. You will find a host of places to see in and around the area with sporting activities close by. Something for everyone.

The Rock Inn

Yelverton, Devon PL20 6DS
Tel: 01822 852022

Whilst parts of **The Rock Inn** date back to the 16th century, it was originally converted from a private residence into a coaching house in the early 19th century and has, since 1880, been owned by the Langton family. Well-established and recognised as Yelverton's premier free house, there has been constant improvements made over the decades and today's proprietors, sister and brother, Sue Callow and Paul Langton, offer their customers three individual bars, a separate games room with pool table, 6ft Sky screen for sporting events, darts, hand football etc, an attractive and sheltered patio garden as well as a warm welcome and excellent hospitality.

A good range of real ales, draught beers, lagers and excellent quality house wines compliment the extensive menu that ranges from light snacks through to heart warming homemade cottage pie and succulent steaks, produced from steer beef raised on the foothills of Dartmoor. Whilst the choice is varied, each dish is individually prepared to order, using where ever possible, all fresh local produce, and certainly all the meat is sourced from the Dartmoor area. A popular place with locals who meet here for a chat and an inn that particularly welcomes children, anyone who has enjoyed a visit here should also try the Whitchurch Inn, Whitchurch, that is also owned by the same family (see page 138).

to be found nearby.

According to local legend, Yelverton is one of very few old settlements to have been renamed by a railway company. Originally called 'Ella's ford town', or Elfordtown, when the Great Western Railway opened its station here in 1859 the company's officials transcribed the locals' dialects pronunciation into Yelverton.

The village is home to the **Yelverton Paperweight Centre** that holds a collection of glass paperweights that contains examples of the work of artists from such renowned studios as Caithness and Whitefriars as well as work by individual artists. Along with the extensive range of paperweights for sale, the centre also displays a range of oil and watercolour paintings by artists who specialise in Dartmoor and moorland wildlife subjects. The centre is open daily from April to October and in December and at weekends for the rest of the year.

Sheepstor

6½ miles SE of Tavistock off the B3212

Surrounded by meadows and woodland, the small church in this attractive little village, is overshadowed by an extraordinary red sarcophagus in its churchyard that is the tomb of the White Raja of Sarawak who retired to nearby Burrator House. Meanwhile, the church itself has a strange feature – the 17th century carving above the church porch.

Just to the northwest lie **Burrator Reservoir** and its **Arboretum**, where footpaths have been carefully laid out to lead visitors through the specimen trees. Although the plantings are relatively recent, the arboretum was begun in 1992, the addition of ponds, bridges over the river and a riverside walk hold the interest as does the wealth of wildlife found here. The trees make an excellent contrast to the open moorland and rugged tors of Dartmoor.

Meavy

5½ miles SE of Tavistock off the A386

Once the home of Sir Francis Drake, Meavy is an archetypal Dartmoor village with a part-Norman church and a delightful old inn, the **Royal Oak**. There are some delightful walks from the village, especially to the northeast through the woods surrounding Burrator Reservoir.

Buckland Monachorum

3½ miles S of Tavistock off the A386

This picturesque village, near the Walkham Valley, is home to **The Garden House** which is open daily from March to mid November (see panel on page 142).

Tucked away in the Tavy Valley, just to the south of Buckland Monachorum, lies **Buckland Abbey** (National Trust) that was founded in 1278 by Amicia, Countess of Devon and, though small, it

The Royal Oak Inn

Meavy, near Yelverton, Devon PL20 6PJ
Tel: 01822 852944
website: www.burrator.gov.uk

Situated in a village on the edge of Dartmoor it is probable that Sir Francis Drake, a local property owner, would have known this charming inn as it dates back to at least 1510 when it was known as the 'Church House Inn'. Unusually this most traditional of pubs is owned by the local parish council and personally run by the tenants, Patrick and Ann Davis. Patrick is a former captain of tall ships such as the famous 'Sir Winston Churchill', whilst Ann, who has a background in catering, has worked at Drakes former home, Buckland Abbey, which is only a few miles from the Inn..

Naturally, Ann has taken charge of the cuisine on offer at the inn and she is fast establishing a reputation for serving excellent and traditional pub food with a difference, that is all freshly prepared and home cooked. The menu changes constantly whilst the choice of beer here always includes a range of local real ales including Princetown Jail Ale. Welcoming at anytime of year the inn has seating outside that overlooks the village green on which stands a 1000-year-old oak tree.

The Garden House

Buckland Monachorum, Yelverton,
Devon PL20 7LQ
Tel: 01822 854769 Fax: 01822 855358
e-mail: office@thegardenhouse.org.uk
website: www.thegardenhouse.org.uk

In 1945 retired Etonian schoolmaster, the late Lionel Fortescue, came to **The Garden House** with the ambition of building the best garden in Britain. He restored a derelict piece of land into what is today The Walled Garden, surrounding the ruins of the medieval vicarage of Buckland Monachorum, demolished at the end of the 18th century to be replaced by the building that is today The Garden House.

The son of a noted artist of the Newlyn school, Lionel inherited a painter's eye for colour. The garden he and his wife Katharine built was once called 'the most beautiful acre and a half in England'.

In 1961 they set up the Fortescue Trust to ensure the survival of the garden for future generations and by the time they died in the 1980's, the volume of visitors was overwhelming. Lionel's successor, Keith Wiley and his wife, undertook to expand the garden into a field and have created a revolutionary garden. It takes inspiration from natural landscapes for a series of interlinked, different garden experiences which offer kaleidoscopic sea of colour from Spring until Autumn. The garden has featured extensively in newspapers and magazines and on television programmes all over the world.

Keith has plans for many more exciting projects in the garden as well as launching a database for use by the public.

went on to become an influential Cistercian monastery. However, it is best known as being the last home of Sir Francis Drake who purchased the former abbey in 1581 from his fellow mariner (and pirate) Sir Richard Grenville, whose exploits in his little ship, the *Revenge*, were almost as colourful as those of Drake himself. The two men were not friends, so Drake bought the property anonymously and Sir Richard is said to have been mortified that his archrival in public esteem had so deviously acquired the imposing old building. The abbey remained in the Drake family until 1947 when it passed into the stewardship of the National Trust. Inside the abbey visitors can see the beautiful plasterwork in the Great Hall, the splendid kitchens and exhibitions that reveal the secrets of medieval monastic life, the Dissolution and the Armada. Also on display is

Buckland Abbey

Drake's Drum that, according to legend, will sound whenever the realm of England is in peril. The drum was brought back to England by Drake's brother, Thomas, who was with the great seafarer when he died (rather ignominiously of dysentery) on the Spanish Main in 1596. Meanwhile, in the abbey grounds there is a new Elizabethan Garden, a herb garden and an impressive 14th century tithe barn that houses an interesting collection of vintage carts and carriages. The village's church of St Andrew contains a tribute to the generations of Drakes who lived at Buckland Abbey whilst, carved on their family pew, is the *Golden Hind*.

Bere Alston

5 miles SW of Tavistock on the B3257

Set back from the River Tamar, which here acts as the boundary between Devon and Cornwall, Bere Alston was, for centuries, a thriving little port that transported the products of Dartmoor's tin mines all over the world. All that commercial activity has long since faded away but the river here is still busy, though nowadays it is mostly pleasure craft riding the waters. Just a few miles upstream from the village is one of the county's most popular visitor attractions – **Morwellham Quay** – an historic port, copper mine and preserved village that lies in a beautiful setting. Now an open-air museum, visitors can experience life in a busy 19th century community as costumed staff give talks and demonstrations in the authentic cottages and in the workshops where craftsmen such as carpenters and blacksmiths continue working in a traditional manner. Meanwhile, deep into the ground below the village is the George and Charlotte Copper Mine and the journey through the mines can be taken on a riverside tramway whilst another highlight here is the restored Tamar ketch *Garlandstone*. Around the village is a nature reserve covering a mixture of marshland, woodland and meadows that provides an opportunity to experience some peace and tranquillity as well as observe a wide variety of wildlife. Morwellham Quay is open daily all year round from February.

Although Morwellham lies some 20 miles upstream from Plymouth the River Tamar was still deep enough here, in the mid 19th century, for 300 tonne ships to load up with precious minerals that included arsenic and half the world's copper. Known as the Devon Klondyke, Morwellham suffered a catastrophic decline when cheaper sources of copper were discovered in South America.

Gulworthy

2 miles SW of Tavistock on the A390

This little village stands in the heart of an area that, in the mid 19th century, had a global reputation as a quarter of the world's supply of copper was extracted from the nearby mines. However, much more alarming is that some 50 per cent of the world's requirement of arsenic was also extracted hereabouts. Mining for copper here has long since been abandoned and Gulworthy's arsenic has also gone out of fashion as an agent of murder.

Milton Abbot

5½ miles NW of Tavistock on the B3362

Situated high above the Tamar Valley, this village is home to the Regency masterpiece, **Endsleigh House** that was designed for the Duke and Duchess of Bedford by the architect Sir Jeffry Wyattville and the landscape designer Humphry Repton. Built in the cottage orné style in around 1810, the house comprises of the main building and a children's wing that are linked by a curved terrace. Meanwhile, the formal gardens were designed to form a setting for the house as well as frame views out across the surrounding countryside. Along with the three terraces, which were restored in 1998, there are less formal garden areas that include a Rock Garden with a mysterious underground grotto that leads to the Dairy Dell. Little altered since it was first created, the grounds also include an internationally famous arboretum containing over 1,000 specimen trees.

Ivybridge

Situated in the beautiful valley of the River Erme, the original bridge here was just wide enough for a single packhorse and the 13th century crossing that replaced it, which is still in use today, remains very narrow. However, when the railway arrived here in 1848, Brunel constructed an impressive wooden viaduct over the valley that was, in 1895, replaced by the equally imposing stone structure that dominates today. The town grew rapidly in the 1860s when a quality paper making mill was established here that made good use of the waters of the River Erme and, since then, Ivybridge has continued to grow as a commuter town for Plymouth.

Serious walkers will know Ivybridge as the southern starting point of the **Two Moors Way**, the spectacular but gruelling 103-mile footpath that runs across both Dartmoor and Exmoor and finishes at Barnstaple. The trek begins with a stiff 1,000 foot climb up **Butterdon Hill**, just outside Ivybridge.

Around Ivybridge

South Brent

5 miles NE of Ivybridge off the A38

Situated on the southern flank of Dartmoor, this is a delightful village of gaily painted cottages that boasts the 13th century Church of St Petrock, with its massive Norman tower. Set beside the River Avon, this was once the main church for a large part of the South Hams as well as a considerable area of Dartmoor. Alongside the River Avon are some attractive old textile mills recalling the days when South Brent was an important centre for the production of woollens. In Victorian times, one of the mills was managed by William Crossing whose famous *Crossing's Guide to Dartmoor* provides a fascinating picture of life on the moor in the late 19th century.

In the days of stagecoach travel the town was a lively place with two posting houses servicing the competing coaches. It was said that four horses could be changed here in 45 seconds and a full three-course meal served in just 20 minutes. The most famous of the coaches, the Quicksilver, left Plymouth at 8.30 in the evening and arrived in London at 4 o'clock the following afternoon – a journey of nearly 20 hours that averaged, with stops, the remarkable speed of 11 miles per hour!

Ugborough

3 miles E of Ivybridge off the A3121

This attractive village, which has regularly won awards in 'Best Kept Village' competitions, has an imposing church more than 130 feet long that stands on top of a substantial prehistoric earthwork. Inside, there are some exceptional features, including a rood screen with a set of 32 painted panels, an unusual monumental brass of an unknown 15th century woman and a carved roof boss in the north aisle depicting a sow and her litter.

Sparkwell

3½ miles NW of Ivybridge off the A38

Just to the north of this village lies the **Dartmoor Wildlife Park** and the **West Country Falconry Centre** (see panel on page 146).

Cornwood

3 miles NW of Ivybridge off the A38

A pleasant village on the River Yealm, Cornwood is a good base from which to explore the many Bronze Age and industrial remains scattered across Dartmoor. One of the most remarkable sights in the National Park is the double line of stones set up on Stall Moor during the Bronze Age. Only accessible on foot, one line is almost 550 yards

long; the other begins with a stone circle and crosses the River Erme before ending at a burial chamber some two miles away. To the north of Cornwood, the rugged landscape of Dartmoor begins in earnest and, from here, there are some 15 miles of spectacular and uninterrupted moorland before the next inhabited place, Princetown, is reached.

Shaugh Prior

7 miles NW of Ivybridge off the A386

Found close to the Plym Valley, this village, of terraced clay workers' cottages, is overlooked by an Iron Age hillfort that stands, to the northwest, on Dewerstone outcrop.

Ashburton

This appealing little town lies just inside Dartmoor National Park and, surrounded by lovely hills, it has the River Ashburn flowing through its centre. An ancient settlement, its municipal history goes back to AD 821 when the town elected its first Portreeve, the Saxon equivalent of a Mayor. The traditional office continues to the present day although its functions are now purely ceremonial and, each year, on the fourth Tuesday in November, officials gather to appoint not just their Portreeve but also the Ale Tasters, Bread Weighers, Pig Drovers and even a Viewer of Water Courses.

Appearing as 'Essebretone' in the *Domesday Book*, when it was recorded as

St Andrews Church, Ashburton

being owned by the Bishop of Exeter, in medieval times Ashburton's prosperity was based on tin. Made one of Devon's four Stannary towns in 1305, Ashburton benefited from the trade generated by the Dartmoor tinners who were obliged to come here to have their metal weighed and stamped, and to pay the duty. Such was the wealth created by this trade that, in 1314, the town's grammar school was founded. Later, the cloth industry took over from tin mining as the major employer and wealth generator and there were several fulling mills along the banks of the River Ashburn producing cloth that the East India Company exported as far afield as China.

Housed in the former home and workshop of a brush maker, the **Ashburton Museum** provides a great insight into the history of this stannary town as well as the domestic and rural life of Dartmoor down the centuries. Most of the items on display have been collected locally and, along with a collection of old farming implements, some Victorian toys (including two of the smallest dolls ever made) and a collection of local minerals, there is a model of the Market Hall that was demolished in 1848 and, most striking of all, a Sioux War Bonnet. The fascinating collection of North American Indian artefacts was donated by the late Paul Endacott whose parents had left Ashburton for Oklahoma at the beginning of the 20th century.

Around Ashburton

Haytor Vale

4½ miles N of Ashburton off the B3387

To the west of this pretty hamlet of white cottages, is the well known tor of **Haytor Rocks**, with Rippon and Saddle Tors nearby, but Haytor is perhaps the most dramatic, particularly when approached from the west, as it rises to a height of almost 1,500 feet and provides a popular challenge for rock climbers. In the early 19th century, the shallow valley to the north of Haytor Rocks was riddled with quarries that have supplied granite for such well known buildings as

Haytor Rocks

was once an important centre of the wool industry and, in the heart of Ilsington, there is a characteristic trio of late medieval buildings – the church, the church house and an inn. The interior of quaint St Michael's Church is well worth seeing with its impressive array of arched beams and roof timbers that seem to hang in mid-air above the nave. Also of interest here are the medieval pew ends that are thought to be the only ones in Devon to be carved with the distinctive poppy head design. The entrance to the churchyard is guarded by an unusual granite lych gate with an upper storey that once served as the village schoolroom. The present structure is actually a replica of the original medieval gate that apparently collapsed when someone slammed the gate too enthusiastically. The nearby church house, dating back to the 16th century, is now sub-divided into residential

London Bridge, the National Gallery and for the pillars of the British Museum. Known as the Templer quarries, they all ceased working by 1858 but the **Templer Way** trail follows part of the old granite shipping route from Haytor to the Teign estuary and, along the way, sections of the old rail track can still be seen.

Ilsington

4 miles NE of Ashburton off the B3387

Like so many Dartmoor communities, this large village of thatched cottages dwellings known as St Michael's Cottages.

Ilsington was the birthplace of the Jacobean dramatist John Ford (1586-1639) whose most successful play, *Tis Pity She's a Whore*, written in 1633, is still occasionally revived.

Bovey Tracey

6½ miles NE of Ashburton off the B3344

This ancient market town takes its name from the River Bovey on which it stands and the de Tracey family who were given the manor by William the Conqueror. The best known member of the family was Sir William Tracey, one of the four knights who murdered Thomas à Becket at Canterbury Cathedral and, to expiate his crime, Sir William endowed the parish church that is dedicated to St Thomas. The original hilltop church was destroyed by fire and the present building dates from the 15th century although its tower was built in the 14th century and it has also undergone some Victorian restoration work. Its most glorious possession is a beautifully carved screen of 1427, a gift to the church from Lady Margaret Beauford, the new owner of the manor and the mother of Henry VII.

Although the church burned to the ground, Bovey Tracey, unlike so many other Devon towns and villages, has never suffered a major fire and this is perhaps just as well as its fire-fighting facilities, until recent times, were decidedly limited. In 1920, for example, the town did have a fire engine, and five volunteers to man it, but no horses were available to pull it! In that year the parish council issued a notice advising "all or any persons requiring the Fire Brigade with Engine that they must take the responsibility of sending a Pair of Horses for the purpose of conveying the Engine to and from the Scene of the Fire."

For such a small town, Bovey is remarkably well served with shops and another interesting place to visit is **Riverside Mill**, the southwest's leading craft showrooms, which is run by the Devon Guild of Craftsmen. Here, in this stunning riverside location, visitors

Willmead Farm, Bovey Tracey

can see the ever-changing craft exhibitions and demonstrations and there is also a Museum of Craftsmanship. Dating back to 1854, this historic mill is also home to the Gallery Café that serves homemade dishes created from largely local sources. Walkers will enjoy the footpath that follows the track bed of the former railway from Moretonhampstead to Newton Abbot, skirting the River Bovey for part of its length.

Another of the town's historic buildings, an old pottery, is now home to the **House of Marbles and Teign Valley Glass**, where an unusual range of games, toys, marbles and glassware has been manufactured for many years. After wandering through the old pottery buildings and seeing the listed kilns, visitors can marvel at the exhibitions in the museum of glass, games, marbles and Bovey Pottery as well as watch glass blowing when work is in progress. The shop sells all manner of glass items, from wine glasses and paperweights to, of course, marbles and there is also a café.

More family fun can be found at **Cardew Teapottery** where the world's most collectable teapots can be seen being made. During the week there is a tour of the factory and visitors are invited to try their hand at decorating and personalizing their own plate, mug or egg cup. The gift shop has a vast selection of pottery and other gift items, including one of the largest displays of teapots in the world, whilst the Teapottery is set in some 10 acres of glorious woodland through which there are footpaths. The Teapottery is open daily all year round expect Christmas.

Just to the north of Bovey is **Parke**, the former estate of the Tracey family but, today, the 19th century mansion, which is owned by the National Trust, is the headquarters of the Dartmoor National Park Authority.

Chudleigh Knighton

7 miles NE of Ashburton on the B3344

Close to this village lies the **Chudleigh Knighton Heath Nature Reserve**, a

The Anchor Inn

Old Plymouth Road, Chudleigh Knighton, Devon TQ13 0EN
Tel: 01626 853123
e-mail: baileygb7@aol.com

Originally a row of cottages that date back to the 16th century, **The Anchor Inn** is situated on the old Portsmouth to Plymouth road and so has, over the years, played host to numerous naval personnel. Today, this cosy and attractive traditional country inn welcomes both locals and visitors alike to come here to enjoy the relaxed hospitality of landlords Geoff and Elizabeth Bailey. Along with all the usual

drinks served at the bar, excellent home-cooked food is served here and, in particular, there are Geoff's authentic Asian dishes.

fascinating area of registered common that provides a variety of heathland habitats for a wide range of wildlife as well as small ponds and areas of woodland. Meanwhile, to the northwest of Chudleigh Knighton is another nature reserve, **Little Bradley Ponds Nature Reserve**, which has been formed around two large ponds in an area that was once a clay works. Best known for its dragonflies – over 20 different species have been recorded here – the reserve has several footpaths that lead visitors around the ponds and boardwalks that cross the muddier part of the reserve.

Buckfast Abbey

Buckfast

1½ miles SW of Ashburton off the A38

This small village, found on the edge of Dartmoor in the valley of the River Dart, is home to **Buckfast Abbey**, a Benedictine monastery that was founded, originally, in the 11th century. The abbey was closed by Henry VIII in the 16th century but, in 1882, the present community of monks returned to the site and began to rebuild their house on the medieval foundations. The magnificent Abbey Church, the last building to be finished here in 1938, was constructed by just four monks and it remains the centrepiece for this enterprising religious community. The Monastic Produce shop, housed in a restored 18th century mill, has a fascinating range of gift items and many are unique as the shop only sells the produce of monasteries and convents. Along with perfumes, soaps and candles there are high quality wines, linens and devotional gifts. Naturally, the Buckfast Abbey monks also sell their own produce that includes their famous tonic wine, honey, fudge and beeswax items. However, it is the peace and tranquillity of the abbey grounds that makes a visit here so special and, along with the sensory garden, there is a Physic Garden where both medicinal and culinary herbs are grown. The gardens are also home to the fragrant National Lavender Collection. Finally, housed in one of the oldest parts of the medieval abbey to have survived, the 12th century arch of the North Gate, is the Grange restaurant.

Buckfastleigh

2½ miles SW of Ashburton on the B3380

Dart Valley Railway, Buckfastleigh

An ancient woollen town that once boasted five textile mills and a tannery, Buckfastleigh has remained relatively unspoilt and, today, there is still evidence of its past industry whilst it is also a good base for walkers and cyclists. Close to both Dartmoor and the South Hams, it lies on the **Dartmoor Way**, a route that was designed specifically for walkers and cyclists. Modes of transport seem to be something of a theme here as this market town is the western terminus and headquarters of the **South Devon Railway** and there is also the **Buckfastleigh Vintage Bus Service**. Formerly known as the Primrose Line, the railway operates steam trains along a seven-mile route through the Dart Valley to Totnes and the line provides an ideal opportunity to discover the delights of this picturesque river whose banks abound with herons, swans, kingfishers, badgers and foxes. At Buckfastleigh station, there is a railway museum, café, model railway and a gift shop as well as ample room for picnics and railway workshops to visit. Meanwhile, the vintage bus service operates a fleet of historic old single and double decker buses that run between the town and various local attractions, namely Buckfast Abbey, on selected days throughout the season.

For anyone looking to stay in one place for a while, there is the **Valiant Soldier Museum and Heritage Centre** that not only provides something of interest for all the family but that has also stood still, in time, for the past 30 years or so. Originally a village inn, the Valiant Soldier closed its doors for the last time in the 1960s and it was not until the 1990s that it was reopened – this time as a museum. With the authentic atmosphere of a working man's pub of the

Salmon Ladder, Buckfastleigh

Buckfast Butterflies and Dartmoor Otter Sanctuary

Buckfastleigh, Devon TQ11 0DZ
Tel: 01364 642916
e-mail: info@ottersandbutterflies.co.uk
website: www.ottersandbutterflies.co.uk

The tropical landscaped gardens at **Buckfast Butterflies and Dartmoor Otter Sanctuary**, with their ponds, waterfalls and exotic plants are home to a wide variety of exotic butterflies from around the world that live, breed and fly freely. The gardens are also home to small birds and other tropical creatures such as leaf cutting ants from Costa Rica, Koi Carp and terrapins.

The complete life-cycle of the butterfly, from chrysalis to drying their wings and making their first flight, can be studied and photographed at leisure. Outside, in another specially landscaped garden is the otter sanctuary where three species of otters, including the shy native British otter, can be seen. A special underwater viewing area allows visitors to observe these playful creatures in their natural habitat and watching them during the thrice-daily feeding times is particularly amusing. Both the otters and the butterflies provide plenty of opportunity for budding wildlife photographers to hone their skills. The butterflies can be seen daily between April and October whilst the otter sanctuary is also open in March.

1940s, this museum offers a unique insight into the lives of ordinary people over the last 60 years or so. Open from April to the end of October, the Valiant Soldier Museum and Heritage Centre also has an exhibition telling the story of the town.

Another popular attraction in Buckfastleigh is the **Buckfast Butterflies & Dartmoor Otter Sanctuary** (see panel above) where a specially designed tropical rain forest habitat has been created for the exotic butterflies. Meanwhile, there is an underwater viewing area that offers a marvellous opportunity to see the otters in their natural habitat. Both the butterflies and otters can be photographed and the otters' thrice-daily feeding times provide some excellent photo-opportunities.

A couple of miles southwest of Buckfastleigh lies **Pennywell**, a spacious all-weather family attraction that offers a wide variety of entertainments and activities. This award-winning centre, which includes numerous rides and slides, is also home to the Dartmoor Pony Centre.

A little further south again lies the little church of **Dean Prior** and, during the time of the Restoration, the vicar here was the poet and staunch Royalist, Robert Herrick, (1591-1674). Herrick's best known lines are probably the opening of *To the Virgins, to make Much of Time*:

"Gather ye rosebuds while ye may,
Old Time is still a-flying
And this same flower that smiles today
Tomorrow will be dying."

Herrick apparently found rural Devon rather dull and much preferred London where he had a mistress 27 years his junior. Perhaps to brighten up the monotony of his Devonshire existence, he had a pet pig that he took for walks and trained to drink beer from a tankard. Herrick died in 1674 and was buried in the churchyard where a simple stone marks his "assumed last resting place."

Holne

3 miles W of Ashburton off the A38

Well known to walkers on the Two Moors Way, this pretty little village, which lies beneath Holne Moor, was the birthplace, in 1819, of Charles Kingsley, the author of *The Water Babies*. In the 14th century parish church is a memorial window to the village's most famous son.

Dartmeet

5½ miles NW of Ashburton off the B3357

This village lies at a famous beauty spot, where the boulder strewn East and West Dart rivers meet in a steep, wooded valley, and, at their junction is a single-span **Clapper Bridge** that dates from the 1400s. Rising in the boggy plateau of north Dartmoor, the River Dart and its tributaries drain a huge area of moor and run for 46 miles before entering the sea at Dartmouth. In the days when the tin

mines were working, this area was extremely isolated, lacking even a burial ground of its own and local people had to carry their dead across the moor to Lydford – "Eight miles in fair weather and fifteen in foul." In good weather this is grand walking country with a choice of exploring the higher moor, dotted with a wealth of prehistoric remains, or following the lovely riverside and woodland path that leads to another fine clapper bridge, near Postbridge.

Clapper Bridge, Dartmeet

The **Dart Valley Nature Reserve**, the largest of Devon Wildlife Trust's reserves and also one of the most spectacular, includes not only areas of unspoilt wooded valley but also upland moorland. The whole area of the reserve can be explored although the going can be rough in places and there are few recognised paths.

To the southeast of Dartmeet and on the southern edge of the National Park lies **Venford Reservoir** that, along with having picnic tables, free fishing and a footpath around the man-made lake, is a good starting point for walks up into the open moorland.

Widecombe in the Moor

5 miles NW of Ashburton on the B3387

Widecombe in the Moor

Enjoying a lovely position in the valley of the East Webburn river, Widecombe in the Moor is a charming and picturesque village with a grand old church that has, with its massive 120-foot high granite tower rising against a backdrop of high moorland, understandably been dubbed the **Cathedral of the Moors**. Dedicated to St Pancras, the church was built with funds raised by local tin miners in the 14th century and enlarged during the next two centuries. A panel inside the church records the disastrous events of the 21st October 1638 when a bolt of lightning struck the tower whilst, inside, a sizable congregation had gathered for a service. Huge blocks of masonry were dislodged and rained down on the worshippers, killing four outright and leaving many badly injured. Local legend maintains that the Devil had been spotted earlier that day spitting fire and riding an ebony stallion across the moor.

In addition to the church there are two other buildings in the village worthy of a mention. **Glebe House** is a handsome 16th century residence that has since been converted into shops whilst **Church House** is an exceptional colonnaded building that was originally built in around 1500 to accommodate those travelling long distances over the moorland to attend church. The house was later divided into almshouses and it served, in succession, as a brewery and then a school. Church House is now home to a National Trust shop and Information Centre.

However, Widecombe is perhaps known for its **Fair**, a jolly occasion that takes place in September and it is known the world over from the song that tells of the adventures of Uncle Tom Cobleigh, his friends and the old grey mare who are on their way to the fair. A succession of Tom Cobleighs have lived around Widecombe over the centuries but the song probably refers to the gentleman who died in 1794. An amorous bachelor, Uncle Tom Cobleigh had a mane of red hair and he refused to maintain any babies that did not display the same characteristic.

Held in the historic hall at Church House, there is, on Thursdays between May and October, a weekly **Craft Market** where craftspeople from the whole of Devon come to sell their wares.

Postbridge

9 miles NW of Ashburton on the B3212

The countryside around this attractive hamlet is littered with numerous Bronze Age remains and this would suggest that Postbridge was, in prehistoric times, one of the main meeting places on Dartmoor. Today it remains an oasis with its beech trees contrasting strongly with the surrounding bleak moorland.

Clapper Bridge, Postbridge

Postbridge is, perhaps, best known for its large **Clapper Bridge** that probably dates from the 13th century and it remains one of the best preserved of all Devon's such bridges. Spanning the East Dart River, the bridge is a model of medieval minimalist construction with just three huge slabs of granite laid across stone piers. Originally built to be used by packhorses making the journey along what was once an essential link from Chagford to Tavistock, the bridge is too narrow for today's traffic. From here there are pleasant walks up the East Dart River although anyone wishing to cross the river during the walk should note that, after heavy rain, this may not always be possible.

To the west of Postbridge lie the ruins of **Powder Mills**, a 19th century gunpowder factory and its isolated position was about the only safety feature at the factory and the batches of gunpowder were tested by firing a proving mortar that can still be seen near the cottages. A little further on lies a low tor, **Crockern Tor**, that, between 1474 and 1703, was the meeting place of the Stannary Court, the administrative body of the Dartmoor miners, and to which each of the four Stannary towns in Devon sent 24 representatives.

Meanwhile, a couple of miles northeast of Postbridge, on the main road to Moretonhampstead, lies **Warren House Inn** that claims to be the third highest tavern in England. It used to stand on the other side of the road but, in 1845, a fire destroyed that building. According to tradition, when the present inn was built its landlord carried some still smouldering turfs across the road to the hearth of the new hostelry and that fire has been burning ever since. It is a pleasant enough sight in summer but it must have been even more welcoming in the winter of 1963 when the inn was cut off by heavy snow drifts some 20 feet deep and for almost three months supplies had to be flown in by helicopter. Such a remote inn, naturally, generates some good tales: like the one about the traveller who stayed here one winter's night and, by chance, he opened a large chest in his room and discovered the body of a dead man inside. "Why!" said the landlord when confronted with the deceased, "tis only feyther! 'Twas too cold to take 'un to the buryin', so mother salted 'un down!"

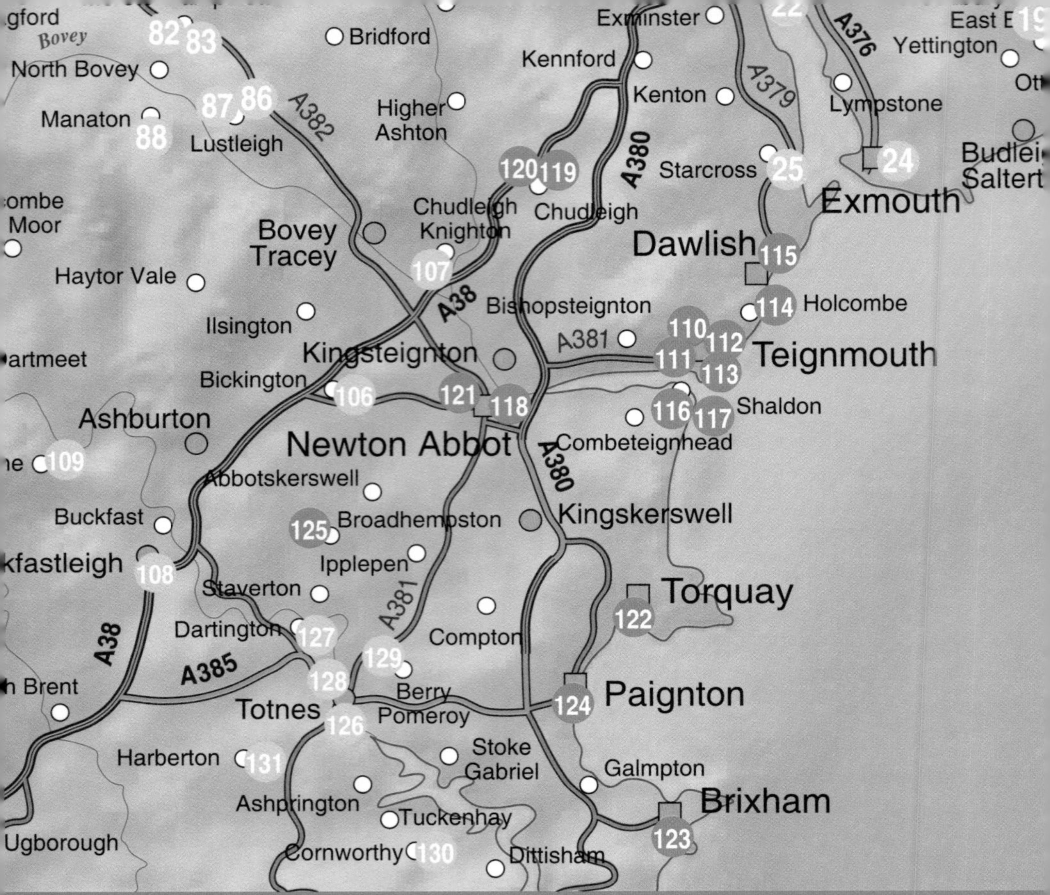

North Bovey
Manaton
Lustleigh
Bridford
Higher Ashton
Kennford
Exminster
Kenton
Starcross
Yettington
Lympstone
Exmouth
Budleigh Salterton
Bovey Tracey
Chudleigh Knighton
Chudleigh
Dawlish
Holcombe
Haytor Vale
Ilsington
Bishopsteignton
Kingsteignton
Teignmouth
Bickington
Shaldon
Ashburton
Newton Abbot
Combeteignhead
Abbotskerswell
Buckfast
Broadhempston
Kingskerswell
Buckfastleigh
Ipplepen
Staverton
Torquay
Dartington
Compton
Totnes
Berry Pomeroy
Paignton
Harberton
Stoke Gabriel
Galmpton
Ashprington
Tuckenhay
Brixham
Ugborough
Cornworthy
Dittisham
A38
A382
A380
A379
A376
A381
A385

PLACES TO STAY, EAT AND DRINK

The Green Room, Teignmouth	110	Restaurant	p161
The Grendons, Teignmouth	111	Self Catering	p162
Lifeboat Inn, Teignmouth	112	Pub with Food	p162
Lyme Bay House, Teignmouth	113	Hotel	p163
The Smugglers Inn, Holcombe, Dawlish	114	Pub and Restaurant	p164
West Hatch Hotel, Dawlish	115	Hotel	p165
La Provence, Shaldon	116	Restaurant	p165
Potters Mooring Hotel, Shaldon	117	Hotel	p166
The Country Table Café, Newton Abbot	118	Café	p167
Coombeshead Farm Cottages, Chudleigh	119	Self Catering	p169
The Ship Inn, Chudleigh	120	Pub with Food	p169
The Mount, Ideford Combe, Newton Abbot	121	Guest House	p170
Dunstone Hall, Torquay	122	Hotel	p173
Sampford House, Brixham	123	Bed and Breakfast	p175
The Roscrea Hotel, Paignton	124	Hotel	p178
The Monks Retreat Inn, Broadhempston	125	Pub with Food	p180

Denotes entries in other chapters

6 The English Riviera

The stretch of Devon coastline between the River Dart and the Exe estuary is known as The English Riviera and this might seem a little presumptuous at first but, as this area has a mild climate, there are palm trees waving in the gentle breeze along the coast. They are not just confined to the public parks and expensively maintained hotel gardens but can be found even growing wild and, along with creating a Mediterranean atmosphere along the coast, they have become a symbol of this area. The first specimen palm trees arrived in Britain in the 1820s and it was soon discovered that this sub-tropical species took kindly to the genial climate of south Devon. To the uninitiated, one palm tree may look much like another, but experts will point out that although the most common variety growing here is Cordyline Australis (imported from New Zealand), there are also Mediterranean Fan Palms, Trachycarpus Fortunei from the East China Sea and Date Palms from the Canary Islands. The oldest palm tree on record in the area is now over 80 years old and it stands more than 40 feet high.

Goodrington Park Sands,

Torbay

The Mediterranean similarities do not end with the trees as Torquay, like Rome, is

Babbacombe

set on seven hills and the red-tiled roofs of its Italianate villas, set amongst the dark green trees, would look equally at home in some Adriatic resort. The Mediterranean resemblance is so close that in one film in the Roger Moore television series, *The Saint*, a budget conscious producer made Torquay double as Monte Carlo.

Still a popular family resort, Torquay lies at the northern point of Tor Bay whilst further round the bay is Paignton, a one time small fishing village that, as its neighbour was developed, also became a popular and elegant resort. Its two sandy beaches, famous zoo and other attractions ensure that plenty of people continue to make this their holiday destination. Here, too, can be found the former home of the sewing-machine manufacturer, Isaac Singer, Oldway Mansion, which was transformed by his son Parish into a fabulously opulent residence that includes a sumptuous ballroom where his mistress, Isadora Duncan, displayed her new, fluid dance style. Close by can be found one of Devon's best kept secrets, the glorious gardens of Greenway, the former home of the novelist Dame Agatha Christie. The world famous crime writer was born in Torquay in 1890 and the town continues to remember its most famous daughter in a special exhibition at Torre Abbey and in the town's museum. At the southern point of Tor Bay lies Brixham, where, in 1688, William, Prince of Orange landed to claim the British throne as William III. On his journey to London he stopped at the ancient market town of

Illuminations and Fireworks, Torquay

Cockington, Near Torquay

Newton Abbot where, in front of St Leonard's Church, he was proclaimed King William III.

Further north, at the estuary of the River Teign lies another elegant resort of fine Regency and Georgian buildings, Teignmouth, but whilst this certainly has everything a resort should have it has also remained a busy port from which, in particular, potters' clay is exported.

Teignmouth

There are two distinct aspects to Teignmouth: the popular holiday resort on the coastal side whilst, on the banks of the River Teign, there is the working port area of the town. With two miles of sandy beaches, a splendid promenade that is almost as long, and a pier, it is easy to see why the town is a family favourite and here, too, can be found a 25-foot high lighthouse that serves no apparent purpose apart from being a rather striking landmark. The residential area of the resort has some fine Regency and Georgian buildings and, in particular, there is the **Church of St James**, with its impressive octagonal tower of 1820, and the former **Assembly Rooms**, a dignified colonnaded building that now houses the Riviera Cinema.

Meanwhile, the port at Teignmouth is reached by the narrowest of channels

The Green Room

The Den, Teignmouth, Devon TQ14 8BD
Tel: 01626 773837

Close to Teignmouth's sea front and the Carlton Theatre, **The Green Room** is a light, bright and airy restaurant that is open all day (but closed on winter Mondays). Owned and personally run by Denny and Pete, who have been here since Easter 2001. The Green Room is well known for its freshly prepared dishes, all created by Pete, and, in particular, its imaginative vegetarian options. From home-made soups and omelettes to lasagne and tuna steak with cous-cous, there is plenty of choice here as well as a children's menu. There is also wheelchair access.

and currents here are so fast and powerful that no ship enters the harbour without a Trinity House pilot on board. Built in 1821 using granite from the quarries on Haytor Down, **The Quay** has withstood the test of time like so many other more famous buildings constructed using the stone. Destroyed by the French in 1690, Teignmouth was once again in the front line when, during World War II, 75 people were killed in German bombing raids. Today, Teignmouth's main export is potters' clay that is extracted from pits beside the River Teign but boatbuilding also continues here although on a much

The Grendons

58 Coombe Vale Road, Teignmouth,
Devon TQ14 9EW
Tel: 01626 773667 Fax: 01626 773667
e-mail: grendonsholapt@cix.co.uk
website: www.cottageguide.co.uk/grendons

Occupying a spectacular situation overlooking Shaldon and the River Teign, **The Grendons** is an impressive early 19th century house that has been tastefully and expertly converted into attractive self-catering holiday apartments. Owned and personally run by Charles Gray, the flats range in size from sleeping two to five people and all are equipped with a fully fitted modern kitchen.The Grendons has its own private garden as well as off street parking.

Lifeboat Inn

6 The Strand, Teignmouth, Devon TQ14 8BW
Tel: 01626 774354 Fax: 01626 777222
e-mail: lifeboatinn@aol.com

Peter and Helly Moffitt, landlords of the **Lifeboat Inn** first moved to Teignmouth nearly 15 years ago with their young family but it was not until 2000 that they came to this inn and started to put it back on the local map. Found tucked away in the town but just a short walk to both the beach and the town centre, the Lifeboat Inn has a lively yet mature atmosphere that is enhanced by the magnificent Wurlitzer juke box that is stocked full of '60s and '70s discs. Along with a very well stocked bar, that includes two real ales and Budweiser on draught, the Lifeboat is renowned for its food.

Freshly prepared by Helly, the daily menu is served throughout the day although not on Tuesday when it's Peter's day off. However, what makes the Lifeboat special is the enthusiastic nature of the hosts who, throughout the week, hold a range of interesting events. On Sundays there is a fun quiz held in aid of the RNLI, whilst on Thurdays there is special themed menu – whatever the day this is always a lively and enjoyable place to visit.

Lyme Bay House

Den Promenade, Teignmouth,
Devon TQ14 8SZ
Tel: 01626 772953

Found next door to Teignmouth's famous 'Church on the Beach', **Lyme Bay House** is a striking former private residence that has been a small private hotel for many years. The sea front lies just across the road and those guest rooms, of which there are 10, at the front have spectacular panoramic views that take in the whole of Lyme Bay. A full home-cooked English breakfast, prepared from humanely produced and hormone free produce starts the day and both children and pets are welcome here.

smaller scale than it once achieved.

Found close to the railway station lies **Teignmouth Museum** that is dedicated to the history of the town and its people. Among the fascinating exhibits here can be seen a collection of artefacts rescued from a ship wrecked near here during the Armada whilst there are also displays on local railway history, the town's boatyards and local lace making.

The Harbour, Teignmouth

Around Teignmouth

Dawlish

2½ miles NE of Teignmouth on the A379

This pretty seaside resort, which boasts one of the safest beaches in England, has the unusual feature of a main railway line separating the town from its sea front. Uninspiring as this may sound, the result is, in fact, quite appealing as, for one thing, the railway keeps motor traffic away from the beach side and also the low granite viaduct that carries the track has weathered attractively in the 150 years or so since it was built. The arches through which beach goers pass create a kind of formal entrance to the beach and the Victorian station has also become something of a visitor attraction in its own right.

However, up until the beginning of the 19th century Dawlish was just a small settlement on the banks of the River Daw that, as it lay about a mile inland, had been protected from seabourne invaders. It is here, surrounded by a small group of thatched cottages, that the original village's 700-year-old church can be found. As the crazy for sea bathing and taking sea air began so Dawlish expanded and, as early as 1803, Regency villas were being built along the Strand as the village was developed into this pretty seaside resort. Right from the start, Dawlish was a fashionable destination and it attracted many distinguished guests including, Jane Austen (one of whose characters could not understand how one could live anywhere else in Devon but in Dawlish) and Charles Dickens, who, in his novel of the same name, had Nicholas Nickleby born at a farm close to the town. Whilst visiting the town in 1818 with his convalescing brother, the poet John Keats was so inspired that he wrote the less-than-immortal lines:

"Over the hill and over the Dale
And over the bourne to Dawlish
Where Gingerbread wives have a scanty sale
And gingerbread nuts are smallish."

Along with developing the Strand, the early 19th century improvers also 'beautified' the River Daw, which flows right through the town, by landscaping the stream into a series of shallow waterfalls and surrounding it with attractive gardens such as The Lawn. Until this time, The Lawn had been a swamp populated by herons, kingfishers and otters but, in 1808, the developer John Manning filled in the marshy land

West Hatch Hotel

34 West Cliff, Dawlish, Devon EX7 9DN
Tel: 01626 864211
e-mail: westhatchhotel@aol.com
website: www.smoothhound.co.uk/hotels/westhatc.html

Found just yards from the seafront, **West Hatch Hotel** is a stylish establishment that dates back to the 1920s and, among the interesting features of the hotel, are its stained glass windows, oak panelled staircase and de luxe four-poster bed. Owned and personally run by Astrid and Ian, along with offering all their guests a friendly and relaxing stay, visitors here will find charming guest rooms with luxurious en-suite facilities, a cosy sitting room, residents only bar and a delicious home-cooked breakfast.

with earth removed during the construction of Queen Street and, today, both areas still retain the elegance of the Regency era.

Housed in an elegant Georgian residence, which is itself an important part of the town's heritage, is the **Dawlish Museum**, where visitors can not only see a Victorian parlour, but there are also rooms displaying collections of china, prints, industrial tools, historically dressed dolls and by-gone toys. However, the most unusual collection here is undoubtedly that of early surgical instruments that was donated to the museum by a retired local doctor.

A couple of miles up the coast, towards the Exe estuary lies **Dawlish Warren**, a mile-long sand spit that almost blocks the mouth of the river. As well as the golf course here this is also a 55-acre nature reserve that is home to more than 450 species of flowering plants and, for one of them, the Jersey lily, this is its only habitat in mainland England.

Shaldon

½ mile S of Teignmouth on the A379

Situated on the opposite bank of the Teign estuary from Teignmouth, this pretty little resort's Marine Parade

La Provence

21 Fore Street, Shaldon, Devon TQ14 0DE
Tel: 01626 872384 Fax: 01626 872384
e-mail: plattken@hotmail.com

Close to the bridge across the River Teign lies **La Provence**, a small and intimate restaurant that was opened by the highly experienced Master Chef Ken Platt in March 2000. Now with an enviable reputation, this impressive restaurant specializes in fish and seafood dishes, although there are other equally impressive items on the menu. However, a must try is the house speciality, Fruit de mar, a wonderful mix of fish, prawns, mussels and squid bound together in the creamy wine sauce and then glazed with cheese.

Potters Mooring Hotel

30 The Green, Shaldon, Devon TQ14 0DN
Tel: 01626 873225 Fax: 01626 872909
e-mail: mail@pottersmooring.co.uk
website: www.pottersmooring.co.uk

Dating back to 1625 and originally a sea captain's residence owned by the Admiralty, **Potters Mooring Hotel** has been lovingly refurbished to create this charming and attractive small hotel that is owned and run by Richard and Dee Harding. Ideally situated just yards from the beach and overlooking the village green, the hotel has six excellent en-suite guest rooms including a cottage that is ideal for families and friends. Breakfast is served in the oak panelled dining room and children are welcome here.

provides an excellent viewing point from which to watch the busy traffic sailing in and out of the river. A good number of Regency houses and villas add an architectural dignity to the town and act as a reminder of an era when affluent Londoners, unable to holiday in Europe because of the Napoleonic Wars, began to discover the gentle charms of England's southwest coast.

A more recent attraction, the **Shaldon Wildlife Trust's** breeding centre for rare, small animals, reptiles and exotic birds, lies just to the north of the town.

Combeteignhead

2½ miles SW of Teignmouth off the A379

Situated across the River Teign from Bishopsteignton, Combeteignhead is a charming place that the poet, John Keats, came to know well when he stayed nearby with his consumptive brother Tom in 1818. In letters to his family, he often enclosed scraps of verse such as:

"Here all the summer I could stay,
For there's Bishop's Teign
And King's Teign
And Coomb at the clear Teign head –
Where close by the stream
You may have your cream
All spread upon Barley bread."

Newton Abbot

5½ miles SW of Teignmouth on the A382

An ancient market town on the southern bank of the River Teign, the town is made up of several medieval manors and one in particular, Wolborough, that in the reign of Henry III became the property of William Brewer, the founder of Torre Abbey. So this area, to the south of the River Lemon (that flows through the centre of the town today), became know as the New Town of the Abbot and, like its rival on the other side of the river, Newton Bushel, it benefited from the wool and leather industries during the Middle Ages. The area once known as Bushel now only exists as a ward on the district council whilst, as the town has expanded, it and the areas it has incorporated have become known as Newton Abbot.

It was here in 1688 that William, Prince of Orange, the "glorious defender of the Protestant religious and the liberties of England", was proclaimed King William III and this Glorious Revolution took place in front of the town's St Leonard's Church (of which only the medieval tower now remains). The new king had landed at nearby Brixham and was on his way to London and, whilst at Newton Abbot, he stayed at **Forde House**. A handsome Jacobean manor, which was completed by Sir Richard Reynell in 1610, the house was no stranger to royalty as, in 1625, Charles I, on his way to and from Plymouth also rested here. Later, during the Civil War, Lady Lucy played a somewhat reluctant hostess to Sir Thomas Fairfax and Oliver Cromwell who stayed here whilst their army was preparing for the second siege of Exeter. Today this house is now used as the district offices and is only open by appointment.

The town's most historic building, and a landmark still today, **St Leonard's Tower** was first mentioned in documentation in 1350 and it once had a small church attached. The church was demolished in 1836, when the new St Leonard's Church was constructed, and this has given rise to Newton Abbot's unique description as having "a tower without a church and a church without a tower."

The Country Table Café

12 Bank Street, Newton Abbot,
Devon TQ12 2JW
Tel: 01626 202120
website: www.thecountrytablecafe.co.uk

The Country Table Café is Newton Abbot's only wholefood café and, since owners Karen and Alan first opened here in 1996, they have grown an enviable reputation that continues to spread across Devon and beyond.

Open daily except Sundays and Bank Holidays, customers at this relaxed and friendly establishment can enjoy all manner of wholesome snacks and light meals that, with the exception of fish, are all vegetarian – even the breakfasts.

However, what makes Karen and Alan's café special are the interesting and highly imaginative dishes: there are sandwiches, filled pitta breads and Italian panini, numerous salads and generously filled jacket potatoes on the regular menu along with an ever-changing daily specials list. Also everything here is home-made from fresh, raw local ingredients and the café is able to cater for special diets.

So popular is The Country Table Café that, when it opens for dinner one Saturday night a month, booking is essential. On these evenings, Karen, Alan and staff put their creative talents to excellent use to offer tempting and enjoyable dishes and customers are asked to bring their own wine to complement their delicious meal.

The whole character of this attractive town changed in the mid 19th century when the Great Western Railway made it their centre of locomotive and carriage repair as well as being the junction for the Moretonhampstead and Torbay branch lines. Tidy terraces of artisans' houses were built along the steep hillsides in the southern areas of the town whilst, to the north, there are the Italianate villas of the well-to-do. Also on the northern outskirts of the town lies **Newton Abbot Racecourse** where national hunt horse racing takes place from the autumn through to the spring and where, for the rest of the year, greyhound races, stock car races and country fairs are held.

For a real glimpse into the past of this historic town there is the **Newton Abbot Museum**, which, through its displays, covers the key moments in the town's rich history as well as celebrating the life and times of some of its great personalities. Along with relics from the Great Western Railway and its interesting collection of recordings made by local people, there is also a tribute to John Lethbridge, the inventor of one of the first diving machines.

Another interesting place worth a visit is **Tuckers Maltings**, the country's only traditional working malt house open to the public, and malt has been made here since 1831. Tours guide visitors around malt house whilst there is also a chance to sample real ale with a further opportunity to buy speciality bottled beer at the maltings shop. The malt house is open Monday to Saturday from Easter to the end of October and also on Sundays in July and August.

On the western edge of Newton Abbot stands **Bradley Manor** (National Trust), a small medieval manor house that is a notable example of the domestic architecture of the time. Most of the house dates from around 1420 and it had a chapel, solar, great hall and a porch but, by the mid 18th century, this quaint style of architecture was decidedly out of fashion and the building became a farmhouse with poultry occupying the chapel. Beautifully situated in the midst of meadows and woodland, the grounds of the manor house contain a spring of fresh water that, so tradition says, has healing properties.

Meanwhile, to the south of Newton Abbot, is a place that all the family will enjoy – the **Hedgehog Hospital** at Prickly Hall Farm. Along with caring for injured hedgehogs, the hospital has a hedgehog village and a hedgehog friendly garden and visitors are encouraged to help feed the little creatures and to hold them. Other animals here include lambs, goats and sheep whilst there is also a café. The hospital is open daily from March to September and also less regularly between November and March.

Bishopsteignton

2 miles W of Teignmouth off the A381

This large village, overlooking the Teign estuary, is noted for its church that

Coombeshead Farm Holiday Cottages

Coombeshead Farm, Coombeshead Cross,
Chudleigh, nr Newton Abbot, Devon TQ13 0NQ
Tel: 01626 853334
e-mail: anne-coombeshead@supernet.com

Found tucked away in the lanes just a mile or so from Chudleigh and surrounded by beautiful rural countryside, **Coombeshead Farm Holiday Cottages** occupy an idyllic and peaceful location that is perfect for a relaxing family holiday. The three cottages, which each accommodate six, have been expertly converted from a massive barn and throughout the atmosphere and character of the original building has been maintained whilst owners, Anne and Bob Smith ensure that every modern comfort and convenience is also provided.

contains some of the finest Norman work in the county. Along with the doorway that is carved with 15 beak-heads, bunches of grapes, birds and a man with a sword, there is an impressive 900-year-old tympanum in the blocked south door that depicts the Adoration of the Magi.

The history of Bishopsteignton and the local area can be discovered at the **Bishopsteignton Museum of Village Life**, a wonderful place that owes its existence to the enthusiasm of local residents. Covering some 2,000 years, the numerous artefacts on display, many of which have been donated by local people, reflect the work, domestic and leisure aspects of past inhabitants. This museum gives visitors a real chance to see what life was like for ordinary folk in rural England and to understand how the 'great and good' influenced their lives and that of the country as a whole.

Chudleigh

5½ miles NW of Teignmouth off the A380

This attractive old town once stood on the main road between Exeter and Plymouth, but the construction of a

The Ship Inn

4 Fore Street, Chudleigh, Devon TQ13 0HX
Te: 01626 853268
e-mail: markmred2301@aol

Ideally placed on the edge of Dartmoor and within easy reach of the south coast, **The Ship Inn** is a charming and traditional small town inn that happily welcomes locals and visitors alike. Dating back to the 18th century, this friendly and lively place is run by sisters, Sue and Lesley White, and as both are excellent cooks, The Ship is a popular place for both lunch and dinner – the specialities here are their home-cooked pies, curries and chillies. Children are welcome here.

bypass in the 1960s has significantly reduced the almost unbearable levels of traffic that were particularly heavy during the summer season. It is now possible to enjoy this pretty town, with its 14th century church that contains some fine memorials to the Courtenay family and its former Grammar School nearby that was founded in 1668 (it is now a private house). It was at the coaching inn here that William of Orange stayed whilst on his journey to London and the new king addressed the people of Chudleigh from one of the inn's upstairs windows. Unfortunately, this Dutchman's English was so bad that his audience was unable to understand what he was saying though they clapped and cheered him all the same. Another royal visitor was Madame Royale, daughter of Louis XIV and Marie Antoinette, who sheltered in the town after her parents' execution.

Clifford Street is named after Sir Thomas Clifford, Lord Treasurer to Charles II and a member of the king's notorious Cabal, a secretive inner Cabinet. As was the custom of the time, Sir Thomas used his official position to amass a considerable fortune and this was later put to good use by his grandson who employed Robert Adam and Capability Brown to design **Ugbrooke House and Gardens**. Situated to the southeast of the town, the house dates from the mid 18th century, when it replaced an early Tudor manor house, and it takes its name from

The Mount

Ideford Combe, near Newton Abbot,
Devon TQ12 3GR
Tel: 01626 331418 Fax: 01626 331418
e-mail: tom@themountguesthouse.co.uk
website: www.themountguesthouse.co.uk

Ideally situated between the rugged moorland of Dartmoor and the coastal resorts of Teignmouth and Dawlish, **The Mount** is a friendly and attractive guest house that is owned and personally run by Tom and Mary Morris. Their spacious house boasts three en suite guest rooms that not only have tea and coffee making facilities but also have been decorated and furnished with their guests' comfort in mind. A delicious home-cooked breakfast is served in the dining room where, from the window, there are superb views over the rolling countryside whilst the cosy lounge, with its large fireplace, is the ideal place to settle down in one of the large armchairs and relax after a day out.

The Mount has a large, well-maintained garden where, in the summer, guests can enjoy afternoon tea out on the patio and there is also a gas barbecue, which they can use. The surrounding countryside offers some excellent walking and horse riding can be arranged from the local stables.

the Ug Brook that flows through the estate and that was dammed to create the three lakes that lie in the beautifully landscaped gardens. In the 1930s, the 11th Lord Clifford left the estate as he could not afford to live here and, during World War II, Ugbrooke was used as a school for evacuated children and as a hostel for Poles, whilst, in the 1950s, some of the ground floor rooms were used to store grain. Today, the house has been beautifully restored by the present Lord and Lady Clifford and the interior is noted for its collections of paintings, furniture, porcelain, needlework and military uniforms. Meanwhile, the gardens include a 200-year-old box parterre, a secluded Spanish garden and unusual semi-tropical trees and shrubs. If Ugbrooke seems familiar it might be as it has appeared in television programmes such as *The House of Elliott* and *Collector's Lot*. The house is open to the public from the second Sunday in July to the first Thursday in September on Sunday, Bank Holiday Monday, Tuesday, Wednesday and Thursday afternoons.

Torquay

Torquay gained the title 'The English Naples' in Victorian times as this genteel resort of shimmering white villas is set amongst dark green trees and spread, like Rome, across seven hills. It was, indisputably, the west of England's premier resort with imposing hotels such as The Imperial and The Grand that catered for people of distinction from across Europe and, at one time, the town could boast more royal visitors to the square mile than any other resort in the world. Edward VII came here on the royal yacht *Britannia*, which was anchored in the bay, and, each evening, he would be discreetly ferried across to a bay beneath the Imperial Hotel and then conducted to the first floor suite where his mistress, Lily Langtry, was waiting.

Still a very popular and elegant resort today, Torquay is best known as being the birthplace, in 1890, of Agatha Mary Clarissa Miller (later Agatha Christie) and she lived here until after her first

Thatcher Rock, Torquay

The Harbour, Torquay

failed marriage in 1914. Agatha came back here in 1916 whilst her second husband, Colonel Archie Christie, was on active service in World War I and it was whilst here that she began her first crime novel. However, it was not until 1926 and the publication of *The Murder of Roger Ackroyd* that Agatha found fame as a writer. Her disappearance a few months later in Harrogate made the national headlines and, following a nervous breakdown and a third marriage, she moved to the country house, Greenway, which overlooks the River Dart. One of the town's most popular attractions can be found in the Abbot's Tower at Torre Abbey that houses the **Agatha Christie Memorial Room**, where a wonderfully personal collection of her memorabilia, donated by her daughter, is on display. Along with her 1937 Remington typewriter, on which she wrote most of her novels, short stories and plays, the rooms contain manuscripts, letters and a photograph taken in 1973 on the occasion of the 21st anniversary of her play *The Mousetrap* – that is still running in London today.

The town's oldest building, **Torre Abbey**, was founded in 1195 but largely remodelled as a Georgian mansion by the Cary family between 1700 and 1750. Within its grounds stand the abbey ruins and the Spanish Barn, a medieval tithe barn so named because 397 prisoners

Torre Abbey, Torquay

Dunstone Hall

Lower Warberry Road, Torquay,
Devon TQ1 1QS
Tel: 01803 293185 Fax: 01803 201180
e-mail: info@dunstonehall.co.uk
website: www.dunstonehall.co.uk

Dating from 1844, when it was built for the Earl of Wicklow, **Dunstone Hall** is a select hotel that offers its guests superb hospitality in an elegant and sophisticated environment. Famous as once being the home of Lillie Langtry, this exceptional hotel is not only well known for its wonderful and stylish accommodation but also for its cuisine. The restaurant, in the Edwardian conservatory, offers a daily menu of Modern English dishes and from here, as with other rooms, there are glorious views over the Bay.

from the Spanish Armada were detained here in 1588. Now open to the public, the house allows visitors a glimpse into the past, from the earliest days of monastic life right up to the time that the last private owners moved out in the 1930s. There are furnished rooms, the family chapel and picture galleries to wander through whilst the grounds contain beautiful formal gardens and an exotic palm house. The abbey is open daily from Easter to the beginning of November.

Meanwhile, at the **Torquay Museum**, there is an exhibition of photographs recording the life of Dame Agatha Christie as well as a pictorial record of Torquay that covers the last 150 years. Amongst the museum's other treasures are many items discovered at **Kents Cavern**, a complex of caves that were first excavated in the 1820s and from where an amazing collection of animal bones, including the remains of mammoths, sabre-toothed tigers, grizzly bears, bison and cave lions, have been recovered. These bones proved to be the dining room debris of cave dwellers who lived here some 30,000 years ago and they are believed to be the oldest known residents of Europe. The caves themselves are open to the public and underground tours of one of Britain's most important Palaeolithic sites can be taken on a daily basis (the cavern is

Cockington Church

closed Mondays from November to March except school holidays). The cavern has attracted the attentions of writers over the years and Agatha Christie refers to it in her novel *The Man in the Brown Suit,* where she describes the mammoth and woolly rhino bones found here during the 1870s whilst Beatrix Potter describes the cave after her visit in 1893 as "... it is very easy to explore and only moderately damp."

Springtime Gardens, Cockington

Another attraction here well worth seeing is **Bygones**, where a fantastic re-creation of a Victorian street of shops, including an ironmongers, grocers and sweet shop, illustrates just what shopping was like a little over 100 years ago. The sights, sounds and smells of World War I are brought to life in the Walk-Through Trench Experience and here is also a gift shop and tea rooms selling home-made cakes. Bygones is open daily all year except Christmas Day.

Just a mile or so from the town centre is **Cockington Village**, a phenomenally picturesque rural oasis of thatched cottages, a working forge and the Drum Inn designed by Sir Edward Lutyens and completed in 1930. From the village there is a pleasant walk through the park to **Cockington Court** that is now a Craft Centre and Gallery. Partly Tudor, this stately old manor was, for almost three centuries, the home of the Mallock family, and, in the 1930s, they formed a trust to preserve "entire and unchanged the ancient amenities and character of the place, and in developing its surroundings to do nothing which may not rather enhance than diminish its attractiveness."

Babbacombe Model Village

Sampford House

57-59 King Street, Brixham, Devon TQ5 9TH
Tel: 01803 857761
e-mail: sampfordhouse@supaworld.com

Overlooking Brixham harbour and the famous *Golden Hind*, **Sampford House**, which dates back to the late 18th century, has an unbeatable location in this pretty coastal town. The home of Chris and Trevor Watson, this charming couple offer bed and breakfast accommodation in a choice of six guest rooms – one of which is in an adjacent cottage and has its own kitchenette. Although no evening meal is served, Sampford House is within easy reach of many good restaurants and cafés.

Just to the north of Torquay is another village but this one is one-twelfth life size! Described as a "unique slice of the Nation's Heritage" by BBC television, **Babbacombe Model Village** has over 400 models and, created by Tom Dobbins, a large number of the beautiful crafted models have been give entertaining names: there is Shortback and Sydes, the gents hairdresser, Walter Wall Carpets and Jim Nastick's Health Farm. Surrounded by delightful gardens, there are also models of Stonehenge and Avebury as well as a laser show, model railway and a spectacular evening light and sound show. The village is open daily.

Around Torquay

Brixham

5 miles S of Torquay, on the A3022

The most southerly of the three towns that make up the great Torbay conurbation, Brixham was, in the 18th century, the most profitable fishing port in Britain and fishing is still the most important activity in this engaging little town, although the trawlers now have to pick their way between flotillas of yachts and tour boats. This is also the place for fresh seafood as, on the quayside, there are stalls selling the boats' daily catch fresh from the sea and, around the harbour, there is a maze of narrow streets that are home to a host of small shops, tea rooms and galleries.

It was at Brixham that the Prince of Orange landed in 1688 to claim the

Brixham Harbour

British throne as William III. Whilst, in 1815, all eyes were focussed on the *Bellerophon*, anchored in the bay, as on board was Napoleon Bonaparte, who got his only close look at England before being transferred to the *Northumberland* and sailing off to his final exile on St Helena. Brixham has another claim to fame as, in the 19th century, the vicar of All Saints' Church, Henry Francis Lyte, composed what is perhaps the best known and best loved English hymn - *Abide with me* – during his last illness.

Berry Head, Brixham

At only 15 feet tall Brixham's **Lighthouse** has been called the "highest and lowest lighthouse in Britain" because, though short, it stands at the top of the 200-foot cliffs at the most easterly point of **Berry Head**. The lighthouse lies within **Berry Head Country Park** that is noted for its incredible views and from here, on a clear day, it is possible to see Portland Bill, some 46 miles away. The park is also home to rare plants, such as the white rock-rose, and colonies of seabirds, including fulmars, kittiwakes and guillemots, which nest on the cliff sides.

This headland has become associated with one of the many flying saucer sightings that have occurred around the world and, in April 1967, at noon, a mysterious

Brixham Harbour

object was reported hovering for about an hour just a couple of thousand feet over the headland. Described as a huge, dome-shaped object with a door on one side, the UFO eventually gained height rapidly and disappeared.

Paignton

3 miles SW of Torquay on the A379

Now merging imperceptibly with Torquay further round Tor Bay, Paignton was, in early Victorian times, just a small fishing village, about half a mile inland, that was noted for its cider and its large, sweet flatpole cabbages. However, the town's two superb sandy beaches and the development of Torquay saw Paignton transformed into a resort, complete with a pier and a promenade, which still has great appeal to families today. Throughout the summer season there is a packed programme of special events including funfairs, firework displays and, in August, a Children's Festival.

The most interesting building in Paignton is undoubtedly **Oldway Mansion,** built in 1874 for Isaac Singer, the millionaire sewing-machine manufacturer. Unfortunately, Isaac died the following year and it was his son, Paris, who gave the great mansion its present exuberant form. Paris added a south side mimicking a music pavilion in the grounds of Versailles, a hallway modelled on the Versailles Hall of Mirrors, and a sumptuous ballroom where his mistress Isadora Duncan would display the new, fluid kind of dance she had created based on classical mythology. Paris Singer sold the mansion to Paignton Borough Council in 1946 and it is now used as a Civic

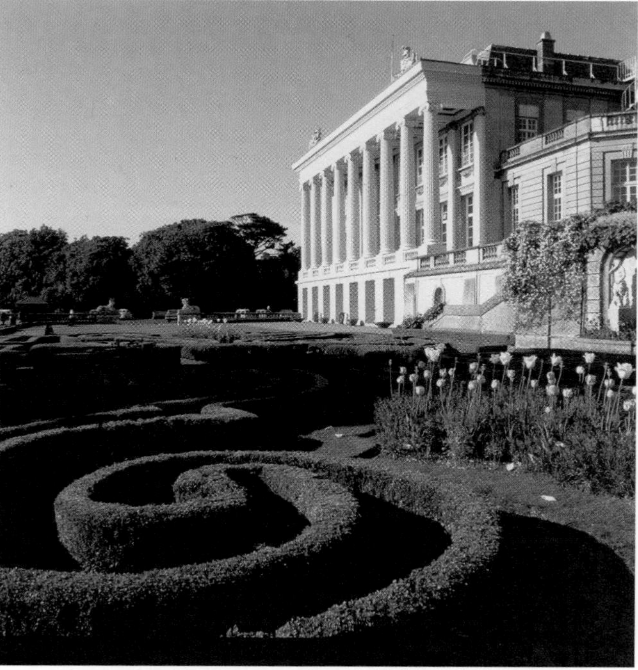

Oldway Mansion, Paignton

The Roscrea Hotel

2 Alta Vista Road, Paignton,
Devon TQ4 6BZ
Tel/Fax: 01803 558706

A large and spacious Victorian villa, **The Roscrea Hotel** occupies one of the most enviable locations in Paignton – situated in the tranquil Roundham area of the town, Paignton's busy little harbour is just a short walk away as is Roundham Head. Although, over the years, alterations to the hotel have been made the distinctive Victorian features of well-proportioned rooms, large windows and high ceilings have remained. The rooms have also been tastefully and individually

decorated and furnished to create a stylish environment in which guests can relax and enjoy the delights of this superb hotel.

Owned and personally run by Chris and Jane Meah, the couple offer excellent accommodation in a choice of 17 en-suite guest rooms, four of which can be found on the ground floor. There are also rooms with balconies from which there are panoramic views out over the sea. Meanwhile, the hotel's glorious garden is an ideal place for soaking up the sun whilst evening drinks can be served here before dinner. There is also a light and airy bar that offers views over Paignton to Torbay as well as stocking a good selection of wines, spirits and beers. During the summer season, Chris and Jane provide entertainment here one evening a week but the main event here is dinner. Served in the spacious surroundings of the dining room, the extensive evening menu offers a good choice of beautifully prepared and presented dishes that not only reflect the high standards that apply at the Roscrea but also the superb range of fresh produce that Devon has to offer. Breakfast too is a feast that is again served in the dining room and guests can choose between a traditional meal and a lighter Continental breakfast.

Open throughout the year, The Roscrea one of Paignton's favourite privately owned hotels and, along with offering a variety of special breaks out of season, this is a popular place at Christmas when Chris and Jane invite guests to book in for their House Party. This is an ideal holiday location for all the family, both children and dogs are welcome, and not only is it well situated for numerous delights of the town but it is within easy reach of many of Devon's attractions.

Centre, but many of the splendid rooms (and the extensive gardens) are open to the public free of charge and guided tours are available.

Of the main attractions here **Paignton Zoo** is, undoubtedly, one of the most popular. Set in 75 acres of attractive gardens, the zoo is home to over 300 species of animals from around the world and, from scorching deserts and African Savannah to rain forests and the frozen poles, they live in as near a natural habitat as possible. Dedicated to protecting the global wildlife heritage, the zoo is particularly concerned with endangered species and over 100 are represented here, including Asiatic lions, Sumatran tigers and gorillas.

Another experience not to be missed in Paignton is a trip on the **Paignton and Dartmouth Steam Railway**, which takes a seven-mile journey along the lovely Torbay coast and through the wooded slopes of the Dart estuary to Kingswear where travellers can board the ferry for the ten-minute crossing to Dartmouth. The locomotives and rolling stock all bear the same green and cream livery and, on certain services, travellers can wine and dine in luxurious Pullman style. At Paignton Station, close to the main line station, there is a gift shop selling all manner of railway gifts, souvenirs and publications, along with a buffet. The railway runs most days from April to October with special services at Christmas and Easter.

Paignton Harbour

Located on Goodrington Sands, **Quaywest** claims to be Britain's "biggest, best, wildest and wettest waterpark," with the hottest, highest and hairiest waterslides in the country. Along with the adult swimming pool and children's play area there are also go-karts, rides, crazy golf, restaurants, cafés and shops. The waterpark is open from May to September whilst the other attractions are open from Easter to October.

Galmpton

5 miles SW of Torquay off the A3022

Close to this village lies **Greenway** (National Trust), the home of Dame Agatha Christie for the last 30 years of her life. Still owned by the family, the house is not open to the public but the glorious gardens, on the banks of the River Dart, are open on certain days in between early March and early October. Renowned for its rare, half-hardy plants and native wildflowers, this charming garden is one of Devon's best kept secrets and it also offers superb views out across the Dart estuary.

Compton

3½ miles W of Torquay off the A380

This village is home to **Compton Castle** (National Trust), a wonderful fortified manor house that dates back to the 1300s and, in Elizabethan times, was the home of Sir Humphrey Gilbert, Sir Walter Raleigh's half brother and the coloniser of Newfoundland in 1583. It remains the home of the Gilbert family and, restored with care in the 20th century, it is a rare example of a late medieval manor house, complete with battlements, towers, portcullis and an impressive Great Hall.

The Monks Retreat Inn

The Square, Broadhempston, near Totnes, Devon TQ9 6BN
Tel: 01803 812203 Fax: 01803 814144

Dating back to the 15th century and formerly called The Church House Inn, **The Monks Retreat Inn** is a wonderful olde worlde establishment that offers customers a chance to travel back in time whilst also experiencing the very best in 21st century hospitality.

Along with the traditional interior – the exposed beams, exposed stone work and the panelled walls – there is a roaring log fire in winter that adds an extra warmth to this already welcoming inn.

In 2000, the highly experienced chef, Ian Durman, took over here and, almost immediately, the inn became a Mecca for anyone who enjoys good food at reasonable prices. Served at both lunchtime and in the evening, the regular menu, which ranges from à la carte to light snacks and sandwiches, is supplemented by the ever-changing specials board and there is also a separate children's menu.

Focusing on locally grown produce, those dining here can complement their meal with a bottle of wine from the far reaching wine list or a glass of real ale from the bar. The Monks Retreat is a delightful inn that is well worth seeking out.

Ipplepen

5 miles NW of Torquay off the A381

The name of this large village is Celtic, it is derived from 'Ippela's hill', and a mile or so to the northwest, crowning an extinct volcano, is the site of **Denbury Fort**, which is often referred to as the fort of the men of Devon. In Ipplepen itself, the most striking building is the 14th century church that has a massive tower and, inside, some fine stained glass and a beautifully carved pulpit.

Abbotskerswell

5 miles NW of Torquay off the A381

At the time of the *Domesday Book*, this attractive village was owned by the Abbot of Horton, in Dorset, which explains the first part of its name while Kerswell refers to watercress, a popular addition to the diet in medieval times and it was grown here in water from a freshwater spring. The village's lovely old **Church of St Mary the Virgin** still bears the scars of the ransacking it received at the hands of Henry VIII's commissioners at the time of the Dissolution.

Outside stands an Elizabethan lych-gate that is believed to be the oldest in the country. When it was built its purpose was to provide a sheltered resting place for coffins that were awaiting the burial service.

PLACES TO STAY, EAT AND DRINK

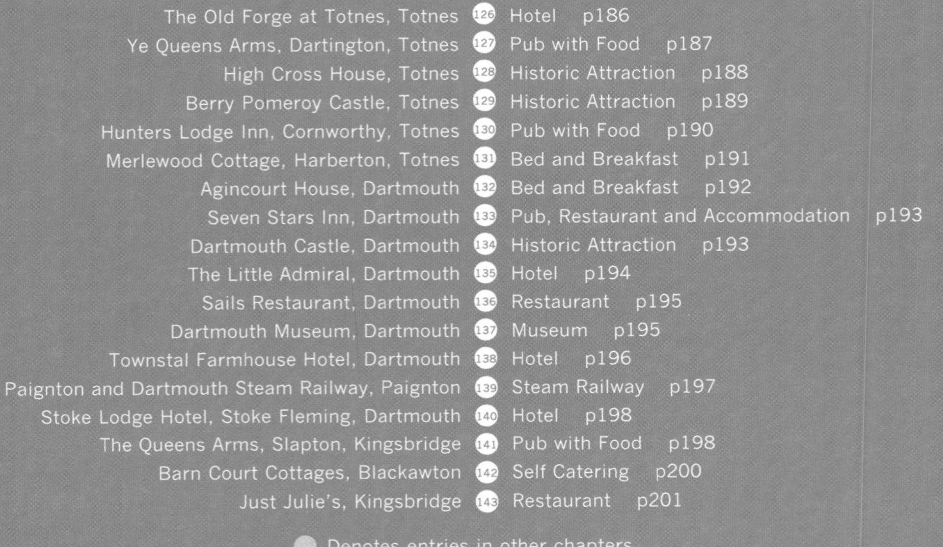

The Old Forge at Totnes, Totnes	126	Hotel	p186
Ye Queens Arms, Dartington, Totnes	127	Pub with Food	p187
High Cross House, Totnes	128	Historic Attraction	p188
Berry Pomeroy Castle, Totnes	129	Historic Attraction	p189
Hunters Lodge Inn, Cornworthy, Totnes	130	Pub with Food	p190
Merlewood Cottage, Harberton, Totnes	131	Bed and Breakfast	p191
Agincourt House, Dartmouth	132	Bed and Breakfast	p192
Seven Stars Inn, Dartmouth	133	Pub, Restaurant and Accommodation	p193
Dartmouth Castle, Dartmouth	134	Historic Attraction	p193
The Little Admiral, Dartmouth	135	Hotel	p194
Sails Restaurant, Dartmouth	136	Restaurant	p195
Dartmouth Museum, Dartmouth	137	Museum	p195
Townstal Farmhouse Hotel, Dartmouth	138	Hotel	p196
Paignton and Dartmouth Steam Railway, Paignton	139	Steam Railway	p197
Stoke Lodge Hotel, Stoke Fleming, Dartmouth	140	Hotel	p198
The Queens Arms, Slapton, Kingsbridge	141	Pub with Food	p198
Barn Court Cottages, Blackawton	142	Self Catering	p200
Just Julie's, Kingsbridge	143	Restaurant	p201

Denotes entries in other chapters

7 Plymouth and the South Hams

The largest centre of population in the southwest peninsula, Plymouth developed at the end of the 12th century when its potential as a military and commercial port was recognised. However, it was not until the 16th century that it became the main base for the English Navy and it was from Plymouth that Sir Francis Drake, after having famously finished his game of bowls, led the fleet against the Spanish Armada. The starting point for the Pilgrim Fathers journey to the New World, Plymouth was heavily bombed during World War II, so much so in fact, that the architect, Sir Patrick Abercrombie was commissioned to redesign a new city centre.

Still an important commercial centre today, situated just a few miles from the city is one of the country's great stately homes, Saltram House, which occupies a grand site overlooking the River Plym. However, this is an area richer in castles

PLACES TO STAY, EAT AND DRINK

Denotes entries in other chapters

than stately mansions as, for centuries, it has been important to protect Plymouth Sound and other river estuaries from foreign invasion. Whilst the Sound is protected by the Citadel, a massive fortification constructed on the orders of Charles II, Dartmouth, once one of the country's major ports, also has a castle. Now in ruins and dramatically sited overlooking the entrance to the Dart estuary, the castle, one of the first to be designed to make specific use of artillery, stands opposite Kingswear Castle on the other side of the River Dart. If these two forbidding defences proved to be lacking, there was another deterrent, and in times of grave danger a heavy chain was strung across the estuary between the two castles. Dartmouth, like Plymouth, also has its links with the Royal Navy and here can be found the Britannia Royal Naval College, the training centre of future naval officers.

Bolt Tail

To the east of Plymouth lies an area known as the South Hams – "the frutefullest part of all Devonshire" according to one old writer. This favoured tract of land, lying to the south of Dartmoor and west of the River Dart, has an exceptionally mild climate, fertile soil and well-watered pastures. The coastline here presents an enormous variety and, along with being home to some of the most spectacular cliff scenery in Devon, it is also an area of long, low-lying sandy beaches. In particular there is Blackpool Sands that has received high praise and awards for its clean water and beaches along with its family facilities. Though the land has been populated since prehistoric times, there are few towns of any size and only Kingsbridge, overlooking the broad and sheltered expanse of the Kingsbridge estuary, and the ancient market town of Totnes, really qualify.

Starehole Bay, Bolt Head

Totnes

Norman Keep, Totnes

Claiming to be the second oldest borough in England, Totnes sent its first Member of Parliament to London in 1295 and elected the first of its over 630 Mayors in 1359. However, this captivating little town also claims a much more ancient heritage as, according to local legends and the fanciful *History of the Kings of Britain* written in the 12th century by the chronicler Geoffrey of Monmouth, it is said to have been founded by a Trojan named Brutus in around 1200 BC. The grandfather of Aeneas, the hero of Virgil's epic poem *The Aeneid*, Brutus sailed up the River Dart, gazed at the fair prospect around him and decided to found the first town in this new country that would take its name, Britain, from his own. The **Brutus Stone**, in the pavement of the town's main shopping street, commemorates this event.

However, the first recorded evidence of a town here, set on a hill above the highest navigable point on the River Dart, does not appear until the mid 10th century when King Edgar established a mint here. The town was fortified by the Saxon kings to defend it from Viking attacks and the name Totnes means 'the fort or lookout (Tot) on the nose or ridge of land (ness)'. A trading and market centre as well as having a mint, the original Saxon town can still be traced by walking around the **Ramparts Walk**. The Saxons also built a castle but the impressive remains of **Totnes Castle** (English Heritage) are of the once imposing Norman fortification that towered over the town and that is generally recognised to be the best preserved motte and bailey castle in Devon. The once great ditch that surrounded the keep is, today, filled with cottages and gardens but the castle still has commanding views over the town and the river that it defended.

The Guildhall, Totnes

A substantial section of Totnes' medieval town wall has also survived and the superb **East Gate**, which

The Old Forge at Totnes

Seymour Place, Totnes, Devon TQ9 5AY
Tel: 01803 862174 Fax: 01803 865385
e-mail: enq@oldforgetotnes.com
website: www.oldforgetotnes.com

Originally the workshops for the Duke of Somerset's Berry Pomeroy Castle, **The Old Forge at Totnes** is now a wonderful hotel with a cosy cottage style atmosphere. Once home to a blacksmith, wheelwright, carpenter and coachbuilder, these ancient but beautifully restored buildings also include an upstairs courtroom and lock-up cell where criminals were first tried by the travelling magistrate and then clapped in irons in the cell by the resident blacksmith.

Owned and personally run by Christine and David, this charming hotel is a lovely and relaxing place to stay and, as well as enjoying the comfort of the stylish reception rooms, guests can also wander around the large and secluded gardens. There are ten individual en-suite guest bedrooms here that all have their own special character, including a cottage suite that can accommodate up to six whilst the Courtroom Suite has its own private roof garden. Dinner too is another highlight of this interesting establishment and, prepared by David, an excellent chef, the dishes are all expertly cooked and presented and can be ordered by prior arrangement.

straddles the steep main street, is part of that wall and, although grievously damaged by a fire in 1990, it has been meticulously restored. Just a little way down the hill from East Gate is the charming **Guildhall**, which was built in 1553 and stands on the site of a Benedictine Priory that was founded in 1088. A remarkable little building with a granite colonnade arching out over the pavement, the Guildhall houses both the Council Chamber and the town's jail (which is not in use today). Open to the public, visitors can see the gloomy cells where prisoners awaited trail and punishment and also the council chamber with its plaster frieze and the table at which Oliver Cromwell sat in 1646. Almost directly across the street from the Guildhall is another magnificent Elizabethan building that was constructed, in 1585, for Nicholas Bell, who had made his fortune from the local pilchard fishing industry. When he died, his wife Anne married Sir Thomas Bodley and it was the profit from the pilchards that funded the world-famous Bodleian Library at Oxford University. However, the town's Elizabethan heritage really comes alive during the summer when, on a Tuesday morning, the people dress up in Elizabethan white ruffs and velvet gowns for a charity market that has, over the years, raised thousands of pounds for good causes.

For an overall view of the history of the town and the surrounding area **Totnes Museum**, housed in another of the town's attractive Elizabethan buildings and whose upper floors overhang the street, is an excellent place to start. Built in around 1575 for Walter Kellond, a cloth merchant, the three floors of his former home contain a wide range of exhibits that illustrate local social history from industry and archaeology to costumes and toys. There are also special exhibits devoted to the life and work of some of the town's famous sons and daughters. The family of the Victorian mathematician and inventor, Charles Babbage, had lived in the town for centuries and, although Charles was born in London, he was educated at Totnes Grammar School. Regarded as the inventor of the computer, Babbage's analytical machine was the forerunner of the modern computer and displays here record his doomed, but inspirational, struggle to perfect a calculator using only mechanical rather than electronic means.

Another inventive Totnes schoolboy was George Jackson Churchward, who became a railway locomotive designer whilst William Willis, along with Burke, was the first European to cross Australia from south to north in 1861. More recently, there is the marathon walker, Ffyona Campbell who was born in Totnes in 1967. Another museum worth a visit is the **Devonshire Collection of Period Costume**, which is housed in 16th century Bogan House, whilst **Totnes Town Mill**, a restored Victorian water wheel and mill, has a display on mill technology and an excellent exhibition showing the development of the town.

In recent years, Totnes has claimed for itself the title of 'Natural Health Capital of the West Country' when, in 1989, the first Natural Health Centre in Britain selected Totnes as its base and, in subsequent years, other practitioners have also arrived, offering a huge range of alternative medicine therapies. In alphabetical order they include acupuncture, the Alexander technique for those suffering from eye problems, aromatherapy, chiropractic, homoeopathy, genuine non-sexual

massage, osteopathy and reflexology. Visitors will also find specialist shops stocked with natural medicines, organic food, aromatherapy products, relaxation tapes and books on spiritual healing. Other craft and antique shops, and a Bear Shop with more than a thousand Teddy Bears in residence all add to the town's appeal.

Around Totnes

Dartington

1½ miles N of Totnes on the A385

When, in 1925, Leonard and Dorothy Elmhirst bought **Dartington Hall** and its estate it had been left to decay for some time and the superb Great Hall had stood roofless for more than a century and the buildings surrounding the two large quadrangles laid out in the 1390s by John Holand, Earl of Exeter, were being used as stables, cow houses and hay lofts. The Elmhirsts were idealists and since Dorothy (née Whitney) was one of the richest American women of her time, they possessed the resources to put their ideals into practice. They restored the Hall, re-opened it as a progressive school and set about reviving the local rural economy in line with the ideology of the Indian philosopher, Rabindranath Tagore. The Irish playwright Sean O'Casey left London and moved close to Dartington so that his children could attend the school that was set up within the cultural community that the couple also created. The Elmhirsts were also

High Cross House

Dartington Hall, Totnes, Devon TQ9 6ED
Tel: 01803 864114 Fax: 01803 867057

A blue and white house that was built in the 1930s on the Dartington Hall estate to the design of architect William Lescaze, **High Cross House** is a wonderful example of a modernist style and it was originally a house for the headmaster of the progressive school that Leonard and Dorothy Elmhirst established at the hall. Although the school is now closed, the ideals of rearing children within a cultural community are remembered here as the house is now an art gallery that is home to the collection put together by the couple and on display here are paintings and ceramics by leading modern artists and craftsmen.

The principal rooms of the house have remained unchanged since Leonard and Dorothy's day and the attraction here are the period pieces of furniture that include the original sofas and tubular steel chairs. There is a display of photographs from archive documents that chart the first 15 years of the estate after 1925 when the progressive school, once known as the Dartington experiment, was founded and also when a range of rural industries were established.

closely involved in the creation of the famed Dartington Glass. Sadly, long after their deaths, their school closed in 1995 as a consequence of financial problems and a pornography scandal, but the Headmaster's house, a classic Modernist building of the early 1930s, which has now been converted into an art gallery, **High Cross House**, is open to the public (see panel opposite).

Dartington Hall hosts more than a hundred music performances each year during its International Summer School, a season which attracts musicians and artistes of the highest calibre from all over the world. All year round, even more visitors are attracted to the **Dartington Cider Press Centre,** a huge gallery on the edge of the estate that displays a vast range of craft products from delicate hand-made Christmas or birthday cards to beautifully modelled items of pottery.

Staverton

3 miles N of Totnes off the A384

Just a short walk down the road from the village, with its riverside walks and famous inn, is a particularly pretty station on the South Devon Railway that is frequently used as film and television locations.

Berry Pomeroy

2 miles E of Totnes off the A385

Arriving with William the Conqueror in 1066, the de la Pomerais family came to this village and they held land here for almost 500 years. In the early 1300s, they built **Berry Pomeroy Castle** (English Heritage) in a superb position on a wooded promontory above Gatcombe Brook and substantial remains still stand there today (see panel below). In 1548, the Pomeroys, as they had become known, sold the estate to Sir Edward Seymour, the brother of Jane who had been the third wife of Henry VIII, and he built a three storey mansion within the medieval castle but, today, this too is a shell. The castle is still owned by a descendant of Sir Edward, the Duke of Somerset. In the village itself, St Mary's Church contains some interesting monuments to the Pomeroys and the Seymours as well as an outstanding rood screen.

Several local legends revolve around

Berry Pomeroy Castle

Totnes, Devon

Reputed to be the most haunted castle in Devon, **Berry Pomeroy Castle** is certainly the county's most romantic. Built by the Norman knight, Ralph de Pomeroy, the castle has barely been touched by the great events of English history, more by those of the family living here and, as a result, it has become enshrined in folklore. Its position, perilously perched on a wooded hillside overlooking the beautiful Gatcombe Valley, give the ruins a tranquil and peaceful air that is far removed from the castle's violent and dramatic past.

Hunters Lodge Inn

Cornworthy, near Totnes, Devon TQ9 7ES
Tel: 01803 732204
e-mail: rog.liz@hunterslodgeinn.com
website: www.hunterslodgeinn.com

Tucked away in the pretty South Hams village Cornworthy, **Hunters Lodge Inn** is a wonderful and traditional country inn where excellent hospitality is assured. Dating back to the mid 18th century, and originally a coaching inn, this charming establishment has lost none of its charm character over the years and, along with the exposed beams, a log fire roars away in the fireplace on winter's nights. Owners, Roger and Liz Little, have only been here a short while, since the summer of 2001, but they have still made their mark and, along with offering good food and drink, they have created a warm and friendly atmosphere that is welcoming for both locals and visitors alike.

From the bar there are always three real ales to choose from including the locally brewed Teignworthy Bitter and, as well as all the usual beers, lagers and spirits, Hunters Lodge Inn is famous for having a range of over 45 malt whiskies. The wine list too is extensive and covers not only old world wines but those from Australia, South Africa and South America.

Food, too, is an important aspect of Hunters Lodge and, served at both lunchtime and in the evening, there is always a superb choice. Liz is the chef here and as well as guaranteeing that each dish is freshly prepared she specializes in using only the finest local ingredients, including freshly caught fish from Plymouth, locally reared meat and Sharpham cheeses. Of the many tempting dishes on offer, the monkfish and scallops in a mushroom and garlic sauce is a particular favourite whilst there are also new and interesting dishes to try. Such is the popularity of dining at Hunters Lodge that it is advisable to book and essential in the evenings.

Meanwhile, this is an inn serving the villagers and, along with cosy environment that makes this an ideal place in which to relax and chat at the end of the day, Liz and Roger also arrange live music one Thursday evening a month. Other entertainment here includes the occasional quiz night, to which all are invited, and themed food evenings that, again, are popular. The Hunters Lodge Inn is certainly a place well worth finding and one that all the family can enjoy as children are welcome.

the castle and the ancient Pomeroy family who lived here and it is said that for their part in the religious rebellion in 1549, Edward VI ordered that their castle's fortifications be greatly reduced. The Pomeroy family would not obey the order and, when troops arrived to enforce the king's decree, two brothers rode over the castle's ramparts to their death. Meanwhile, another story concerns two Pomeroy sisters, Eleanor and Margaret, who were in love with the same man. Eleanor, jealous of her beautiful sister, imprisoned Margaret and starved her to death and Margaret's ghost is said to haunt the castle ruins.

Ashprington

2½ miles SE of Totnes off the A381

An attractive village, with a 15th century church, Ashprington lies next to the Sharpham estate, a 1,000-year-old farm with a house, designed by Sir Robert Taylor in 1770, that overlooks the surrounding fields and the wooded slopes above the River Dart. The estate is home to **Sharpham Vineyard** where both old and new World techniques are used to produce their wine that has unique regional characteristics. A full range of wines is stock in the vineyard's shop, wine tastings are available and the beautiful grounds, home to an abundance of wildlife, have footpaths and picnic tables. The vineyard is open from March to Christmas, non Bank Holiday Mondays to Saturday and every day from June to August.

Tuckenhay

3 miles SE of Totnes off the A381

Situated on Bow Creek, the largest tributary of the River Dart this delightful waterside retreat was once an important industrial village with busy quays, mills and limekilns. Just to the west are two ancient hill forts, Halwell Camp and Stanborough Camp.

Harberton

2½ miles SW of Totnes off the A381

This delightful village is regarded as absolutely typical of the South Hams

Merlewood Cottage

Tristford Road, Harberton, near Totnes,
Devon TQ9 7SD
Tel: 01803 864261
website: www.merlewoodcottage.co.uk

Once part of the old village hall, **Merlewood Cottage** is a particularly attractive house that is the home of Alick and Peggie Whittle and, from here, this welcoming couple offer superb bed and breakfast accommodation. Both guest rooms are beautifully decorated and furnished, have private or en-suite bathrooms and one even has a balcony. Alick's home-cooked, hearty breakfast is served in either the family kitchen or on the terrace that overlooks the cottage's delightful garden and the surrounding countryside beyond.

and Devon with its church and pub adjacent to each other. It lies cradled in a fold of the hills with the striking 78-foot high tower of its Perpendicular church rising high above the cottages and houses. Inside the church there is an outstanding example of a 15th century wooden screen and one of the last remaining medieval stone pulpits to be found in Devon. An ancient inn stands beside the church and, at the heart of the village, there is still a working dairy farm.

Dartmouth

For centuries, this entrancing little town, clinging to the sides of a precipitous hill, was one of the country's principal ports and, in the 12th century, it was from here that crusaders on both the second and third Crusades, mustered before sailing. Here, too, in the shelter of the harbour, Elizabeth I's men o' war lay in wait to see off stragglers from the Spanish Armada. Millions of casks of French and Spanish wine have been off-loaded on to the quayside here over the centuries and, in 1620, *The Mayflower* put in here for a few days for repairs before hoisting sail on August 20th for Plymouth and then on to the New World where the pilgrims arrived three months later. However, it was Alfred the Great who developed Dartmouth as a strategic base and the town has a long connection with the Royal Navy, the oldest of the British services. Dartmouth's famous and historic

Agincourt House

27 Lower Street, Dartmouth,
Devon TQ6 9AN
Tel: 01803 839278

Grade II listed and dating back to 1380, **Agincourt House** is documented as the second oldest building in Dartmouth. It is a wonderfully ancient and historic building that is not only close to the Dartmouth to Kingswear ferry but also it is just a few yards from the harbourside where *The Onedin Line* was filmed and the Pilgrim Fathers left for the New World.

The open fireplaces, exposed beams and wooden floors of the original building have remained but owners, Liz and Peter Croad who have been here for three years, have decorated the house in a style that is sympathetic to its age but also in a manner that creates a light and airy atmosphere.

There are two charming guest rooms here which the couple let on a bed and breakfast basis and it is certainly one of the most interesting such establishments in the area as well as being one of the most hospitable. The quality of decoration and furnishings is outstanding.

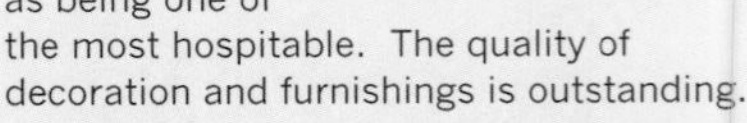

Along with the excellent breakfasts guests will be greeted with each morning, Liz and Peter are soon to open a seafood restaurant that will enable more people to enjoy their culinary skills whilst also being able to sample some of the freshest fish and seafood in Devon.

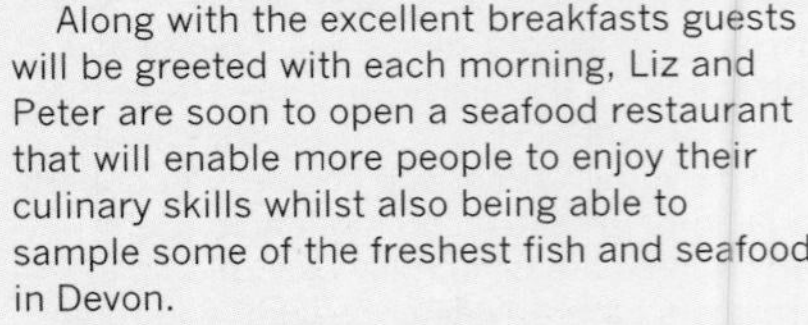

Agincourt House is open all year round and accepts cash or cheques only.

Seven Stars Inn

8 Smith Street, Dartmouth, Devon TQ6 9QR
Tel: 01803 832575

Dating back to the late 16th century and found in the heart of Dartmouth, the **Seven Stars Inn** is a warm and friendly place that welcomes locals and visitors alike. Certainly a place for those who enjoy real ale, landlady Sue Brown makes sure there is always a good selection that increases during the summer months. This, too, is a popular place to eat and chef Tracey's delicious dishes make it necessary to book throughout the summer.

Finally, the inn has five guest rooms and children are welcome in the restaurant area.

quayside has been used as a major location by programme and film makers over the years and, in particular, for the BBC television series *The Onedin Line* and the feature film *Sense and Sensibility* starring Emma Thompson and Hugh Grant.

In his capacity as Inspector of Customs, Geoffrey Chaucer visited the town in 1373 and he is believed to have modelled the Shipman in his *Canterbury Tales* on the character of the then Mayor of Dartmouth, John Hawley. An enterprising merchant seafarer, Hawley was also responsible for building the first **Dartmouth Castle** (English Heritage - see panel below), the dramatically situated fortress that guards the entrance to the Dart estuary although the building seen today is one that was erected by Edward IV after the War of the Roses. Along with the castle, the town had another defence against invasion and, in times of danger, a heavy chain was strung across the harbour to Kingswear Castle on the opposite bank.

There is a striking monumental brass to John Hawley and his two wives in the part 14th century **Church of St Saviour**, which lies down by the quayside and against the walls of which ships used to tie up before the New Quay was built in the 16th century. Here, too, lies the **Custom House**, a handsome building of 1739 that has some fine internal plasterwork ceilings. The harbour is still

Dartmouth Castle

Dartmouth, Devon

Jutting out into the narrow entrance to the Dart estuary and with tidal waters lapping at its foot, **Dartmouth Castle** is well placed to guard what was once one of England's most important ports. The first castle in the country to be constructed specifically with artillery in mind, the additional fortifications built over the last 500 years show a fascinating history of coastal defences right up to World War II when a pillbox was

constructed. A medieval castle full of atmosphere, its spectacular setting provides an equally compelling reason to visit.

The Old Front, Dartmouth

busy with naval vessels along with pleasure boats and ferries, and it is particularly colourful during the June **Carnival** and the **Dartmouth Regatta** in late August.

Away from the quayside is another of the town's old buildings, **The Butterwalk**, a timber-framed former merchant's house dating from 1640 that is now home to the **Dartmouth Museum** (see panel opposite). Along with holding a fine local history collection that, naturally, centres on the town's maritime history, the museum has a working steam pumping engine that was built to a revolutionary design by

The Little Admiral

27/29 Victoria Road, Dartmouth,
Devon TQ6 9RT
Tel: 01803 832572 Fax: 01803 835815
e-mail: info@little-admiral.co.uk
website: www.little-admiral.co.uk

Close to Dartmouth's famous harbour and just a short, level walk from the River Dart, **The Little Admiral** is an elegant town house Hotel that provides its guests with comfortable but stylish accommodation right in the heart of the town.

The house dates back to the Georgian era and the beautifully decorated rooms, including the ten en-suite guest bedrooms and the residents' lounge, have been given a contemporary twist, using modern furniture, paintings and furnishings which combine relaxation with style

The Little Admiral is owned and personally run by Clare and James Brown, (with their two young sons, Ben and Jack never being far away). Along with their superb hospitality, the couple have also opened an excellent and stylish tapas restaurant to residents and non-residents on Thursday, Friday and Saturday evenings.

James is the chef and the restaurant menu has gained such a reputation that it is advisable to book at all times. The relaxed style of The Little Admiral makes it a pleasure to visit. Children too are welcome here.

Sails Restaurant

First Floor, 22 South Embankment,
Dartmouth, Devon TQ6 9BB
Tel: 01803 839281
e-mail: lornaperman@hotmail.com

With fantastic views out over Dartmouth harbour and across to Kingswear, **Sails Restaurant**, situated above Dartmouth Yacht Club, has an unbeatable position. Owned and personally run by Lorna and Don Perman, this superb, small restaurant has an excellent reputation and each evening experienced chef, Malcolm Whybrow, creates a mouth-watering menu that features a tantalising range of imaginative dishes including, naturally, some of the freshest fish in Devon. This popular restaurant is open 6 nights a week in season and booking is essential.

Thomas Newcomen. Newcomen was born in Dartmouth in 1663 and it was at his ironmongery business that he designed and built an atmospheric steam engine to pump water out of coal mines. However, the engine wasted a lot of the energy it produced and it was years later that, whilst he was repairing an old Newcomen engine, James Watt became interesting in designing a more efficient machine. The museum is open Monday to Saturday throughout the year though the hours are more limited in winter.

The town's curious railway station is also worthy of a mention as it is possibly the only station in the world that has never seen a train. It was built by the Great Western Railway as the terminus of their line from Torbay but the actual railway line ended at Kingswear and passengers completed their journey to Dartmouth by ferry.

However, there is, of course, one building that continues to dominate this town – **Britannia Royal Naval College**, a sprawling red brick and Portland stone construction that represents Edwardian architecture at its very best. Completed in 1905, this land-based college replaced the series of moored ships that, up until then, had been the Royal Navy's training base for potential officers. Continuing the traditions of the Royal Navy, the college is still its officer training centre and, though on land, the jargon of a ship is still used throughout the building. The **Britannia Museum** tells the history of the college, from its

Dartmouth Museum

The Butterwalk, Duke Street, Dartmouth,
Devon TQ6 9PZ
Tel: 01803 832923
e-mail: dartmouth@devonmuseums.net
website: www.devonmuseums.net/dartmouth

People come to Dartmouth today to enjoy the splendour of her scenery, but mariners have been visiting the Dart for centuries because of its sheltered deep water. The Museum has a strong nautical theme with a large collection of models illustrating the developement of ships from early dugouts to 20th century liners and naval craft, and a large collection of photographs etc. maps the history of the ancient town. The Museum is housed in a spectacular Grade I listed building with carved ceilings and wall panels both inside and out.

Townstal Farmhouse Hotel

Townstal Road, Dartmouth, Devon TQ6 9HY
Tel: 01803 832300 Fax: 01803 835428
Website; www.smoothhound.co.uk/hotelstownstal.html

A 16th century farmhouse that was mentioned in the Domesday Book, over the past 20 years or so owner Jean Hall has tastefully extended this charming old building to create **Townstal Farmhouse Hotel** that offers guests olde worlde charm along with modern comforts. The magnificent residents' lounge and the attractive dining room still retain many features of the original farmhouse whilst the 16 en-suite guest rooms are superbly decorated and furnished to provide the perfect environment for a relaxing nights' sleep.

beginnings in the mid 19th century and through the building of the college to the present day, whilst there is also a gift shop selling memorabilia.

One of the loveliest rivers in England, the River Dart rises in the great central bogs of Dartmoor and flows for some 46 miles before entering the sea here. Called the 'English Rhine' by Queen Victoria, the river, along with its tributaries drain much of the moorland. Meanwhile, much of the coastline around the Dart estuary is now in the hands of the National Trust and, as well as being a valuable nesting area for seabirds, it also contains some ancient oak woodland and the remains of lime kilns.

Around Dartmouth

Dittisham

2½ miles N of Dartmouth off the A3122

This pretty yachting village of atmospheric cottages, whose narrow streets drop down to the River Dart, was once famous for its plums but is now best known as the home of the Dimbleby family.

Dittisham

Stoke Gabriel

4 miles N of Dartmouth off the A385

A charming village of narrow lanes and alleys, Stoke Gabriel stands on a hillside above a tidal spur of the River Dart and, traditionally, it was known for its salmon fishery and apple orchards. A weir was built across the neck of the creek in Edwardian times and this traps the water at low tide, giving the village a pleasant lakeside atmosphere. The part 13th century Church of St Gabriel has a restored late medieval pulpit whilst, in the churchyard, are the rather forlorn remains of an oak tree, which is reputed to be more than 1,500 years old, as well as a huge yew tree. The steam locomotive designer, George Jackson Churchward, was born here.

Kingswear

1 mile E of Dartmouth on the B3205

Situated on the steeply rising east bank of the River Dart, from Kingswear there are panoramic views of Dartmouth that is stretched out across another hillside on the opposite bank. Kingswear is the terminus of the **Paignton and Dartmouth Steam Railway** (see panel below) and, from here, passengers alight and can take a ferry for the ten-minute journey to Dartmouth. Meanwhile, above the estuary stand the impressive remains of **Kingswear Castle** that, together with its twin across the river, Dartmouth Castle, guarded the wide estuary of the River Dart. The castle is now owned by the Landmark Trust and has been converted into holiday flats.

Just to the northeast of the town lies **Coleton Fishacre House and Garden** (National Trust), a wonderful house that was designed in the 1920s for Rupert and Lady Dorothy D'Oyly Carte of Gilbert and Sullivan fame. Reflecting Arts and Crafts style from outside but with refreshingly modern Art Deco interiors, the house is surrounded by a luxuriant coastal garden that the couple created in this beautiful stream-fed valley. Along with a wonderful array of exotic and rare plants, the garden contains formal arrangements, wooded areas with wild flowers and water features and there is something of interest here all year round – from spring bulbs to the rich autumn colours.

Stoke Lodge Hotel

Stoke Fleming, near Dartmouth,
Devon TQ6 0RA
Tel: 01803 770523 Fax: 01803 770851
e-mail: mail@stokelodge.co.uk
website: www.stokelodge.co.uk

Known as The Country House Hotel by the Coast, **Stoke Lodge Hotel** is a charming and attractive family run establishment that offers guests first class hospitality in a warm and friendly environment. Managed by Chris and Steven Mayer and Steven's mother Phyl, this superb hotel has plenty to keep guests occupied – a beautiful garden, tennis court and indoor and outdoor swimming pools. However, the hotel is best known for its Garden Restaurant where chef Steven Wood creates tempting menus for both residents and non-residents.

Stoke Fleming

2 miles S of Dartmouth on the A379

One of the most delightful villages in the South Hams, Stoke Fleming is perched on top of the 300-foot cliffs that overlook Start Bay and its prominent church has served generations of mariners as a reassuring landmark. Inside the church is a brass dating from 1351 that is reckoned to be one of the oldest in Devon whilst another commemorates the great-grandfather of the celebrated engineer, Thomas Newcomen.

Just a mile to the south of the village are **Blackpool Sands**, one of south Devon's most beautiful beaches. Set in an unspoilt and sheltered bay and with a backdrop of magnificent pines, the sands are an ideal family beach as there is swimming in clean water, sandpits, a boating pond, a bathing raft and a beach café along with beachside shops.

Slapton

5 miles SW of Dartmouth off the A379

To the south of the village lies a remarkable sand and shingle bank that

The Queens Arms

Slapton, near Kingsbridge, Devon TQ7 2PN
Tel: 01548 580800
website: www.slapton.org/queensarms

Dating back to the 14th century, **The Queens Arms** is a traditional Devon local that was once famous for producing its own 'white ale', a local speciality though sadly the recipe for this has been lost over the years. Now offering a choice of four real ales, including Dartmoor IPA, landlords Sandra and Kevin Watson have also gained a fine reputation for their meals and Kevin, who does the cooking, specialises in home-made pies. Along with the extensive menu there are themed food nights in the winter. Children and dogs welcome.

Slapton Ley Nature Reserve

divides the saltwater of Start Bay from **Slapton Ley**, Devon's largest natural freshwater lake that is fed by three small rivers. The shallow lake, and the land around it, is designated a Site of Special Scientific Interest and also a nature reserve that is home to a large number of fresh water fish, insects, water-loving plants and native and migrating birds. The Slapton Ley Field Study Centre, located in the village, has leaflets detailing the delightful circular nature trails through the reserve.

Normally, the four-mile stretch of sand and shingle beach on the seaward side of Slapton is too extensive to ever become crowded but, in the lead up to the D-Day landings of World War II, it was a very different scene as rehearsals for the invasion were carried out here. As live ammunition was used some 3,000 people from seven villages were evacuated and Slapton became deserted save for the rats that roamed the streets. The events of those days were recorded by Leslie Thomas in his novel *The Magic Army* whilst, in 1954, a tall stone obelisk was unveiled on the beach that commemorates the activities that took place here and the part that the people of the area played in the preparations for the invasion.

Torcross

6½ miles SW of Dartmouth on the A379

Another village who saw its beach used for the D-Day preparations, while the exercises were in progress here, an enemy E-boat attacked the landing forces on Torcross Beach and more than 600 Allied servicemen lost their lives. Beside the Sherman tank, recovered from the sea in 1984 and now displayed in the car park, there are memorial tablets to the men who died during the little-publicised military tragedy and to the many who trained here and later perished on the Normandy beaches.

Beesands

7½ miles SW of Dartmouth off the A379

Easy to reach on foot by taking the coastal path from Torcross, the journey by road to Beesands is a four-mile detour through a series of narrow country lanes.

Barn Court Cottage

At Dreyton Cross. Blackawton,
Devon TQ9 7DG
Tel: 01803 712131 Fax: 01803 712797
e-mail: ruthcoe@barncourt.com
website: www.barncourt.com

At the end of a short lane and surrounded by farmland, **Barn Court Cottages** offer superb self-catering holiday accommodation in a tranquil rural setting. In 1997, Ruth and Vic purchased this wonderful site and started renovation of the farmhouse and out buildings, which had become derelict over the previous 20 years. The two cottages, Barn Owl and Orchard, have been converted to an exceptionally high standard from an old stable block whilst the couple have also renovated the farmhouse as their family home.

The larger of the two cottages, Barn Owl, has glorious views over open country and woodland from its first floor lounge and dining areas whilst here too is a fully fitted kitchen and a spacious en suite double bedroom. Meanwhile, on the ground floor are an en suite family bedroom and an en-suite double bedroom, the double having it's own entrance, potentially being a self-contained unit. While Barn Owl sleeps up to seven in comfort, Orchard Cottage can take up to six adults in the same degree of luxury. Again the reception rooms are on the first floor to take full advantage of the views that, from here, take in a local golf course. Here again all three bedrooms have en suite shower or bath facilities. As well as providing superb family holiday accommodation in a quiet setting, ideally placed for many of south Devon's attractions, Ruth and Vic ensure that all their guests feel welcome and even provide a 'Welcome shopping list' of provisions that are ready for guests when they arrive.

As well as renovating the farmhouse and buildings, Ruth and Vic are also very environmentally conscious and the surrounding grounds, in which they have created a small wetlands habitat, contain many varieties of birds, butterflies and wild flowers. The reed beds and willow plantations in the wetlands area have another purpose as they process all the waste water from the house and cottages whilst water for the washing machines and toilets is recycled rain water. Similarly Barn Court Cottages are self-sufficient when it comes to drinking water and this comes from a system of bore holes, is treated by UV filter and is tested annually.

Finally, Ruth and Vic also own the local pub, The George Inn, in Blackawton Village, – an ideal place to spend an evening catching up with the local gossip.

Today, this is a tiny hamlet with just a single row of old cottages lining the foreshore of Start Bay but, as recently as the 1920s, this was a busy fishing village where boats laden with lobster, crab and mullet were drawn up the beach almost to the cottages by the fishermen. Sadly the fishing fleet is no longer operating but the mile-long shingle beach is as appealing as ever and is known for its clean, clear water.

From here the **South West Coast Path** continues to follow the coastline to the ruined village of **Hallsands** that was almost completely demolished by a violent storm in January 1917. A little further along the footpath lies the **Lighthouse** at **Start Point**, which was built in 1836 and, open throughout the year on specific days and daily during school summer holidays, there are visitors tours of this interesting building.

Capton

2½ miles NW of Dartmouth off the A3122

Tucked away in the hills above Dartmouth and well off the beaten track, excavations here in the 1980s revealed that the nearby hilltop was occupied in Neolithic times and the remains of a chambered tomb were discovered along with a number of artefacts dating from Palaeolithic to medieval times.

Kingsbridge Harbour

Kingsbridge

A pretty town, situated at the head of the Kingsbridge estuary, Kingsbridge's name reflects the fact that there has been a bridge here since the 10th century. However, **Kingsbridge Estuary** is not, strictly speaking, an estuary

Staunton Lodge

Embankment Road, Kingsbridge,
Devon TQ7 1JZ
Tel: 01548 854542 Fax: 01548 854421
e-mail: miketreleaven@msn.com
website: www.stauntonlodge.co.uk

Found in the outskirts of Kingsbridge and with uninterrupted views across the Kingsbridge estuary, **Staunton Lodge** is a spacious late Edwardian house that is the home of Mike and Elaine Treleaven. A warm and friendly bed and breakfast establishment with two charming guest rooms, each with their own bathroom, Staunton Lodge not only comes highly recommended but it has also won awards for its breakfasts. An idyllic location, Staunton Lodge is an ideal holiday base but the house is only suitable for children over eight.

at all as no river flows into it, but it is a ria, or drowned valley. This does not take away the fact that this broad expanse of water provides an attractive setting for this busy little town and its quayside. A place of narrow alleyways, some of which bear such descriptive names as Squeezebelly Passage, this is a pleasant place for a quiet stroll.

In Fore Street stands the mostly 13th century parish Church of St Edmund that is well known for the rather cynical verse inscribed on the gravestone of Roger Phillips who died in 1798:

"Here lie I at the chancel door
Here lie I because I'm poor
The further in the more you pay
Here lie I as warm as they."

Close by is **The Shambles**, an Elizabethan market arcade, whose late 18th century upper floor is supported on six sturdy granite pillars, and this acts as a reminder that Kingsbridge was once an important market centre serving the surrounding towns and villages.

Meanwhile, the town's rather modest Victorian Town Hall has an unusual onion-shaped clock tower that adds a touch of glamour to the building. Above the church, and housed in the former Grammar School that was founded in 1670, is the **Cookworthy Museum** (see panel opposite) that is named after William Cookworthy who was born in Kingsbridge in the early 18th century.

Working as an apothecary in Plymouth, Cookworthy encountered traders from the Far East who had brought back fine porcelain from China. English pottery makers despaired of ever producing such delicate cups and plates, but Cookworthy identified the basic ingredient of the porcelain as kaolin, huge deposits of which lay in the hills just north of Plymouth and, ever since then, the more common name for kaolin has been China clay. Meanwhile, the museum, which is open from Monday to Saturday from the end of March to October, tells the story of the

Cookworthy Museum

Kingsbridge, Devon
Tel: 01548 853235

The Cookworthy Museum of Rural Life, housed in Thomas Crispin's Old Grammar School, which was built in 1671, is a must for the visitor to the South Hams. There is so much to see. First you enter the boy's door and go upstairs into the original panelled schoolroom where the story of Kingsbridge unfolds. You move on to the Costume Gallery with its new exhibition 'And So To Bed' which illustrates life in the Victorian era and early 20th century. Then on to view the 'Your School Days' display. A time for nostalgia! Move on again to an Edwardian pharmacy, a

Victorian kitchen and out to the Farm Gallery and walled garden. Finally the Gift Shop and photographic collection to view and order prints.

town along with having re-creations of a 17th century schoolroom, a Victorian kitchen and an Edwardian pharmacy.

Around Kingsbridge

Loddiswell

3 miles N of Kingsbridge off the B3196

After the Norman Conquest, Loddiswell became part of the 40,000 acre estate of Judhel of Totnes, a man who had an apparently insatiable appetite for salmon and, instead of rent, he stipulated that his tenants should provide him with a certain number of the noble fish: Loddiswell's contribution was set at 30 salmon a year.

The benign climate of south Devon has encouraged several viticulturists to plant vineyards in the area and the first vines at **Loddiswell Vineyard** were planted in 1977. Since then its wines have been laden with awards from fellow wine-makers and consumer bodies. The vineyard welcomes visitors for guided tours or walkabouts on weekday afternoons from Easter to October, and

The Ring o' Bells

West Alvington, near Kingsbridge,
Devon TQ7 3PG
Tel: 01548 852437 Mobile: 07976 053749

Found high above the Kingsbridge estuary, **The Ring o' Bells** is an attractive Victorian inn that is owned and personally run by George and Rosemary Holdsworth. Along with offering a good selection of drinks, including real ales, from the bar, their warm and friendly inn has a well-deserved reputation for its cuisine. Available at both lunchtime and in the evening, the extensive menus offer a whole host of dishes but each is prepared to order

from the freshest of local ingredients. Accommodation is also on offer here and children are welcome.

The Fortescue Arms

East Allington, near Totnes, Devon TQ9 7RA
Tel: 01548 521215 Fax: 01548 521215
e-mail: tinakerswell@hotmail.com
website: www.fortescue-arms.co.uk

Found in the heart of this pretty South Hams village, **The Fortescue Arms** is a wonderful, traditional English inn that still has its original flagstone floors, exposed beams and roaring log fires in winter.

Named after a long ago lord of the manor, this charming and delightful country inn has not only gained a reputation for its excellent choice of real ales from the bar but also for its cuisine. Served at both lunchtime (though not during weekdays in the winter) and in the evening, both the à la carte menu, served in the attractive restaurant, and the bar snacks list offer customers a tantalising choice of meat, fish and game dishes.

Everything here is home-cooked and such is the fame of The Fortescue's food that it is necessary to book at all times. Along with the success of their food and drink, owners Robin and Tina Kerswell also extend a warm welcome to guests looking for accommodation and here there are three charming en-suite bedrooms that are let on a bed and breakfast basis.

A relaxed and friendly inn, The Fortescue Arms is well worth visiting.

also Sunday afternoons in July and August.

To the north of the village les **Andrew's Wood**, a nature reserve of woodland and grassland that also includes the ruins of the hamlet of Stanton. There are two circular way-marked trails through the reserve.

Frogmore

3½ miles E of Kingsbridge on the A379

A small cluster of houses and rather more than a hamlet but hardly a village, Frogmore stands at the neck of **Frogmore Creek**, a two-mile long

The Globe Inn

Frogmore, near Kingsbridge, Devon TQ7 2NR
Tel: 01548 531351 Fax: 01548 531375
e-mail: info@theglobeinn.co.uk
website: www.theglobeinn.co.uk

Overlooking Frogmore Creek, **The Globe Inn**, a picturesque 18th century coaching inn, offers wonderful, traditional hospitality tailored to the needs of modern families. The landlords, Lynda and John Horsley, ensure that this is a friendly place with a relaxed atmosphere and a place, too, where customers can be sure of an excellent range of real ales and beers. The inn is also renowned for its cuisine, from the

traditional bar lunches through to the regular curry evenings. Children are welcome and there is comfortable en-suite guest accommodation.

Saddlestones

Well Farm, Chillington, Devon TQ7 2LQ
Tel: 01548 580083 e-mail:
saddlestones@tinyonline.co.uk

Surrounded by the gentle countryside of the South Hams and close to both Kingsbridge and Start Bay, **Saddlestones** is a striking barn conversion found in an idyllic and peaceful location.

Once part of a working farm and dating back, in parts, to the 13th century the barn was expertly converted nearly 20 years ago and, today, it is the home of Jan and David Long,their daughter Sarah and the family cats who came here in 1997.

A charming and picturesque home that is decorated and furnished in a traditional cottage style, Jan and David started to offer bed and breakfast accommodation at the beginning of 2002 and they have already met with great success – several satisfied visitors have already returned.

There are two pretty and comfortable double guest rooms and, along with a full home-cooked English breakfast, Jan and David also offer evening meals by prior arrangement. Saddlestones is open all year and a discount is given on stays of 3 nights plus.

Perfectly placed for those looking for a quiet and tranquil setting where they can unwind from the rigours of modern life, Saddlestones is also ideally placed for anyone wishing to spend their holiday touring the south Devon coast, Dartmoor and beyond.

waterway that flows into the Kingsbridge estuary.

Chivelstone

4½ miles SE of Kingsbridge off the A379

One of Devon's most hidden places and certainly off the beaten track, Chivelstone is an unassuming village tucked away in a maze of country lanes in the extreme southwest of the county. It is the tranquil, rural surroundings that make this such an appealing place but the village does also have a fine parish church, the only one in England dedicated to the 4th century pope, St

Maelcombe House

East Prawle, near Kingsbrigde,
Devon TQ7 2DE
Tel: 01548 511521 Fax: 01548 511501
e-mail: barber.maelcombe@talk21.com

Set in its own extensive grounds and surrounded by land designated an area of outstanding natural beauty, **Maelcombe House** is one of Devon's hidden treasures. This glorious turn of the century house, owned by Sally and Peter Barber, not only has stunning views out across its private beach to the sea but also three exceptional self-catering holiday apartments as well as limited bed and breakfast accommodation. Along with the views, guests here can enjoy the indoor heated swimming pool, sauna, tennis and, above all, supreme comfort.

Sylvester. Historically, Sylvester was a mysterious figure but an old story claims that his saintly ministrations cured the Roman emperor, Constantine, of leprosy. Chivelstone church was built in the 15th century, at a time when this disfiguring disease was still common in England: it seems likely that the parishioners hoped that, by dedicating their church to him, St Sylvester would protect them from the ravages of the illness that, once contracted, imposed total social exclusion on its innocent victims.

Salcombe

3 miles S of Kingsbridge on the A381

Standing at the mouth of the Kingsbridge estuary, this captivating town enjoys one of the most beautiful natural settings in the country. Sheltered from the prevailing west winds by steep hills, the town basks in one of the mildest micro-climates in England. In the terraced gardens rising up from the water's edge, it is not unusual to see mimosa palms and even orange and lemon trees bearing fruit.

Like other small south Devon ports, Salcombe developed its own special area of trading and, whilst Dartmouth specialised in French and Spanish wines, at Salcombe high-sailed clippers arrived carrying the first fruits of the West Indian pineapple harvest and oranges from the Azores. Although that traffic has now ceased, the harbour now throngs with pleasure craft while a small fishing fleet still operates from **Batson Creek**, a picturesque location where the fish quay is piled high with lobster creels.

To the south of the town lies **Overbecks Museum and Garden** (National Trust), a charming Edwardian house that was built in 1913 for Captain George Vereker and, after his death, it was bought by the research chemist, Otto Overbeck who lived here between 1918 and 1937. The house now holds the wide ranging collection of items put together by Overbeck and of the many items on display are late 19th century photographs of the area, local shipbuilding tools, model boats and toys. Meanwhile, the beautiful, sheltered

Salcombe

The Fortescue Inn

Union Street, Salcombe, Devon TQ8 8BZ
Tel: 01584 842868

Tucked away in a quiet part of Salcombe yet just 50 yards from the sea lies **The Fortescue Inn**, a charming and quaint old place that dates back, in parts, to the early 18th century and, indeed, one of its bars was once the old stables. The interior of this traditional old inn has retained much of its original character and, along with the olde worlde atmosphere, there are numerous artefacts, memorabilia and old photographs hanging on the walls.

Landlords, Mike and Val Rowlands, who have been here since 2001, offer a warm welcome to both locals and visitors alike as well as ensuring that all receive the very best in English inn hospitality. Along with a well stocked bar that includes a choice of five real ales, the couple have gained an enviable reputation for the food that is served here at both lunchtime and in the evening. There is a separate evening menu and an ever changing specials board from which to choose but, whilst there are a whole host of mouth-watering dishes, it is for its fish that The Fortescue is justly popular.

gardens, which benefit from Salcombe's mild micro-climate, are planted with many rare trees, shrubs and plants and, along with the views out over the Salcombe estuary, this garden has a Mediterranean feel.

The coastline to the south and west of Salcombe, some of the most magnificent in Britain, is now largely owned by the National Trust. Great slanting slabs of gneiss and schist tower above the sea, making the Clifton walk here both literally and metaphorically breathtaking. At **Bolt Head,** the rock forms a jagged promontory protruding onto the western approaches to the Kingsbridge estuary, and further west, the spectacular cliffs between Bolt Head and **Bolt Tail** are interrupted by a steep descent at Soar Mill Cove.

The Castle, Salcombe

The Port Light Hotel, Restaurant and Inn

Bolberry Down, near Salcombe,
Devon TQ7 3DY
Tel: 01548 561384 Mobile: 07970 859992
e-mail: info@portlight-salcombe.co.uk
website: www.portlight.co.uk

Originally a wartime RAF Radar station, The **Port Light Hotel, Restaurant and Inn** not only has an interesting history but also much to offer to both visitors and locals alike. Well known for its fabulous views of the sunsets over Bigbury Bay, this excellent establishment is also well renowned for its chef, Tasmanian David Singline. Add to this the six luxury en-suite guest rooms, the cosy bar and the welcoming atmosphere and owners Sean and Hazel certainly have a success on their hands.

Malborough

3 miles SW of Kingsbridge on the A381

The lofty spire of this pretty village's 15th century church has been acting as a local landmark for centuries and it is a broach spire rising straight out of the lower tower. Inside the church is wonderfully light so much so in fact that the splendid arcades built in Beer stone seem to glow.

Hope Cove

Hope Cove

4½ miles SW of Kingsbridge off the A381

There are two Hopes here: Outer Hope, which is more modern and so gets less attention, and Inner Hope which must be one of the most photographed villages in the

The Old Inn

Higher Town, Malborough, near Kingsbridge,
Devon TQ7 3RL
Tel: 01548 561320 Fax: 01548 561814
e-mail: oldinnmalborough@hotmail.com

Found just outside the centre of Malborough, **The Old Inn** is a former coaching inn that dates back to the early 18th century and, today, it continues to offer both locals and visitors a warm and friendly welcome. Surprisingly light and airy inside, guests here cannot only enjoy an excellent selection of drinks from the bar but also tuck into some delicious food. Specialising in fresh fish dishes, both the lunchtime and evening menus are popular here and it is essential to book at weekends.

Hope Cove

country. A picturesque huddle of thatched cottages around a tiny cobbled square, Inner Hope once thrived on pilchard fishing but nowadays only a few fishermen still operate from here, bringing in small catches of lobster and crab.

Thurlestone

4 miles W of Kingsbridge off the A381

Another attractive coastal village, Thurlestone can boast not just one, but two beaches that are separated by a headland. Both beaches are recommended, especially the one to the south with its view of the pierced, or "thyrled", stone, the offshore rock from which the settlement gets its name and that was specifically mentioned in a charter of AD 846. The village itself stands on a long, flat-topped ridge above the beaches and is an attractive mixture of flower-decked cottages, old farm buildings and long-established shops and inns. The parish Church of All Saints is worth a visit to see its

Thurlestone Sands

impressive 15th century south porch, Norman font and Lady Chapel.

Bantham

4 miles W of Kingsbridge off the A379

This small village has a long history that goes back to the days of the ancient Britons when Bantham was a centre of early tin trading between these people and the Gauls. By the 8th century, the Saxons were well established here and were farming the fertile soil whilst the sea also provided a major source of income in the form of pilchard fishing. A small fleet of boats were kept busy during the boom years and the humble fish were both cured and even exported from here. Bantham continued to be a busy little port until the early 20th century with sailing barges bringing in coal and building stone for the surrounding area. The village has also seen its fair share of shipwrecks and the bay on which it stands has yielded some fascinating finds over the years whilst some of the timbers from the wrecks have been incorporated into houses in the village.

Bigbury on Sea

5½ miles W of Kingsbridge on the B3392

Found in the heart of an area of outstanding natural beauty, this popular family resort nestles in Bigbury Bay and has not only acres of fine sand but also spectacular views across some of the most glorious South Hams coastline. An excellent place for windsurfing, canoeing and dramatic coastal walks, there is also the added attraction of **Burgh Island** that is actually only an island at high tide as, when the sea recedes, it can be reached by walking across the sandbank or by taking an exciting ride on the Sea Tractor. The whole of the 28-acre island, complete with its 14th century Pilchard Inn, was bought in 1929 by the eccentric millionaire Archibald Nettlefold. He built an extravagant Art Deco hotel on the island that attracted many visitors including Noel Coward, the Duke of

Burgh Island

Windsor and Mrs Wallis Simpson and Agatha Christie. The Queen of Crime used the island as the setting for two of her novels: *And Then There Were None* and *Evil Under The Sun*.

Just to the northeast lies the small hilltop village of **Bigbury** that enjoys grand views over Bigbury Bay and Burgh Island.

Aveton Gifford

3½ miles NW of Kingsbridge off the A379

A pleasant small village (whose name is pronounced 'Awton Jiffard'), which is little more than one main street, had one of the oldest churches in Devon until it was almost completely destroyed by a German bomb in 1943. The modern replacement is surprisingly pleasing but no buildings here can compare with the grandeur of those designed by Aveton Gifford's most famous son. Born here in 1790, Robert Macey first learnt his father's trade of stone masonry before training to become an architect. He then walked all the way to London where he successfully established himself in his chosen profession and went on to design many hospitals, factories, churches and theatres, of which the most notable are the Adelphi and the Haymarket in London.

At the southern end of the village, just before the three-quarter mile long medieval causeway, a lane on the right is signposted to Bigbury. This very narrow road runs right alongside the River Avon and is very beautiful but drivers should beware as the river is tidal here and when the tide is in the two fords along the way are impassable.

Modbury

7 miles NW of Kingsbridge on the A379

This pretty little market town has a long and rich history that dates right back to the 8th century although it was at its most powerful and prosperous during Tudor times. Then the most influential family were the Champernownes and, in particular, there was Katherine Champernowne whose children by her first marriage included Sir Humphry Gilbert, who established the colony Newfoundland, and Aidrian Gilbert, who discovered the North West Passage, and, by her second marriage, Sir Walter

Raleigh. Although the family's fortunes and influence has declined over the years they have left a constant reminder – the granite fireplace lintel set into the pavement outside the old White Hart Inn.

Sutton Harbour, Plymouth

During the Civil War the local peace was disturbed when two battles were fought in and around Modbury but, today, the many Georgian buildings give the town a gentle air of quiet elegance that is far removed from the violence that went before. However, the town does come very much alive during its popular eight day **May Fair** that was first held in 1329.

Plymouth

Perhaps the best way to get to know this historic city is to approach **Plymouth Hoe** on foot from the main shopping area, along the now pedestrianised Armada Way. It was, of course, here on the Hoe, a park and promenade overlooking **Plymouth Sound**, that on Friday 19th July, 1588, the Commander of the Fleet and an erstwhile pirate, Sir Francis Drake, was playing bowls when he was told of the approach of the Spanish Armada – an historical event that is known to every schoolchild. With true British phlegm, Sir Francis completed his game before boarding *The Golden Hind* and sailing off to harass the Spanish fleet. The Hoe is still an open space from where there are superb views of the sea and the wooded headlands and here, too, is a statue of Drake who strikes a splendidly belligerent pose and looks proudly out to the horizon.

Just offshore, in the waters of the mouth of the River Tamar, lies the striking shape of **Drake's Island**, an English Alcatraz that, in medieval times, was known as St Nicholas' Island. However, its name was changed when Sir Francis Drake was appointed governor and he began to fortify the island. In its day, this stark island has been used as a gunpowder repository (it is said to be riddled with underground tunnels where the powder was stored), a prison and a youth adventure centre. Further out into the Tamar estuary lies Plymouth's remarkable **Breakwater** that protects the Sound from the destructive effects of the prevailing south-westerly winds. Built by prisoners between 1812 and 1840, this massive mile-long construction required around four million tons of limestone and its upper surface was finished with enormous dovetailed blocks of stone and there is also a lighthouse at one end to ward ships off the obstruction.

From the Hoe, on a clear day, it is possible to see the famous **Eddystone Lighthouse** that stands on a rock some 12 miles out in the English Channel. The present lighthouse is the fourth to be built here and the first, made of timber, was swept away in a huge storm in 1703, taking with it the man who had built the lighthouse, the ship-owner Winstanley. In 1759, a much more substantial stone lighthouse was built by John Smeaton and this stood for 120 years before the rock on which it was built began to collapse. Dismantled and re-erected on Plymouth Hoe, **Smeaton's Tower** is now one of the city's most popular attractions and from the top there are excellent views of Millbay Docks, Plymouth's busy commercial port. The tower is open to the public daily from the end of March to the end of October (but closed on Sundays and Mondays for the rest of the year) and, along with climbing the 93 steps to the top of the tower, visitors can see how the lighthouse keepers lived. Close to the tower is **Plymouth Dome**, a stunning attraction that vividly captures Plymouth's long history. The imaginative exhibitions here allow visitors to experience the stench and grime of an Elizabethan street, brave the seas with Drake and Cook and witness the devastation of Plymouth's port by the Luftwaffe. The dome, which also contains a gift shop and café, is open daily from the end of March to the end of October.

Plymouth's oldest quarter, **The Barbican**, is, today, a lively area of restaurants, pubs and an innovative small theatre, but it was once the main

The Hoe, Plymouth

trading area for merchants exporting wool and importing wine. Close by is **The Citadel**, a massive fortification built by Charles II as a defence against a seaborne invasion. Perhaps bearing in mind that the city had resisted a four-year siege by his father's troops during the Civil War, Charles' Citadel has a number of gun ports that bear down directly on Plymouth. It remains military base but there are guided tours around the building during summer.

Nearby are the **Mayflower Steps** where the Pilgrim Fathers boarded their famous ship for their historic voyage across the Atlantic to Massachusetts. The name of the *Mayflower's* company are listed on a board on nearby Island House. Many other emigrants were to follow in the Fathers' footsteps, with the result that there are now more than 40 communities named Plymouth scattered across the English-speaking world. Other significant events in Plymouth's history are also remembered here: the sailing, in 1839, of the *Troy*, an early emigrant ship to New Zealand, and the return of the Tolpuddle martyrs who were transported to Australia. Adjacent to the Steps and opened in 2002 is the **Plymouth Mayflower**, which takes people on a unique journey through Plymouth's world famous harbour and Barbican. From its earliest days as a rocky natural harbour through the numerous historical voyages that have started from here to the ravages of World War II bombing, the very latest

audio and visual technologies brings all these events very much to life. The Plymouth Mayflower is open every day except Christmas Day.

Another recent addition to the Barbican's visitor attractions is the **National Marine Aquarium** that takes visitors on a fascinating journey through an underwater world. There are over 4,000 animals and fish here including the largest collection of seashore species in the world but it is, perhaps, its massive tank, Britain's deepest, that is home to a mass of predatory sharks that is its most spectacular draw. Open daily throughout the year, the aquarium also looks at the diversity of life in the lakes, rivers and seas that make up over seventy per cent of the world's surface.

A number of interesting old buildings around the Barbican have survived the ravages of time and the terrible pasting the city received during World War II: **Prysten House,** behind St Andrew's Church, is a 15th century priest's house; the **Elizabethan House** in New Street has a rich display of Elizabethan furniture and furnishings; and the **Merchant's House** in St Andrew's Street, generally regarded as Devon's finest Jacobean building, is crammed full of interesting objects relating to Plymouth's past. A particularly fascinating exhibit in the Merchant's House is the **Park Pharmacy**, a genuine Victorian pharmacy, complete with its 1864 fittings, which is stocked with such preparations as Ipecacuanha Wine (one to two tablespoonfuls as an emetic) and Tincture of Myrrh and Borax "for the teeth and gums". The city is also home to **Jacka's Bakery** that claims to be the oldest commercial bakery in the country and it is reputed to have supplied *The Mayflower* with ships' biscuits.

The blackest date in Plymouth's history is undoubtedly March 21st, 1941 and, on that night, the entire centre of the city was razed to the ground by the combined effects of high explosive and incendiary bombs dropped by the Luftwaffe. More than a thousand people were killed whilst another 5,000 were injured. After the war, the renowned town planner Sir Patrick Abercrombie was commissioned to design a completely new town centre. Much of the rebuilding was carried out in the 1950s, which was not British architecture's Golden Age, but half a century later the scheme has acquired something of a period charm. This new city centre has some excellent facilities, including a first-rate **Museum and Art Gallery,** near Drake Circus, the **Theatre Royal** (see panel opposite) with its two auditoria in Royal Parade, the **Arts Centre** in Looe Street, and the **Pavilions** complex of concert hall, leisure pool and skating rink at the foot of Western Approach. One place that did survive the World War II bombs was England's oldest working gin distillery, **Plymouth Gin Distillery**, where gin has been distilled since 1793. Formerly a Dominican monastery dating from the early 15th century and the final lodgings of the Pilgrim Fathers before they set

Mount Edgcumbe, Plymouth

sail, there are tours of this fascinating place that has provided gin to the Royal Navy for over 200 yeas. A favourite of Churchill, Roosevelt, Ian Fleming and Alfred Hitchcock, Plymouth Gin is considered to be the original base for a Dry Martini and it constantly features in the Savoy Cocktail book – the bible of mixed drinks.

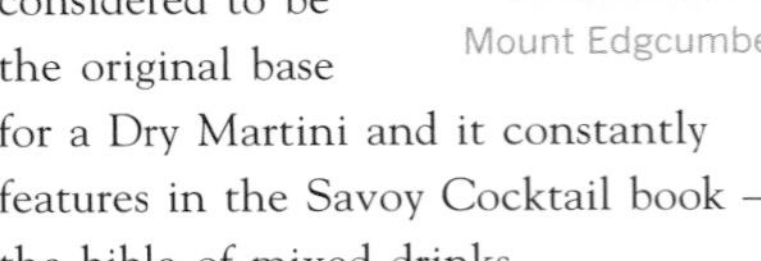

Locally, the Tamar estuary is known as the Hamoaze, (pronounced ham-oys), and it is well worth taking one of the boat trips that leave from the Mayflower Steps and Phoenix Wharf. This is certainly the best way to see the Devonport Dockyard, while the ferry to Cremyll on the Cornish bank of the Tamar drops off passengers close to **Mount Edgcumbe Country Park** and the old smuggling village of Cawsand.

Just a few miles to the north of the city centre lies **Crownhill Fort**, one of the largest and best preserved of Plymouth's many fortifications. Well hidden from the outside world, the fort was built between 1863 and 1872 and, with its massive earth ramparts, hidden gun emplacements and tunnels it was one of the most advanced of Lord Palmerston's fortresses that were built to defend the country from a French invasion. A wonderful place to explore, on certain days throughout the year the fort comes alive again when the original Victorian drill is followed and a wide range of canon are fired.

Around Plymouth

Tamerton Foliot

3 miles N of Plymouth off the B3373

Set on a hillside overlooking a large creek that runs into the River Tamar, Tamerton Foliot was the birthplace of Gilbert Foliot who was to hold the position of Bishop of London for 35 years, from 1153 to 1188. He was an arch-adversary of Thomas à Becket who excommunicated him, a punishment that was overturned by the Pope. The village has a 15th century church with some outstanding monuments to the local landowners, the Copleston, Gorges and Radcliffe families, and an interesting Tudor pulpit with linen fold panelling.

Overlooking the Tavy and Tamar estuary, **Warleigh Point Nature Reserve** covers one of the finest examples of coastal oak woodland in Devon and, along with magnificent views, it is home to a wealth of wildlife.

Plym Bridge

3½ miles NE of Plymouth off the B3432

To the north of the village lie the luxuriant oak woodlands of **Plym Bridge Woods** that can be found beside the River Plym. At their best during the spring, when the woods are carpeted with flowers, there are way marked paths through the woods that provide visitors with an opportunity to see the wealth of bird and animal life contained here. In the 17th century, this was a less than peaceful place as tons of slate were quarried from the exposed rock here and the woods are littered with fascinating industrial archaeological remains.

Plympton

5 miles E of Plymouth on the B3416

Now more of a suburb of Plymouth than a town in its own right, in early medieval times, Plympton was larger than its neighbour and the earthwork of a medieval castle can still be seen. However, Plympton is home to one of Devon's grandest mansions, **Saltram House** (National Trust) that was built in the 18th century around a Tudor core and it is surrounded by an estate near the tidal creek of the Plym estuary. The house, which contains fine period furniture, china and a fantastic Georgian collection of paintings, was the home of the Parker family who, in the 1790s, commissioned Robert Adam to create the magnificent state rooms that contain some exceptional plasterwork. Along with the Great Kitchen, Chapel Gallery and Orangery, there are superb 18th century gardens and an amphitheatre that is a relic of the opulence of the

The Boringdon Arms

Turnchapel, near Plymouth,
Devon PL9 9TQ
Tel: 01752 402053 Fax: 01752 481313
e-mail: liz@boringdon.btinternet.co.uk
website: www.bori.co.uk

Found at the lower end of Turnchapel village, in a row of listed Georgian houses, is **The Boringdon Arms**, an exceptional and traditional inn that is owned and personally run by Liz and Barry Elliott. Dating back to the early 18th century, this striking building, that is believed to have been constructed by Lord Boringdon (one of the Parkers of Saltram), was originally a quarry master's house but, by around the 1770s, it had become a public house.

A friendly and popular local that offers an equally warm welcome to visitors, The Bori, as it is known in the village, is highly regarded for both its real ales and its food. Recognised by CAMRA, the range of handpulled real ales here draws connoisseurs from far and wide and the traditional surroundings of the bar, with wooden or flag-stoned floors, provide the perfect environment to enjoy a freshly pulled pint. The old photographs of the village, including its now defunct ferry, that hang on the walls add further to the atmosphere here of an old fashioned inn and meeting place for the locals. Meanwhile, visitors here can also enjoy a wonderful array of home-cooked meals that, along with the printed menu, include a range of daily specials. Annette Taylor helps Liz in the kitchen and it is Annette's home-made pies that have become legendary in this part of Devon whilst the inn's cod in beer batter, served with chips and mushy peas, is also popular. Meals are served in both bars and also in the conservatory and, when weather permits, in the secluded walled beer garden.

The superb hospitality offered by Liz and Barry extends beyond their excellent food and drink and, along with the comfortable guest rooms that are offered on a bed and breakfast basis, the couple plan a wealth of entertainment throughout the year. There is live music each week, on a Wednesday and Saturday evening, and along with the usual pub games many enjoy taking part in the weekly Sunday evening quiz. However, the most well attended, and most eagerly anticipated event at The Bori is the bi-monthly beer festival, held over the last weekend of the month starting in January, when over 20 different real ales are available on tap for customers to sample.

Georgian era. Anyone who saw the film of Jane Austen's novel *Sense and Sensibility* will recognise the mansion as it was used as the location for Norland House.

From the village the **Plym Valley Railway** carries passengers on a restored part of the former Great Western Railway to the local beauty spot of Plym Bridge in rolling stock that re-creates the 1950s and 1960s.

To the east, and almost in Dartmoor, is another Georgian mansion that is often overlooked. **Hamerdon House**, which is still occupied by the original family, contains family and other portraits, silver, books and period furniture and is open on a limited basis in May, June and August.

Turnchapel

3 miles SE of Plymouth off the A379

Enjoying views across Cattewater to Plymouth, this waterside village was, until the end of the 18th century a small fishing village but, in 1797, the 2nd Baron Baringdon, John Parker of Saltram, enclosed its dry dock and, for a time, it was the busiest shipyard in the area.

Turnchapel was declared a Conservation Area in 1977 and, with its two pubs, church and waterfront, it is a very pleasant place to wander around. Nearby, there are ex-RAF Cataline flying boats to see and, from Mountbatten Peninsula, there are grand panoramic views over Plymouth Hoe and Drake's Island. Incidentally, it was at RAF Mountbatten that Lawrence of Arabia served as a humble aircraftman for several years.

A short distance to the south is a stretch of coastline known as **Abraham's Garden** and a local story goes that, during the fearful plague of 1665, a number of Spanish slaves were buried here. In their memory, the shrubbery always remains green – even in winter.

Elburton

4½ miles SE of Plymouth on the A379

Located on the very edge of the South Hams, Elburton was once a separate village but is now effectively a suburb of Plymstock and a popular residential centre for commuters into Plymouth who only have to travel a few miles in the other direction to find themselves in the soft, rolling hills of the South Hams.

Wembury

6 miles SE of Plymouth off the A379

Wembury church makes a dramatic landmark as it stands isolated on the edge of the cliff, and the coastal path here provides spectacular views of the Yealm estuary to the east, and Plymouth Sound to the west. The path is occasionally closed to walkers when the firing range is in use and red flags are displayed as a warning. A mile offshore, in Wembury Bay is the **Great Mew Stone**, a lonely islet that was inhabited until the 1830s when its last residents, the part-time

The Volunteer Inn

Fore Street, Yealmpton, Devon PL8 2JN
Tel: 01752 880463

Found in the centre of Yealmpton, **The Volunteer Inn** is a traditional early 18th century former coaching inn that is now a popular local inn with Bridy Malin at the helm. Although Bridy has only been here since November 2002, both she and her able manager, David Prout, have certainly put their mark on this well known local.

In the cosy surroundings of the friendly bar, customers have a choice of real ales, as well as all the usual drinks, whilst there is also an excellent choice of delicious home-cooked food available at both lunchtime and in the evening (food is served all day from April to October). The Sunday roast lunches are particularly popular here and it is necessary to book to avoid disappointment. Other innovations that this forward thinking couple have put into action include the Thursday fish and chip nights, the Friday curry nights and, on occasion, live entertainment. When the weather is pleasant, customers can make use of the secluded beer garden to the rear of the inn and children are welcome for Sunday lunch.

smuggler Sam Wakeham and his family, gave up the unequal struggle to make a living here. The Mew Stone is now the home of seabirds that surely cannot take kindly to its use from time to time by the HMS Cambridge gunnery school on Wembury Point.

Newton Ferrers

7½ miles SE of Plymouth off the B3186

A picturesque fishing village of whitewashed cottages sloping down to the river, Newton Ferrers is beloved by

Bugle Rocks

Battisborough, nr Mothecombe, Holbeton, Devon PL8 1JX
Tel: 01752 830422 Fax: 01752 830558
e-mail: buglerocks@hotmail.com

Overlooking the sea and the South West Coastal Path and close to the famous Mothecombe beach, **Bugle Rocks** is a charming late 19th century coach house that has been imaginatively and sympathetically converted into a magnificent family house by owners Jan and Nick Stockman. Others too can share in the beauty and charm of this delightful house as the couple offer bed and breakfast accommodation of an exceptionally high standard. Experience some of the finest views in the area from the guest lounge.

THE SWAN INN

Pillory Hill, Noss Mayo, Devon PL8 1EE
Tel: 01752 872392

Overlooking the River Yealm, **The Swan Inn** is an attractive old inn that was once used to house prisoners from the Napoleonic Wars but, today, is not only a popular local but also a favourite with yachtsmen, walkers and tourists.

Along with the excellent range of drinks here, landlords, Paul and Elise Stafford, offer a superb range of home-cooked traditional pub dishes whilst there are also occasional live music evenings. Children are welcome and there is a small beer garden that overlooks the river.

artists and is also one of the south coast's most popular yachting centres. Part of the village sits beside the River Yealm (pronounced Yam) whilst the rest lies alongside a large creek and, when the creek dries out at low tide, it is possible to walk across to **Noss Mayo** on the southern bank. (When the tide is in, a ferry operates, but only during the season).

TOURIST INFORMATION CENTRES

DEVON INFORMATION HOLIDAY LINE

P.O. Box 55
Barnstaple
Devon
EX32 8YR
Tel: 0870 6085531 (calls charged)
e-mail: tourism@devon.gov.uk

AXMINSTER

The Old Courthouse
Church Street
Axminster
Devon
EX13 5AQ
Tel: 01297 34386
Fax: 01297 34386

BARNSTAPLE

Tourist Information Centre
36 Boutport Street
Barnstaple
Devon
EX31 1RX
Tel: 01271 375000
Fax: 01271 374037
e-mail: barnstapletic@visit.org.uk

BIDEFORD

Tourist Information Centre
Victoria Park
The Quay
Bideford
Devon
EX39 2QQ
Tel: 01237 477676
Fax: 01237 421853
e-mail: bidefordtic@visit.org.uk

BRAUNTON

Tourist Information
The Bakehouse Centre
Caen Street
Braunton
Devon
EX33 1AA
Tel: 01271 816400
Fax: 01271 816947
e-mail: brauntontic@visit.org.uk

BRIXHAM

Tourist Information Centre
The Old Market House
The Quay
Brixham
Devon
TQ5 8TB
Tel: 0906 680 1268
Fax: 01803 852939

BUDLEIGH SALTERTON

Tourist Information Centre
Fore Street
Budleigh Salterton
Devon
EX9 6NG
Tel: 01395 445275
Fax: 01395 442208

COMBE MARTIN

Tourist Information Centre
Seacot
Cross Street
Combe Martin
Devon
EX34 0DH
Tel: 01271 883319
Fax: 01271 883319
e-mail: combemartintic@visit.org.uk

CREDITON

Tourist Information Centre
The Old Town Hall
High Street
Crediton
Devon
EX17 3LF
Tel: 01363 772006
Fax: 01363 772006

(DARTMOOR) HIGH MOORLAND VISITOR CENTRE

Duchy Building
Tavistock Road
Princetown
Devon
PL20 6QF
Tel: (01822) 890414

DARTMOUTH

Tourist Information Centre
The Engine House
Mayor's Avenue
Dartmouth
Devon
TQ6 9YY
Tel: 01803 834224
Fax: 01803 835631
e-mail: enquire@dartmouth-tourism.org.uk
website: www.dartmouth-information.co.uk/

DAWLISH

The Lawn
Dawlish
Devon
EX7 9PW
Tel: 01626 215665
Fax: 01626 865985
e-mail: dawtic@Teignbridge.gov.uk
website: www.southdevon.org.uk

EXETER

Tourist Information Centre
Civic Centre
Paris Street
Exeter
Devon
EX1 1JJ
Tel: 01392 265700
Fax: 01392 265260
website: http://www.exeter.gov.uk

EXMOUTH

Alexandra Terrace
Exmouth
Devon
EX8 1NZ
Tel: 01395 222299
Fax: 01395 269911
e-mail: exmouth@btinternet.com

HONITON

Lace Walk Car Park
Honiton
Devon
EX14 1LT
Tel: 01404 43716
Fax: 01404 43716

ILFRACOMBE

Tourist Information Centre
The Landmark
The Seafront
Ilfracombe
Devon
EX34 9BX
Tel: 01271 863001
Fax: 01271 862586
e-mail: Ilfracombe Tic@aol.com

IVYBRIDGE & SOUTH DARTMOOR

St Leonards Road
Ivybridge
Devon
PL21 0SL
Tel: 01752 897035
Fax: 01752 690660

KINGSBRIDGE

Tourist Information Centre
The Quay
Kingsbridge
Devon
TQ7 1HS
Tel: 01548 853195
Fax: 01548 854185
website: www.kingsbridgeinfo.co.uk

LYNTON

Tourist Information Centre
Town Hall
Lee Road
Lynton
Devon
EX35 6BT
Tel: 01598 752225
Fax: 01598 752755
website: www.lynton-lynmouth-tourism.co.uk/
e-mail: info@lynton-lynmouth-tourism.co.uk

MODBURY

Tourist Information Centre
Poundwell Meadow Car Park
Modbury
Devon
PL21 0QL
Tel: 01548 830159
Fax: 01548 831371
e-mail: modburytic@lineone.net

NEWTON ABBOT

6 Bridge House
Courtenay Street
Newton Abbot
Devon
TQ12 4QS
01626 215667
01626 369260
e-mail: natic@Teignbridge.gov.uk
website: www.southdevon.org.uk

OKEHAMPTON

Tourist Information Centre
Museum Courtyard
3 West Street
Okehampton
Devon
EX20 1HQ
Tel: 01837 53020
Fax: 01837 55225
e-mail: oketic@visit.org.uk

OTTERY ST MARY

Tourist Information Centre
10b Broad Street
Ottery St Mary
Devon
EX11 1BZ
Tel: 01404 813964
Fax: 01404 813964
e-mail: tic.osm@cosmic.org.uk

PAIGNTON

Tourist Information Centre
The Esplanade
Paignton
Devon
TQ4 6ED
Tel: 0906 680 1268
Fax: 01803 551959
e-mail: Paignton.TIC@torbay.gov.uk

PLYMOUTH

Tourist Information Centre
Island House
9 The Barbican
Plymouth
Devon
PL1 2LS
Tel: 01752 304849
Fax: 01752 257955

PLYMOUTH

Tourist Information Centre
Plymouth Discovery Centre
Crabtree
Plymouth
Devon
PL3 6RN
Tel: 01752 266030
Fax: 01752 266033

SALCOMBE

Tourist Information Centre
Market Street
Salcombe
Devon
TQ8 8DE
Tel: 01548 843927
Fax: 01548 842736
e-mail: info@salcombeinformation.co.uk
website: www.salcombeinformation.co.uk

SEATON

Tourist Information Centre
The Underfleet
Seaton
Devon
EX12 2TB
Tel: 01297 21660
Fax: 01297 21689
e-mail: inf@seatontic.freeserve.co.uk
website: www.eastdevon.net/tourism/seaton

SIDMOUTH

Tourist Information Centre
Ham Lane
Sidmouth
Devon
EX10 8XR
Tel: 01395 516441
Fax: 01395 519333

SOUTH MOLTON

Tourist Information Centre
1 East Street
South Molton
Devon
EX36 3BU
Tel: 01769 574122
Fax: 01769 574044
e-mail: mail@visitsouthmolton.co.uk

TAVISTOCK

Tourist Information Centre
Town Hall
Bedford Square
Tavistock
Devon
PL19 0AE
Tel: 01822 612938
Fax: 01822 618389
e-mail: tavistocktic@visit.org.uk

TEIGNMOUTH

The Den
Sea Front
Teignmouth
Devon
TQ14 8BE
Tel: 01626 215666
Fax: 01626 778333
e-mail: teigntic@Teignbridge.gov.uk
website: www.southdevon.org.uk

TIVERTON

Phoenix Lane
Tiverton
Devon
EX16 6LU
Tel: 01884 255827
Fax: 01884 257594
e-mail:
tivertontic@devonshireheartland.co.uk

TORQUAY

Tourist Information Centre
Vaughan Parade
Torquay
Devon
TQ2 5JG
Tel: 0906 680 1268
Fax: 01803 214885
e-mail: Torquay.TIC@torbay.gov.uk

TORRINGTON

Tourist Information Centre
Castle Hill
South Street Car Park
Great Torrington
Devon
EX38 8AA
Tel: 01805 626140
Fax: 01805 626141
e-mail: info@great-torrington.com

TOTNES

Tourist Information Centre
The Town Mill
Coronation Road
Totnes
Devon
TQ9 5DF
Tel: 01803 863168
Fax: 01803 865771

WOOLACOMBE

Tourist Information Centre
The Esplanade
Woolacombe
Devon
EX34 7DL
Tel: 01271 870553
Fax: 01271 870553
e-mail: woolacombetic@visit.org.uk

INDEX OF TOWNS, VILLAGES AND PLACES OF INTEREST

A

B

C

D

R

S

T

U

W

Y

LIST OF ADVERTISERS

A

Acorns Café and Tea Rooms, Hatherleigh	Café and Tea Rooms	p114
Agincourt House, Dartmouth	Bed and Breakfast	p192
Allhallows Museum, Honiton	Museum	p13
The Anchor Inn, Chudleigh Knighton	Pub with Food	p150
Arlington Court, Arlington, Barnstaple	Historic House and Gardens	p83

B

Barn Court Cottages, Blackawton	Self Catering	p200
Barnfield House, High Bickington, Umberleigh	Bed and Breakfast	p67
Barnstaple Heritage Centre, Barnstaple	Historic Attraction	p58
The Bay Tree Guest House, Seaton	Guest House	p26
Becky Falls Woodland Park, Manaton	Scenic Attraction	p122
The Bell Inn, Monkleigh, Bideford	Pub, Food and Accommodation	p94
Berry Pomeroy Castle, Totnes	Historic Attraction	p189
Bicton Park Botanical Gardens, East Budleigh	Gardens and Museum	p28
The Black Venus Inn, Challacombe, Barnstaple	Pub and Restaurant	p80
The Boringdon Arms, Turnchapel, Plymouth	Pub, Food and Accommodation	p218
Bramble Barn & Willow Barn, Holsworthy Beacon	Self Catering	p98
Braunton Museum, Braunton	Museum	p75
Buckfast Butterflies and Dartmoor Otter Sanctuary, Buckfastleigh	Wildlife Attraction	p153
Budleigh Farm, Mortonhampstead	Self Catering	p116
Bugle Rocks, Battisborough, Holbeton	Bed and Breakfast	p220
Burrow Farm Gardens, Dalwood, Axminster	Gardens	p11

C

Cadhay Manor, Ottery St Mary	Historic House and Gardens	p16
Carlton Inn Restaurant, Honiton	Pub and Restaurant	p13
Castle Drogo, Drewsteignton	House and Gardens	p117
The Castle Inn, Axminster	Pub with Food	p5
Chambercombe Manor, Ilfracombe	Historic House and Gardens	p70
Chipley Mill Cottages, Bickington, Newton Abbot	Self Catering	p148
The Cleave at Lustleigh, Lustleigh, Newton Abbot	Pub with Food	p120
Cobbaton Combat Collection, Chittlehampton	Historic Attraction	p63
Coldharbour Mill, Uffculme, Cullompton	Historic Attraction	p20
Combe Martin Wildlife and Dinosaur Park, Combe Martin	Wildlife Attraction	p84
Cookworthy Museum, Kingsbridge	Museum	p203
Coombeshead Farm Holiday Cottages, Coombeshead Cross, Chudleigh	Self Catering	p169
The Copper Key Inn, North Tawton	Pub and Restaurant	p110
The Cornish Arms, Tavistock	Pub and Restaurant	p133
The Country Table Café, Newton Abbot	Café	p167

D

The Dartmoor Wildlife Park, Sparkwell	Wildlife Attraction	p146
Dartmouth Castle, Dartmouth	Historic Attraction	p193
Dartmouth Museum, Dartmouth	Museum	p195

HIDDEN PLACES ORDER FORM

To order any of our publications just fill in the payment details below and complete the order form. For orders of less than 4 copies please add £1 per book for postage and packing. Orders over 4 copies are P & P free.

Please Complete Either:

I enclose a cheque for £ ______ made payable to Travel Publishing Ltd

Or:

Card No: ______ Expiry Date: ______

Signature: ______

Name: ______

Address: ______

Tel no: ______

Please either send, telephone, fax or e-mail your order to:

Travel Publishing Ltd, 7a Apollo House, Calleva Park, Aldermaston, Berkshire RG7 8TN

Tel: 0118 981 7777 Fax: 0118 982 0077 e-mail: karen@travelpublishing.co.uk

	Price	Quantity
Hidden Places Regional Titles		
Cambs & Lincolnshire	£7.99	....
Chilterns	£7.99	....
Cornwall	£8.99	....
Derbyshire	£8.99	....
Devon	£8.99	....
Dorset, Hants & Isle of Wight	£8.99	....
East Anglia	£8.99	....
Gloucs, Wiltshire & Somerset	£8.99	....
Heart of England	£7.99	....
Hereford, Worcs & Shropshire	£7.99	....
Highlands & Islands	£7.99	....
Kent	£8.99	....
Lake District & Cumbria	£8.99	....
Lancashire & Cheshire	£8.99	....
Lincolnshire & Notts	£8.99	....
Northumberland & Durham	£8.99	....
Sussex	£8.99	....
Yorkshire	£8.99	....
Hidden Places National Titles		
England	£10.99	....
Ireland	£10.99	....
Scotland	£10.99	....
Wales	£9.99	....

	Price	Quantity
Hidden Inns Titles		
East Anglia	£5.99	....
Heart of England	£5.99	....
Lancashire & Cheshire	£5.99	....
North of England	£5.99	....
South	£5.99	....
South East	£5.99	....
South and Central Scotland	£5.99	....
Wales	£5.99	....
Welsh Borders	£5.99	....
West Country	£5.99	....
Yorkshire	£5.99	....
Country Living Rural Guides		
East Anglia	£9.99	....
Heart of England	£9.99	....
Ireland	£10.99	....
Scotland	£10.99	....
South of England	£9.99	....
South East of England	£9.99	....
Wales	£10.99	....
West Country	£9.99	....

Total Quantity ______

Post & Packing ______

Total Value ______

Easy-to-use, Informative Travel Guides on the British Isles

THE HIDDEN PLACES OF
Lancashire & Cheshire
including the Isle of Man
An informative guide to the more secluded and less well-known places to visit
■ Places of interest ■ Accommodation ■ Food ■ Drink

HIDDEN INNS OF THE
SOUTH EAST
INCLUDING KENT, SURREY AND SUSSEX
AN INFORMATIVE GUIDE TO THE MORE SECLUDED PUBS AND INNS OF THE SOUTH EAST

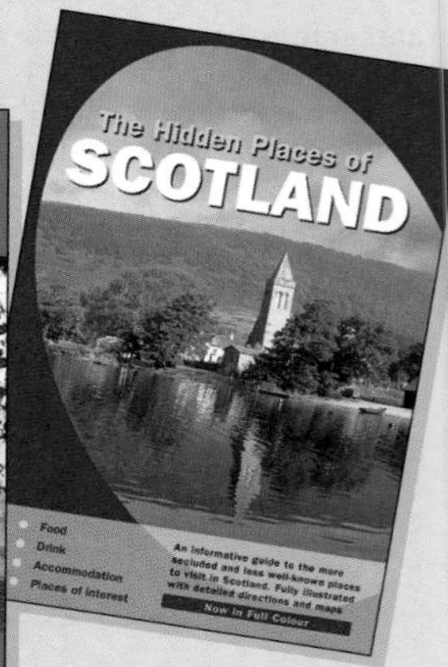

The Hidden Places of
SCOTLAND
• Food • Drink • Accommodation • Places of interest
An informative guide to the more secluded and less well-known places to visit in Scotland. Fully illustrated with detailed directions and maps
Now in Full Colour

COUNTRY LIVING MAGAZINE
GUIDE TO RURAL ENGLAND
THE HEART OF ENGLAND
• Where to go • Where to stay • What to see • Where to eat • What to do • Where to buy
Fully illustrated with detailed directions and maps

THE GOLFERS GUIDE to Ireland
Packed with information on Golf Courses and where to stay, eat and drink
Dermot Gilleece

COUNTRY LIVING MAGAZINE
GUIDE TO RURAL SCOTLAND
• Where to go • Where to stay • What to see • Where to eat • What to do • Where to buy
Fully illustrated with detailed directions and maps

Travel Publishing Limited

7a Apollo House • Calleva Park • Aldermaston • Berkshire RG7 8TN
Phone: 0118 981 7777 • **Fax:** 0118 982 0077
e-mail: adam@travelpublishing.co.uk • **website:** www.travelpublishing.co.uk

READER REACTION FORM

The *Travel Publishing* research team would like to receive reader's comments on any visitor attractions or places reviewed in the book and also recommendations for suitab le entries to be included in the next edition. This will help ensure that the *Country Living series of Rural Guides* continues to provide its readers with useful information on the more interesting, unusual or unique features of each attraction or place ensuring that their visit to the local area is an enjoyable and stimulating experience. To provide your comments or recommendations would you please complete the forms below and overleaf as indicated and send to:

The Research Department, Travel Publishing Ltd,
7a Apollo House, Calleva Park, Aldermaston, Reading, RG7 8TN.

Your Name:

Your Address:

Your Telephone Number:

Please tick as appropriate:

Comments ☐ Recommendation ☐

Name of Establishment:

Address:

Telephone Number:

Name of Contact:

READER REACTION FORM

Comment or Reason for Recommendation:

READER REACTION FORM

The *Travel Publishing* research team would like to receive reader's comments on any visitor attractions or places reviewed in the book and also recommendations for suitab le entries to be included in the next edition. This will help ensure that the *Country Living series of Rural Guides* continues to provide its readers with useful information on the more interesting, unusual or unique features of each attraction or place ensuring that their visit to the local area is an enjoyable and stimulating experience. To provide your comments or recommendations would you please complete the forms below and overleaf as indicated and send to:

The Research Department, Travel Publishing Ltd,
7a Apollo House, Calleva Park, Aldermaston, Reading, RG7 8TN.

Your Name:

Your Address:

Your Telephone Number:

Please tick as appropriate:

Comments ☐ Recommendation ☐

Name of Establishment:

Address:

Telephone Number:

Name of Contact:

READER REACTION FORM

Comment or Reason for Recommendation:

READER REACTION FORM

The *Travel Publishing* research team would like to receive reader's comments on any visitor attractions or places reviewed in the book and also recommendations for suitab le entries to be included in the next edition. This will help ensure that the *Country Living series of Rural Guides* continues to provide its readers with useful information on the more interesting, unusual or unique features of each attraction or place ensuring that their visit to the local area is an enjoyable and stimulating experience. To provide your comments or recommendations would you please complete the forms below and overleaf as indicated and send to:

The Research Department, Travel Publishing Ltd,
7a Apollo House, Calleva Park, Aldermaston, Reading, RG7 8TN.

Your Name:

Your Address:

Your Telephone Number:

Please tick as appropriate:

Comments ☐ Recommendation ☐

Name of Establishment:

Address:

Telephone Number:

Name of Contact:

READER REACTION FORM

Comment or Reason for Recommendation:

....

....

....

....

....

....

....

....

....

....

....

....